HOW TO MAKE IT IN
MUSICALS

THE INSIDER'S GUIDE TO A
CAREER AS A SINGER-DANCER

Michael Allen

Foreword by
Donna McKechnie

Back Stage Books
An Imprint of Watson-Guptill Publications
New York

Dedicated to Breanna Joy Moritz.
Destined for Broadway, taken from us at the tender age of 12,
she's now performing in her Castle in the Clouds.

Published in 1999 by Back Stage Books, an imprint of Watson-Guptill Publications,
a division of BPI Communications, Inc., 1515 Broadway, New York, NY 10036-8986

The publisher thanks the following for the use of their copyrighted materials: Page 17: Photo courtesy
of Brian Biggs Photography • Page 21: Photo courtesy of the American Boychoir, Princeton, N.J. •
Page 98: Photo courtesy of John Bedford • Pages 104-105: Photo courtesy of Actor's Casting and
Talent Services • Page 117: Courtesy of Alberto Stévans • Page 166: Cedar Point photo by Dan Feicht
• Page 178: Photo courtesy of Michelle Rosen and Garold Gardner • Page 197: Photo courtesy of Stan
Barouh, the Troika Organization • Page 221: Photos by Eric Weber • Page 246: Photo of Michael Allen
by Eric Weber; photo of Jo Rowan by John Bedford.

Editor for Back Stage Books: Dale Ramsey
Book design: Cheryl Viker
Production manager: Ellen Greene

Library of Congress Cataloging-in-Publication Data
Allen, Michael, 1955-
   How to make it in musicals : the insider's guide to a career as a singer-dancer / Michael
Allen ; foreword by Donna McKechnie.
     p. cm.
   Includes bibliographical references and index.
   ISBN 0-8230-8815-4
   1. Music--Vocational guidance. 2. Dance--Vocational guidance. 3. Music
trade--Vocational guidance--United States. I. Title.

ML3795 .A737 1999
792.6'028'023--dc21   99-049420

Manufactured in the United States of America
1 2 3 4 5 6 / 04 03 02 01 00 99

CONTENTS

ACKNOWLEDGMENTS

I would first like to thank Jo Rowan for being my chief researcher and contributor. Her help was inspiring and invaluable. I also thank Michael C. Kronholm, my right-hand man, for giving form and focus to this book; Michelle DeLong for providing an incredible amount of information; and Michelle Womack for her persistence in getting this project started in the first place. I greatly appreciate the contribution of a Foreword to this book by the supremely talented Donna McKechnie.

How to Make It in Musicals could not have been realized without the interviews and support of the following performers, agents, managers, casting directors, and others who shared their experiences and knowledge, so that I could pass it on to all the young hopefuls and parents who read these pages: Scott Allegucci, Sharon Allyson, Maceo Anderson, Witt and Sharon Andrews, Rebecca Berstler, Wayne Bryan, Florence Birdwell, Mary Price Boday, Clarence Brooks, Kathy Carney, Christy Carson, Lewis R.Chambers, Irene and William Chapman, Christy Coachman, Jeff Corrick, Lyn Cramer, Robert Crowder, Pat Criscito, Debbi Dee, Nancy Derby, Matthew Dickens, Richard DiSarno, Harvey Evans, Rusty Frank, Garold Gardner, Al Gilbert, Kenneth Green, Rob Geers, Jim Halsey, Marcia Hendricks, Lisa Holtz, Kenneth Huber, Melba Huber, Geoffrey Johnson, Jan Johnson, Caryn Kocel, Kathryn V. Lamkey (AEA), Tracey Langram, Kathleen Mann, Amanda McTique, Lili Mori, Gail Nelson-Holgate, Bev Newcomb, Heather Olive, Gerald Otte (AGMA), Destin Owens, Ruben Permel, Jay Pouhe, Scott Prough, Ken Prescott, Ginger Prince, Gerard Purcell, Lee Roy Reams, Erin Robbins, Jamie Rocco, Murray Ross, Michelle Rosen, Martille Rowland, Don Risi, Jonathon Rummel, Kay Sandel, John Sawyer, Vickie Sheer, Joshua Siegal, Thomas Sinclair, Will Small, Michael Stansbery, Alberto Stévans, John Miller Stephany, Steven Stockdale, Ashley Stover, Melanie Stovall, Mary Ellen Stuart, Charlie Suggs, Katie Swan, Erin Swanson, Jerry Teske, Cullen Titmas, Kristin Tuder, Jack Tygett, Steve Unger, Michelle Van Doeren, Eric Weber, Marcel Wilson, Judy Wish, Brian Wolf, and members of the staffs at the Broadway Dance Center in New York, Steps Studio in New York, the Troika Organization, and Upstage Dancewear in Colorado Springs.

My thanks to you all!

Michael Allen
Colorado Springs, Colorado
September, 1999

FOREWORD

"It's called Show Business, not Show Art!" said Bob Avian, co-creator of *A Chorus Line*.

"New York is a city full of NOs! So when you get a job, save your money!" said Bob Fosse, the brilliant director and choreographer of stage and film shows such as *Sweet Charity* and *Chicago*.

"Don't go into this business! They will use you up, then discard you!" said Geraldine Fitzgerald, the great Irish actress of stage and film, speaking to students during a lecture series by performing artists at New York University. "But if you have to, then you have to," she concluded.

On the other hand, as Michael Bennett, Pulitzer Prize–winner and creator of *A Chorus Line,* put it: "Talent inspires me!"

I think of these quotes when I'm called upon to talk to students about choosing a career in musical theater. While it's very hard to give advice about a profession in which facing rejection daily is the norm and heartbreak is a given, I know that dreams do come true. Prayers can be answered, and great joy can be found in a life devoted to theater.

Of course, the best way to learn how to have a career in musical theater comes through firsthand experience. Lessons learned the hard way have staying power. But . . . wouldn't it be nice to save yourself some time, money, and certain grief by taking advantage of someone else's hard-earned experience?

This is why I admire and appreciate what Michael Allen has done in this book by compiling so much valuable information about "what it takes" to create a career in musical theater.

I don't believe there is a subject or category Michael misses. Whether you're a parent searching for the right training for your child, or a young hopeful in need of audition skills, there are great guidelines for you in this book. He even tells you how to negotiate a contract if you don't have an agent.

As I read through each chapter, I hear the voice of a teacher, scholar, performer, and big brother—in short, someone who is passionate and truly committed to the performing arts. He embodies the very qualities that create success in what is called "show business."

Thank you, Michael, for such a complete, up-to-date handbook for our theater library, bedside table, or that special place in our dance bag.

Donna McKechnie

Donna McKechnie won the 1975-76 Tony Award for her performance in the landmark hit musical A Chorus Line.

INTRODUCTION

Broadway bound! Is that you? Are you ready to make your way to New York City and prove yourself? Are you willing to take all the vocal, dance, and acting lessons you'll need to equip yourself for that big chance, when it finally comes along? Until then, are you prepared to endure the audition process, call after call? When I consider these questions, a story comes to mind, of a young girl just arriving in Manhattan, the obstacles she encounters, and her ultimate triumph on the Broadway stage. Many, many songs in countless shows and movies over the years have dramatized her struggles. Two of the most memorable are "I'm the Greatest Star," from *Funny Girl*, and "Some People," from *Gypsy*. As long as musical comedy has been around, there have been scripts written whose main theme has centered on stage life and the hardships involved in getting into show-biz, such as *A Chorus Line, Seesaw, My Sister Eileen, The Goodbye Girl, 42nd Street, The Jazz Singer*.

What is this fascination aspiring performers have with New York City? Why is it that, when you place young hopeful singer–dancers in a room and ask them about their goals, they will instantly say, "I want to be on Broadway"?

Well, why shouldn't they? Haven't *you* ever imagined walking down Broadway dreaming that it was your picture hanging in each theater lobby you passed? Haven't *you* imagined looking at the cast list of a Broadway play and seeing your name on the evening performance chart? Haven't *you* imagined entering the stage door of a Broadway theater and walking to the glorious place we call "backstage" to *your* dressing room and preparing for the matinee or evening performance? Haven't *you* imagined hearing the audience applauding after a performance—sounds that will echo in your mind and keep you connected, until the next performance, to what you love to do? For a performer these are the signs that mark your complete success in life, signs that say, "You did it . . . you made it!"

What allows this success to happen for one talented performer but not another? Is it being in the right place at the right time? Is it dreaming bigger than the next person? Is it never letting anything get in the way of your dreams, never letting anyone discourage you in any way? Never giving up?

The answer is "Yes!" . . . to each of these questions.

My favorite ride at Disney's Epcot Center is the "World of Imagination." As you enter your car and the ride gets underway, you are greeted by your host, who then takes you on this glorious adventure of imaginative exploration. The ride lasts a few minutes, and you don't even have to be an active participant. All you have to do is sit there, watch, and enjoy the ride as it takes you from the start of your journey to its successful finish.

Wouldn't it be great if life were an amusement park ride? If you could say, "I want to be on Broadway" and then simply get into a little car that would take you on a journey where all you had to do was experience the adventure? You could let everything happen without your active participation. Around the first corner, you could get your headshot taken. At the next corner, someone would write and design your resume, and on and on until, bingo, you were watching yourself audition for the Broadway show *Beauty and the Beast*—and, lo and behold, you found yourself a member of the cast.

Well, it's just not going to happen the way it does at Epcot. You are not going to be able to sit back and hope your success will just magically appear. You must become involved in planning for your success. You must read and ask questions about the path you want to take. You must learn as much as you can so your road doesn't turn into a maze where you become lost.

REALITY

First, let's consider the realities of the business. There are about 40,790 members of Actors' Equity Association (AEA; usually called Actors' Equity, or simply Equity). The average annual earnings of those members recorded in the 1997 *Equity Report* were only $13,967. The median annual earnings were $5,705. The median number of working chorus members per week were 1,209, and the median number of working principal performers per week were 3,024. What does this mean? Simply put: At any given time, about eighty-five percent of the performers who belong to Actors' Equity are unemployed, and most of those who are working earn at the poverty level. These figures do not take into account the fact that members of Equity may also be members of the Screen Actors Guild (SAG) or the American Federation of Television and Radio Artists (AFTRA) and finding paid work in commercials or movies. But the truth of the matter is that the employment and income statistics for SAG and AFTRA members are no better than they are for members of Equity.

When I was a kid, I wanted nothing more than to be a dancer. I lived, ate, and breathed my art. I thought about it all the time. The only thing I lacked was talent. I took my weekly lessons with some of the best known teachers in the business, only to watch their hair turning grayer by the week. I must have driven my teachers into other professions as they tried patiently to get me to stop tripping over my own feet as I danced. They shook their heads and wondered why this Jewish boy from Cleveland Heights, Ohio, kept coming back for more.

Well, on the positive side, those teachers never discouraged me. At the age of 19, I auditioned and was accepted for the United States International School of Performing and Visual Arts, in San Diego, California. I didn't get into that college based on my talent, though. I was accepted because the school had a need for male dancers. I guess they had to meet a quota!

In the first year I was at that school, I was put on a six-month probation: Either I worked hard and showed great improvement or I wouldn't be coming back for the next semester. Well, I did work hard and spent the next four years there—two years as a ballet major and two years as a musical theater major. In the first two years of college,

I quit tripping over my feet and developed some coordination, and by the third year, things started to come together. I was getting better. Teachers actually smiled when they gave me corrections, and their voices actually lowered an octave. Being able to attend this college meant so much to me, and just the fact that I received training in ballet, tap, jazz, and Spanish dance—as well as studying voice, acting, and just about everything else a performer could wish for—was icing on the cake. The teachers were terrific, and I wanted to stay there forever.

But eventually it was time to graduate and go off into the world of performing—to Las Vegas, to New York, to—well, to where? There were so many choices, so many decisions to make. But what did I know? I knew how to sing and dance. But what did I know of the business? For four years, I had spent my time in classes but never once did the school offer a class on the nuts and bolts of show business. But who cared? I had what it took to succeed, it seemed to me, and the performing world was going to open up its arms unconditionally to me, or so I thought.

So after college, I headed for Las Vegas, and for two years struggled to break into the business. But I was clueless about *how*. I had no knowledge of the trade papers. I had no idea what to wear to an audition or how to present myself in a marketable way.

One day, however, I happened to learn of an audition that was going to take place at the Sahara Hotel about thirty minutes after I heard about it. In my jeans and T-shirt, I rushed over to the hotel and tried out for the show. Because there was a shortage of men at the audition and we just had to perform piqué turns across the floor, and a time step, I got my first job. The show was a musical comedy called *The Great American Dream*, starring Dick Shawn. Boy, what a relief! I was finally in a show.

I thought this job would last forever. I had no idea I was supposed to be making contacts from that job to get more jobs. I had no idea that you should be nice to everyone in the cast and staff because this helps you obtain future work. When it came to knowing anything about the business, I was lost.

The years went on, and I continued to struggle. I found myself picking up work here and there, learning one lesson at a time . . . the hard way. I closed doors all over the place and was too embarrassed to approach people to ask for help. I wasted many years struggling unnecessarily!

BREAKING INTO THE BUSINESS

It's amazing to me that people who want to be a doctor or a nurse, an attorney or an accountant, have a plan already laid out for them from beginning to end: college or trade school, internship, certification, job hunting, and finally, job placement. The road has already been tested and proven over and over again. Yet if a young person chooses to be a dancer or a singer, an actress, a musician or anything else related to the performing arts, the procedure is vague. Few people know where to start, what to do, and what to avoid—and, curiously enough, little has been written about all this in a systematic way. The aim of this book is to change that.

Breaking into show business is a long and difficult process that requires specific kinds of knowledge and a lot of work. You can't just sit back and assume it's going to happen. Let me show you the way and give you some direction.

In preparing this book, I interviewed more than forty of the best-known and best-respected performers, agents, managers, and teachers in the business. With the insights they have provided, you will learn first-hand all the information you need to move toward and at last experience a long and successful career as a musical theater performer. Among the more important topics covered:

- How to pick the right dance, vocal, and acting teachers and methods of instruction
- How to manage your career and make yourself marketable so that show business "power people" take notice
- How to write an effective resume and have headshots photographed that hit will home
- When and how to join performers' unions
- What agents, managers, and casting directors do
- How to audition for a musical—the right *and* the wrong way

This book is for beginners and for those who are already on the road toward performing careers. And since the first steps toward such a career usually take place in childhood, it is also for parents whose kids want to be performers. I'll teach you how to take all the *next* steps, too—how to hone your skills and build your career working on cruise ships, in theme parks, in Las Vegas, and with touring companies—all the way to your first Broadway show.

By the way, my own career did finally take off. In Vegas, I met Maceo Anderson, one of the original Four Step Brothers and one of the greatest tap dancers of our time. He took me under his wing, and as a mentor and friend, showed me the performing "ropes." He introduced me to contacts and took me on stage with some of the biggest stars in show business. He gave me guidance and helped me develop my performing skills until they became exceptional. Today, as a performer, I tap dance and do a standup-comedy trick-roping cowboy act with orchestras and many other shows throughout the country. And Maceo, at 88 years old, is still there for me as my mentor and friend.

So dream big, and remember, it is more important to lead the life you wish to lead than to worry about being rich and famous. With these words, and the chapters that follow, we'll see you on Broadway!

1
Managing Your Road to Success

Walt Disney once said, "If you can dream it, you can do it." We all have dreams, don't we? "I want to be a movie star." "I want to be on the Broadway stage." "I want to be famous and have lots of money." "I want to co-star with Leonardo DeCaprio in his next film." Yet without a plan, without a map to guide you toward your ultimate destination, dreams alone won't bring success.

The truth is, most would-be performers—and even many performers who have taken the first steps and actually landed themselves jobs—never achieve their full potential because, as easy as it is to say you want something, it's much harder to act on those desires. A dream may seem unrealistic or unreachable, out of our league. We procrastinate, thinking we probably don't have the talent it takes to achieve what we want. We tend to think the ordinary rules of creating a career for ourselves don't apply to us—that talent is enough. But performers in one sense are simply self-employed business people, and like business people of all stripes have to devise a plan that makes them and their talents marketable. They have to develop their own success packages.

There have been hundreds—perhaps thousands—of self-help books published over the years for mainstream America teaching people how to shape their own destinies. Think of this book as a self-help manual aimed specifically at those interested in a career in musical theater. Think of it as a guidebook that will help you build and sustain a career that will last you a lifetime.

Have you ever walked around in a candy store, really paying attention to the vast selection? Candy by the pound, imported candy, cheap candy, expensive candy. Whatever you choose, whatever you have a craving for, you want the most for your money. Think of yourself as candy—not on a shelf, of course, but on a stage, where you'll be on display for the agents, clients, and production companies of the performing world. As with candy, the secret of being desirable as a performer is having the right combination of ingredients, so that someone will step up and say, "I want *you!*"

In this chapter we'll discuss basic career elements and the approaches that will help you to be taken seriously by agents, directors, and production people, and thus help you achieve your life's dream of being a success in musical theater. So first we take up the topic of goals.

GOALS

Your Super Goal
Get some paper and a pencil. I'll wait.

Now, at the top of the paper, write your goal. Not a short-term, interim goal, but the big one. For example, you might write, " I want to be a Broadway star." Or "I want to be a top fashion model on all the magazine covers." This is your super goal, the one you'll be working toward, your final destination. Then take the piece of paper and post it where you'll see it every day—on the wall in your bedroom or in your school notebook which you carry to class. Spend the next week thinking about what you wrote. Ask yourself the following questions: Is this what I really want? Will this make me happy? Is there anything else in the world I'd rather do? If I do want this, what will I have to do to get there? Do I have the talent it will take to achieve this goal? Do I have the will and the drive to go for it?

These are important questions. After a week of thinking about them, if you decide your super goal isn't right for you, get a new sheet of paper and start again. On the other hand, if you feel the goal *is* right for you, that that's the place you want to move toward, it's time for the next step.

Your Stepping Stone Goals

On that same piece of paper, I want you to write small goals, stepping stones to your super goal. Limit them to five, and make them realistic and achievable, steps you can attain within a year's time. Remember, if you set your sights too high for the little goals, you might become discouraged over your super goal.

Let's say you're age 15 and want to perform on Broadway someday. Your initial five stepping stones might be as follows:

1. Find good teachers for voice, dance, and acting lessons. Study weekly, taking at least one private lesson in voice, along with classes in ballet, jazz, and tap dancing and an acting class.
2. Go to a photographer for a professional headshot and put your resume together.
3. Get involved with a community, high school, or college theater in your area.
4. Subscribe to *Back Stage* magazine and read it regularly.
5. Read the rest of this book.

As you can see, all these goals are within your reach. When you reach age 16, you can decide on another five small steps . These might be:

1. Audition to work as a performer at a theme park during the summer. Whether you're selected or not, this will help you start familiarizing yourself with the audition process.
2. Read a book specializing in your craft.
3. Update your resume and make sure your headshot still looks like you. Don't forget, you're growing and changing physically. If you're looking different at age 16 than at age 15, have the photographer shoot another picture.
4. Prepare for professional auditions. Put together your dance bag (see Chapter 15) and practice singing a ballad and some up-tempo songs so you're ready to try out for any shows that may come your way.

5. Throughout the year, continue your involvement with community, high school, and college shows.

I think you get the idea. When you reach the age of 17, your annual goals may include researching colleges you'd like to attend because they offer degrees in musical theater. Just remember to take one step at a time, accomplishing specifically what you set out to do. If you find yourself ahead of schedule, completing your goals before the year is up, set five new goals. The point is, you have to work on your career every day. As David J. Schwartz, Ph.D., in his book, *The Magic of Thinking Big*, states: "The person determined to achieve maximum success learns the principle that progress is made one step at a time. A house is built a brick at a time. Every big accomplishment is a series of little accomplishments."

Telling People About Your Goal

Now that you've established your goal, know what you want to achieve, and have started working toward it on a daily basis, don't be afraid to tell people about it. Of course, other people may not approve of your decision and may not back you up, but you must believe in yourself enough to go for it anyway. You can't let someone else decide your future for you.

Ashley Stover, a prominent Los Angeles casting director, notes: "Although it is the toughest business to be in, show business is probably the most rewarding career one can have. Not only is it creative for the performer, but it gives others enjoyment as well. To have the ability to pull an audience into your world is the most wonderful experience."

I believe there is a flame in everyone lighting destiny's way. Performers are aware of it already in childhood. Sometimes it burns out by itself, but too often it is extinguished by the people closest to us. You must find in yourself the intensity to pursue your goal regardless of the response from others.

Why do others try to extinguish that flame? Are they jealous? Are they frustrated with their own lives? Are they too conventional to appreciate the ambitions of those unlike themselves?

Let's look at a couple of examples.

Susan's father owned a clothing business. It had been in the family for generations. When Susan let her parents know she wanted to be a singer, they sat her down and said, "Dear, you know we love you very much, but you're living in a fantasy world. Nobody makes a living in that profession. The success rate is so low as to not even exist, and we think you should do something more practical."

Carol's story was similar but more complicated. It was time for her to apply to college. She had been interested in theater since her first role in the musical *Peter Pan* when she was in eighth grade. She sang throughout middle school and high school, and at age 17, landed her first professional job, as a performer at a theme park. Calling a family meeting one evening, Carol had a heart-to-heart talk with her parents about her future. She eagerly told them about how excited she was about working in theater and how she wanted to continue. Her father listened as she spoke, but appeared irritable. At the end of Carol's presentation, when he himself spoke, she understood why. He began by telling her how proud he was of her, but he thought that this "theater thing" was just a phase, something she would eventually grow out of. When Carol told him again how much she loved it and wanted to pursue it in college, he let her know, sternly, that this "would not do." If he was going to financially support her education, he told her, she'd have to major in something different from theater. Otherwise, she would be on her own.

How many times have children approached older people they trust, describing their dreams and goals and what they feel is their calling in life, only to have their hopes crushed by the limiting assumptions passed down from one generation to the next? Do adults forget they were once young themselves, that they had their own dreams and goals? How many of them work at jobs they now hate, working day after day with no real enthusiasm for what they do? How many of them, when they are sitting in their recliners at home with the TV on, wonder "what if" about some dream they had and gave up on earlier in their own lives?

Why should anyone have to wonder "what if?" about their lives?

The reason for setting your super goal is to make clear to yourself the type of life that will make you happy. One of the biggest problems people can run up against is working day to day at a job they dislike, just to survive. Working to pay the mortgage and the car loan, they are actually fulfilling the boss's dream, not their own. Setting a super goal and going after it will help you avoid getting into a rut, finding yourself stuck in a miserable job and unable to break free. Life is too short and precious to waste in *that* way.

People may not agree with your goals, but you can't allow them to get away with putting down the very things you live for. When you hear that kind of criticism, do the following:

1. Listen to what the person has to say and thank them for their advice. But tell them you've thought about what you want to do and will be pursuing it with or without their support.

2. If the person cites a list of why you shouldn't pursue your goal, remind them that in no profession is success a sure thing, and it's better to do something you love than something other people think is "right" for you. Also, assure them that you've done your homework (like reading this book). Tell them you know the difficulties connected with achieving success in show business, but you also know how the business works and are willing to spend the energy it takes to succeed. (Note: Going into this career blindly is a very dangerous thing to do, so really *do* the homework you need to do to educate yourself about it fully.)

3. If parents threaten to cut their financial support, look for ways to fund your goals yourself. If you want a performing career badly enough, you'll find

those ways. You can always go to a voice, acting, or dance teacher and ask, "What can I do for you at your studio in return for lessons?" You might have to work your way through college. But take responsibility for your own ambitions. It always pays off in the long run.

As a child, Jennifer was a talented dancer. She was proficient in all the dance styles, had a wonderful singing voice, and was just beginning her acting training. She had a strong desire to be a musical comedy star, took her lessons seriously, and practiced fervently. Her teachers had no doubt she had what it took to succeed. Then about seven years into her training, she gradually withdrew from her studies. She quit her lessons altogether at age 17 and decided instead to become a kindergarten teacher.

What happened to Jennifer? The significant people in her life kept telling her, on a daily basis, that pursuing a musical theater career was difficult, unwise, and impractical. She heard this criticism so many times she came to believe it. Her spirit was broken. "I probably won't make it," she finally thought, and the flame of her ambition went out.

Don't let the basic need we all have for love from parents and other significant people in our lives destroy the momentum that keeps you moving toward your goals. The most important thing to realize is that you can't always expect support from others. You might have to develop a circle of friends who share your enthusiasm. If your parents, friends, or school counselors think you're crazy, so be it. You might have to develop a whole new circle of friends who share your enthusiasm. You have to find ways of continuing to believe in yourself and your ambitions.

SUCCESS FACTORS

There are several key requirements necessary to achieve success. These include personal traits like persistence, self-discipline, and a positive attitude. Other factors involve knowing how to manage stress, maintaining your health through good nutrition, developing a sense of timing, being able to network, and knowing how to make that imponderable quality called luck work for you.

Persistence

Webster's New Collegiate Dictionary defines the word "persist" as "to take a stand, to stand firm. To go on resolutely or stubbornly in spite of opposition or warning." Without persistence, you'll sink slowly into a morass of quicksand, unable to break free to continue your journey.

Chelsie had auditioned for seven shows. She had tried out for a variety of theme parks, cruise ships, and theaters, but had not landed one callback. Feeling discouraged, and wondering if she had the goods to succeed, she began to think of a career change. She lapsed into depression, beating up on herself because she didn't get any of the jobs she'd auditioned for. She'd recently been offered a full-time position in a clothing store and was considering accepting, knowing full well that it would limit the auditions she could attend in the future. In the end she turned down the job and forged ahead, continuing her acting and singing lessons and living on a meager amount of money while she kept going to auditions. The rejections were hard on her. She found living day to day increasingly difficult. But she was determined not to give up. Two months later, she landed a performing job in a nonunion bus-and-truck tour.

There is a lesson here on how to avoid defeat. If you think you're beaten, you *are* beaten. You'll encounter plenty of obstacles and rejections, but you have to keep going, picking yourself up after each negative experience and moving on to the next opportunity. You might lose a battle here and there, but you don't have to lose the war. By preparing yourself and continuing to move forward, you'll eventually reach your objective.

Chelsie could have taken that safe job, but it was more important for her to figure out why she wasn't getting any callbacks. Was it her headshot? Was she wearing the wrong kind of clothes to the auditions? Was she trying out for the wrong parts, or was she just not well prepared with her audition material? Chelsie had to learn from her setbacks and to turn them into victories.

David J. Schwartz, in *The Magic of Thinking Big*, recommends blending persistence with experimentation. "Stay with your goal but don't beat your head against a stone wall. Try new approaches. Experiment," he writes.

What Schwartz means by "experiment" is that, if something isn't working for you, find another path to take. "Someone trying to go through a locked door will never get to the other side no matter how many times he or she turns the handle. Find an open window instead."

Self-Discipline

A strong work ethic is essential to success. You have to be dedicated to your craft and strive for excellence. You must have the discipline to put in the time, the persistence to practice and improve, and the perseverance for the long haul. You must work to transcend the average. It's going to take a lot of time. A person who wants a career in musical theater but does not want to put in the time or effort required to succeed is indulging in a pipe dream with no chance of success.

Attitude

A positive attitude is one of the most important qualities you'll need for a successful career in the performing arts. Attitude reflects how you look at life. Where some people look for the bad side of everything, others look for the good. Attitude also has to do with how you treat people, which in turn affects your reputation. A good reputation will help your career enormously; it can even affect how long you live. People enjoy working with others who are pleasant to be around. Establish a good reputation, and they'll continue wanting to work with you.

A negative reputation, on the other hand, will cause you nothing but harm. If you are known as someone who is late all the time, who always causes problems, or who likes to gossip or bad-mouth people, you're not likely to be hired or sought for return engagements. Directors and producers want to avoid trouble and won't risk the friction you might bring to a show. An unhappy cast is much harder to work with, and troublemakers just aren't hired.

Michelle DeLong, a casting director, tells an anecdote that demonstrates how a bad attitude affects the way others perceive you. It's the story of a New York actress, a member of the Screen Actors Guild (SAG), who moved to Oklahoma. Michelle remembers:

I first spoke with this actress in January, after she had been referred to me. She lived in Tulsa and left a message on my voice mail. I returned her call, long distance, and spoke with her for about twenty minutes, at my expense, and offered some suggestions for marketing herself in the mid-southwest. I encouraged her to mail a headshot and resume directly to me, since she was listed with a Tulsa agent known for being a bit lax when it came to promoting talent.

In lieu of sending these items herself, she contacted her agent and asked him to forward them—ignoring my advice, and my goodwill. I never received either of them. And she lost out.

Then last week, a different agent in Tulsa contacted me about arranging a meeting with a new talent he was representing. He mentioned I'd spoken with this woman before. When he told me her name, I remembered the New York actress from earlier in the year. I set up another appointment, with instructions for her to confirm it the day before we were set to meet, since my life changes daily, depending on production schedules, and those changes have priority. I never received the confirmation call and had to make other plans. I even called her agent the day before our meeting and told him to remind her to call me, but she didn't.

She showed up at 10:40 A.M. for a 10:30 appointment which was never confirmed. I wasn't in the office, and my associate casting director, who works in the office full time, called to notify me of her arrival. I was expecting a couple of important calls at my home office before a scheduled 12:30 lunch engagement and had no intention of visiting the casting office until afterwards. Through my associate casting director, I offered to meet the actress at 2 P.M., when I would be in that office. But the actress asked if there was any way I could see her right then since she was already at the casting office. Once again I explained that I couldn't.

My casting associate called me back five minutes later, absolutely livid. Now, this is not someone who blows her top easily, but she was totally offended by what happened after I hung up. Apparently this New York City actress expressed her disgust with the whole situation—how rude and inconsiderate I was of her and her schedule—and treated my associate like she was nothing!

Now this associate is the very girl who pulls all the headshots, works with the talent agents daily, and frequently advises producers and directors as to which actor or actress might be better for one job than another. I usually come in just to direct the big auditions or meet with the big producers. In short, with her intolerable behavior, this actress bit the hand that may potentially have fed her. My associate's feelings about her were so strongly negative that she said, "I'd have a hard time recommending her for any job."

The moral of the story is never assume anyone is a little person and, even if they are, never underestimate the power of a bad impression. Even if my casting coordinator were a lowly receptionist, she still has my respect as an employee and, more importantly, my ear in terms of the stories she tells me about clients. A report from her regarding bad behavior carries a lot of weight. It works in reverse, too. I've had receptionists and assistants remark on "how nice" or "how pleasant" a talent behaves, and I've given those individuals a second look based on these positive plugs.

As a professional, it's your job to act professionally, presenting your credentials, being pleasant, and working as part of a team. Putting on a show is hard work. Consequently, directors and production people look for performers who are easy to work with, whose attitudes are upbeat and positive, and who don't bring any negativity with them into the theater.

Everyone who worked in the original cast of *Song and Dance*, on Broadway, said that Bernadette Peters was a thoughtful and generous person who was always considerate of others. She used her position as a star to create an environment the rest of the cast enjoyed being a part of. They all admired her, and her consideration of others created a sense of family among the cast members.

Because producers have an ever-increasing range of talent to choose from, they simply won't tolerate people who are difficult to get along with. Always aim to leave a show with a good reputation, where people say, "I'm glad I worked with that person."

Stress

The performing arts business is filled with stress, and you'll have to learn how to deal with it. At times you may not have enough money to pay the bills or to live comfortably. You may find yourself being rejected at one audition after another, having to learn a new role in an impossibly short period of time, or not knowing where your next job is coming from. No kidding, it can be rough.

The following anecdote dramatically demonstrates a stressful entrance into the world of professional theater, from an actual cast member of a touring production of the musical *West Side Story*. The person to whom it happened we'll call Megan.

Megan was fortunate enough to land the role of Maria. But during rehearsals, she found herself having problems with her asthma after one of the musical numbers because of the demands of the new role. She used an inhaler to get through it, which, unbeknownst to her, caused upper gastrointestinal irritation. This, in turn, caused acid reflux problems after eating. She assumed this physical chain reaction was stress-related, which is only natural. But the continued use of the inhaler and the recurring stomach acid problems caused her vocal chords to go. Between the inhaler dehydration, the stomach problems, and the rigorous demands of the show itself, Megan's body was damaged.

Assuming she had strained her voice, Megan checked in with a vocal coach. Of course, the problem didn't lie there. Finally, after losing her voice for three days, she went to a doctor, who determined that using the inhaler was at the root of all the problems.

By this point, Megan had risked permanent damage to her voice. Stressed beyond belief at her failing health, she had an important decision to make. Making a brave move, she went on medical leave to rest and to allow her vocal chords to heal. She wanted to get her asthma under control by less radical means. Did she lose her job in *West Side Story*? Did this hurt her career? Surprisingly, the production company worked with her, and Megan rejoined the cast two weeks before they left Los Angeles to start the tour.

This story illustrates only one of the many stress factors that are a natural part of the business, and you'll need to develop coping mechanisms. If you don't learn to roll with the punches, you will be constantly stressed out, sick, irritable, and hard to work with.

Health and Nutrition

You have to stay healthy in this business and to treat your body as a temple. You're going to have to dance, sing, and act with it as long as possible, so staying physically well is more important for performers than for those in most other professions. You don't want to get voice nodes, sprain your ankles, or catch colds. You shouldn't share food with just anyone or hang around people who are sneezing and coughing. If you have to be around someone who is ill, make sure to wash your hands after any contact with the person. And you can't be a perpetual night owl, staying out all night. It will definitely affect your ability to train and perform.

You shouldn't smoke, drink, or take drugs of any kind. With all the information available about the damage they do to the body, why would you want to do any of them anyway? Some people smoke to keep off weight, but intelligent eating to keep fit is by far the better choice.

You have to take care of your voice and your body with healthy eating, so learn to make the correct dietary choices. You shouldn't settle for eating smart just eighty percent of the time; aim for one hundred percent. Of course, you may fall off the wagon every now and then, but you just need to get back on as quickly as possible. Remember, food is fuel for your body, so you'll have to be strict about what you put in your mouth.

You'll also be setting yourself up for disastrous results if you rely on gum or starvation dieting to maintain your weight. Chewing gum may seem like an innocent enough habit. But it's a nonfood and a heavy sugar hit. When you chew gum, your stomach begins to contract because it thinks food is on the way, even though nothing actually goes into the stomach. People who chew gum constantly think about food, because they are ingesting sugar all day. They'd be better off, instead, going cold turkey and quitting. Ironically, when people rely on the gum routine to remain thin, they begin to develop muscles near their ears. You can see that certain kids are hooked on gum by their enlarged chewing muscles.

Going on starvation diets is also bad for your health and fitness. It changes your metabolism. The body shuts down as it tells itself to conserve energy. So instead of losing weight, your body conserves calories, and when you start eating again, you tend to gain weight. Unfortunately, this leads many people into "yo-yo" dieting, where eating too much food or avoiding it altogether becomes an all-consuming lifestyle.

Simply put, you should never use gum or go on starvation diets to lose a few pounds. Doing so will deplete your energy and eventually affect how you perform on stage.

Timing, Networking, and Luck

I would like to tell you that the road to stardom is based one hundred percent on talent, but that wouldn't be honest. Certainly, talent is required, but it's not the most important element. What really makes success happen is timing and networking—being in the right place at the right time. With the millions of talented people out there, have you ever wondered why there are so few stars? First off, there's only a need for so many stars. Second, most people don't have the qualities necessary for stardom—the dedication, commitment, desire, or any of the other attributes we've discussed in this chapter. If you lack those qualities, and your timing in being at the right place at the right time is off as well, it's not likely that anything will happen with your career.

Jamie, an actress from Colorado, was attending the University of Southern California (USC) when the Los Angeles auditions were scheduled to begin for the national touring company of the musical *Grease*. She was an acting student with ten years of experience in voice and dance, but without an agent or union affiliation. She mailed in her headshot and resume to the casting director but heard nothing.

Her father was acquainted with a screen writing instructor from USC, so he e-mailed the teacher, seeking advice. As luck would have it, the teacher knew the casting director fairly well, and was able to arranged an appointment for Jamie. She was given the opportunity to audition along with the agent-represented, nonunion performers.

Jamie auditioned, and, because the producers liked her, made it through two levels of callbacks. Now she had to audition a third time, this time for the director. When she showed up, all the producers were assembled, but one of them was on the phone. The director asked her if she wouldn't mind waiting outside until they were done conducting business. He said he would call her when they were through.

Once Jamie was out of the room, the director turned to the producers and said, "Look guys, I know you like this girl for the part of Sandy and I'm sure she's talented, but she's not the right type. Let's not waste her time or ours." The casting director asked the director if, as a personal favor to him, he would audition her anyway. She had come this far and prepared herself according to the producer's request. The director nodded okay but went back to writing on his note pad.

Jamie came in and auditioned her prepared selection, and, lo and behold, the director stopped what he was doing and looked up. "Well, we have our Sandy," he said to the producers.

It is important to point out that Jamie had the talent required for the job. But it was ultimately the networking, the timing, and being in the right place at the right time that got her the job.

And what about luck? Is there good luck and bad luck? I think luck is really preparation meeting opportunity. It isn't simply handed to you. Instead, by taking all the steps we've discussed and sticking to them, you can reap good fortune.

Coming out ahead of someone else in an audition or in any competitive situation has little to do with luck. It has everything to do with being well prepared and well qualified. It has to do with working harder than your competition. Dr. Schwartz writes in *The Magic of Thinking Big*: "When someone has 'good luck,' you'll find not luck, but preparation, planning, and success-producing thinking preceded his good fortune." When good fortune does come your way, it's probably because you worked for it, using self-discipline and persistence in pursuit of a concrete goal.

BECOMING A TRIPLE THREAT

In order to survive in musical theater for any length of time, you're going to have to become what is known as a "triple threat." If you really want to reach the heights this business has to offer, you'll have to learn to sing, dance, and act. Not just competently but superbly, learning everything you can about each of them, in as many different styles as possible. That's the only road to long-term success.

Most people starting out don't believe being a triple threat is important. They think they can concentrate in one category or another. But they're really shortchanging themselves. The truth is, in any market, but especially in New York, you have to be equally adept at all three areas of singing, dancing, and acting to achieve success. You also need to know something about acrobatics, ballroom dancing, modern dance, and musical theater dance, as well as specialty dancing like folk, flamenco, African, and other ethnic styles. If you neglect your development, directors will simply see you as a dancer who can't speak, a singer who can't dance, or an actor who can't do anything else. You'll be limited in the business, and your career may be over before it even gets started.

I'm not saying it's impossible to get cast in a Broadway show if you're just a one- or two-talent performer. Obviously, it depends on the show. But, as in all things, it's best to be prepared and, if you want longevity as a performer, you'll have to train in all three areas. Otherwise, you may find yourself singing in the same musical, as a member of the chorus, for nine years. Being well rounded as a performer will generate more work, create more opportunities, and help you achieve better financial security.

In conclusion, setting goals, strengthening your success factors, building your network of contacts, and putting together a good package of skills at the beginning of your career will ensure your chance of succeeding in an overcrowded market, where thousands of young people are pursuing the same goals. And once your career is off and running, all these skills will give it longevity. If you have what it takes, don't settle for less than your best. Take your talents to the limit. You owe it to yourself and your ambitions!

2
VOCAL TRAINING

ave you ever rented a video, something special for your family? Everyone piles in the car and off you go. Walking into the video store, you're faced with what seems an impossible choice. Everything from action movies to romances, science fiction to classics, animated features to documentaries is available. New releases add to the dilemma. Scanning the shelves, you spot one that looks like a possibility. Turning it over in your hands, you read the front and back covers. Who's in it? Is the plot interesting? Is it suitable for everyone in the family to watch? So far so good, but there's one final hurdle to be cleared. You ask for the others' approval. If it's "yes," you take your selection to the counter, present your rental card, and head home. If it's "no," you start again, going up one aisle and down another. Finally, after thirty minutes, everyone agrees on something. At this point, you just hope the cassette doesn't jam in your videotape player.

How come we are willing to make such an effort to rent a video for $3, yet are so casual about finding a voice teacher? I've often asked parents and performers how they found an instructor, and the answers ranged from picking the teacher with the biggest ad in the Yellow Pages, to saying, "Eenie meenie minie mo," to picking an instructor based on location. The closer the teacher is to where you live the better, right? *Wrong!* A career is at stake here, and deserves more consideration than renting an action film.

Everyone loves to sing. We sing in the shower, we sing in our car as we drive around, we sing babies to sleep. Singing can stimulate us and express the joy in our lives. It can also comfort us and lift our spirits when things aren't going so well.

How many times have you seen *Fiddler on the Roof* just to hear Tevye sing "If I Were a Rich Man" one more time, or *Les Misérables* to hear little Cossette, with her bucket and broom, stir your soul with "Castle in the Clouds"? Whether it's happy or sad, emotion expressed through song captures us, transporting us to a different time and place.

Remember Kristine in *A Chorus Line*, how depressed she was because she really couldn't sing? We felt her anguish as she confessed her lack of talent, while at the same time admiring her will to try. In *Peter Pan*, instead of singing, Peter crows about how clever he is, delighting us with his smug self-confidence. In *The Roar of the Greasepaint, the Smell of the Crowd*, Cocky's dream girl appears before him as he confesses his feelings in "My First Love Song." Rising above his insecurities, he pours his heart out and breaks our own. And who could ever forget the Glee Club rehearsal in *You're a Good Man, Charlie Brown*, when Lucy, all the way through "Home on the Range," demands her pencil back from Linus? Everyone becomes angry and, one by one, walks off the stage. Only poor Schroeder, the lonely conductor, remains while Snoopy howls and blows him a kiss.

Funny or poignant, we embrace these moments and make them part of our lives.

How do you go about finding a good vocal teacher? Where do you begin? What should you look—and look *out*—for? If you don't have any experience in this field, if you know more about the dark side of the moon than about a singing career, you're not alone. You may not even know what questions to ask, much less where to get the answers. In this chapter, we'll address those concerns.

Professional voice training usually starts in childhood, long before the person interested in a singing career is able to make informed choices for himself or herself. So this chapter is addressed largely to parents, who will be making the decisions early on.

STARTING OUT

Say the young person is eight years old and has an obvious vocal gift, something beyond the ordinary. You're anxious to enroll her or him in some kind of program. Now what? My first advice is to relax. Everything depends on having a cool head, as you will be making very important, long-term decisions. Let's start with some specific questions:

1. Should the student take private voice lessons, or become a member of a non-school choral group?
2. Should he or she be involved in school programs or in community theater?
3. Should he or she take piano lessons prior to voice lessons?
4. How much will private lessons cost?
5. Should you go back to bed, hoping all these issues are nothing more than a bad dream?

It can all seem overwhelming at first. There is, however, a clear and logical approach to finding vocal training.

First, a note on cost. You've heard the cliché "You get what you pay for." In the vocal world, this is certainly true, and it boils down to this: In New York City and Los Angeles, private vocal lessons can run as high as $60 to $300 a lesson. Outside major metropolitan areas, they are considerably cheaper—$15 to $60 per lesson—but they still cost. While a good teacher won't overcharge for lessons, training for a vocal career doesn't come cheap. But then, neither does anything worthwhile in life.

THE FOUNDATION YEARS: AGES 8 TO 13

Private Lessons

It is critical that kids from 8 to 13 years old get the best voice evaluation and training possible. Otherwise, they can be ruined vocally for the rest of their lives.

It's best to begin with a voice evaluation. Only a highly skilled, properly trained voice teacher has the credentials to do this. Be advised that anyone with a year or two of vocal training can hang out a sign claiming to be a voice teacher. So take care to find the best instructor you can. Start by calling the musical organizations in your town, or ask any friends and acquaintances involved in the music scene. You might check local music stores to see if they have a list of teachers. Or call the local symphony orchestra, high school music teachers, or nearby colleges that have music programs and can offer sound advice. Keep your eyes and ears open to find out where others in your town are taking voice lessons.

Once you have gathered the names of instructors, notice if any appear more often than others, or if any come especially recommended. Make appointments with the top two or three individuals.

You're going to a vocal teacher for the young student to learn techniques for using his or her voice in a healthy manner. Early testing is important, as children have a tendency to imitate other artists, whether rock 'n' roll, country and western, or pop. Through imitation, they can pick up bad vocal habits, something you really don't want them to continue. Jerry Teske, an expert on the child's voice, says, "Muscle memory is the strongest memory we have. Once learned early on, it's set in cement." A good voice teacher can assess a singer's vocal direction and determine the type of training needed.

If the young singer is developing bad habits, he or she needs the guidance a teacher can provide. On the other hand, if he or she is singing naturally and without bad habits, there is no reason to start private voice training so early. To keep on the safe side and avoid the development of bad habits, the singer should be checked out every six months to a year by a reputable teacher. And he or she can be allowed to gain some vocal training simply by singing in a school choir or stage production, or in a nonschool choral group.

I'm aware that some people think private training as early as possible is the only way to go. Your impulse may be to follow that course. No matter at what age you decide the singer should pursue private lessons, though, the issues involved in finding the best vocal teacher remain the same, so we turn to those now.

The Interview I first recommend that, in arranging for private voice lessons, you interview all the potential teachers. There's nothing worse than a teacher who doesn't really like to teach—and, believe me, they're out there. They can be cranky and hard to get along with, raising their own voices, attempting to dominate their students, and disregarding others' right to ask questions. But you have every right to thoroughly understand a teacher's regimen and how it can affect the student, and the student has every right to study with a teacher he or she likes and feels comfortable with.

If you notice a teacher doesn't relate well with kids or, worse yet, doesn't like them, get away as fast as you can. Teachers should be enthusiastic about their work. It should be a calling that energizes them and, consequently, their pupils. A love for their profession and the skill to carry it out are perhaps the most important factors to consider when making your choice.

Never sign on with the first teacher you interview. Interview several before committing. Make sure they are familiar with the age range of the given student and his or her vocal needs. Teachers have different training approaches, and what works with one student may not work with another. Implementing advanced techniques before the student is ready can be difficult and dangerous to the development of his or her voice. It can also kill motivation.

You will be asking some basic questions at the initial interview. Some of them involve what a parent and the young singer can expect from the teacher—the types of materials used to teach and whether parents can observe the lessons—but you also need to find out what the teacher will expect from the parent and the student in terms of practice time each week, studio policy regarding cancellations, and billing payment dates. Ask these questions up front. You'll sense if something isn't right.

Parents, once they have selected a teacher and feel comfortable with the choice, should ask him or her if they can attend a few lessons as a quiet observer. Most good vocal instructors will welcome parents to the studio to observe. They appreciate the family involvement, knowing that their professionalism can rub off on the parent and help guide students in taking care of their voices and practicing at home. If, however, the teacher doesn't allow this, or if at any time you feel that things aren't going right, don't hesitate to look for someone else. It's your money.

Parents should also realize that one of their main responsibilities is taking the student to the voice lessons, and that in itself involves some issues. This is an exciting time for the young singer, so the transportation time shouldn't be treated as a nuisance. The student's morale, along with his or her training, could suffer if parents are not supportive. Be energetic and upbeat about this important time and make getting to the lessons as pleasant as possible. Make sure not to argue in the car. If you upset a student just before a lesson, the time in the studio is sure to be wasted.

What to Look for in Results First of all, realize that vocal development takes time. If you expect some kind of overnight miracle, be prepared for disappointment. The student's voice took a while to get where it is. It'll take a while longer to get where it should be.

There are, however, good and bad signs to watch out for in observing lessons. Most parents aren't familiar with vocal technique, so I offer them some specific signs here.

One of the best involves tension versus relaxation. As you observe a lesson, is the teacher asking the student to do anything that causes tension? Is his or her body shaking? Is his or her jaw shaking or protruding? Does the teacher tell the student to make funny faces, or to holler when singing? Does the teacher ask for a vibrato or tell the student to tilt his or her head or lift the chin to reach high notes? Is there any tension visible around the student's throat, or audible in the sound produced? William Chapman, of the national touring production of *Sunset Boulevard*, says, "Any abnormal physical attitude in singing is going to be wrong." He also points out that if there is too great an emphasis on breath control, or any extensive physical control at all, it is counterproductive and can immobilize a singer. Actors don't act with physical restrictions, so why would singers sing with them?

If the student returns from a lesson with a hoarse, scratchy, or fatigued voice, something is definitely wrong. You might want to start looking for another teacher. The goal at this stage of voice training is to build good technique and develop stable singing habits with no forcing of tone or physical constrictions.

Another sign involves body alignment, or posture. Vocal lessons concentrate on voice production, or how sound is produced. Good sound production means good posture. Rounded shoulders and bad posture can cause voice problems, and good vocal teachers will address these problems early on.

Teachers should also work with students on relaxed breath management, pure vowel delineation, and intonation (singing on pitch). Students should learn how their vocal chords work. For example, what happens physically when you sing a high note versus a low note? Most people don't know the physiology involved, and the vocal teacher should provide a simple overview that is both enlightening and fun for the student to learn.

At this point students should also learn about the tongue, one of the largest muscles in the body, and often a big problem for singers. It gets quite a workout throughout life. It enables you to speak, chew, and swallow, and helps to prevent choking. As a result it becomes very strong. While you can see the tip of your tongue, you can't see most of its base, which reaches all the way back into the throat. But the base of the tongue is where much of the problem lies for singers in terms of developing good technique. Voice teachers try to teach students to manage the front of their tongues so the back doesn't get too tight. Since you can't actually see the back of your tongue, you can't see it tense up visually. So voice teachers also help students learn how to perceive or sense tension at the back of their tongues and alleviate it without visual aids. It's not an easy lesson to learn.

Pushing a young voice to extremes can cause permanent damage. Voice teachers remind us of this over and over. So at this stage of development, it is well to remember that no development of interpretation or singing style is necessary, or even desirable, unless the student is working in professional theater. The goal of voice instruction at this point should be simply learning *how* to sing—and that means learning how to sing *properly*. Technique and interpretation are two separate things, and technique must precede interpretation. As Laura Browning Henderson notes in her book *How to Train a Singer*, without technique there is no interpretation. It is vital that young vocalists learn how to sing, not how to overinterpret. A good teacher won't let interpretation become their students' technique.

Another sign of good teaching involves repertoire. It is important that the songs students learn be appropriate in terms of singing difficulty to the developmental level of their voices. Kids' voices should not be forced to adapt to something too strenuous for them to sing. Nevertheless, learning to perform in a variety of styles helps expand and extend one's vocal ability, and in today's musical singing market, where an incredible number of people are vying for the jobs available, versatility is a great asset. A young student's voice is best served by singing church music, folk songs,

Groups like Kids to Go offer young performers a high-energy musical theater experience along with training in voice, acting, and dance performance techniques. Based in Colorado Springs and under the direction of Michael Allen and Krista Reynolds, Kids to Go has a repertoire that includes Broadway, country & western, and other styles.

Broadway tunes, and jazz standards. Some Broadway shows like *Les Misérables, Jekyll and Hyde*, and *Phantom of the Opera* feature highly trained singers with extensive vocal training. So by all means get the best voice training possible, and concentrate on versatility. But at the start, learn the basics.

To sum up: Young people 8 to 13 years old should not be "cutting loose" or being reckless with their voices. Nor should they attempt to make grand vocal statements. Lessons at this age should be no more than thirty to forty-five minutes long, once a week. (Once children reach the age range of 14 to 18, one-hour lessons twice a week are acceptable.) And while teachers can help them work through small voice problems and teach them the basics of singing technique, they can't begin to train any voice as an adult instrument until there is enough physical development. Generally, this means after puberty.

Degree of Parental Involvement Again, parents need to get involved in their children's vocal lessons, but they must allow the teacher the necessary space to teach. The following incident illustrates an important point regarding teacher/parent responsibilities. Once, during a high school production of 42nd Street, I had scheduled a specific rehearsal time in order to choreograph a musical number, and a handful of students took issue with it. Instead of bringing the problem to my attention and discussing it with me, they went directly to the principal, and some went so far as to have their parents call the principal's office with complaints. Consequently, I had to come in and explain the situation. I did so and was able to proceed according to my original plan, thanks to the principal's support.

The point is that parents can be *too* involved in the day-to-day operation of schools, and in how their kids are taught. (If a young person managed to get into a prestigious university, such as Harvard or Stanford, what parent would argue about the curriculum?) This can also happen with vocal lessons. Parents have the right to ask questions, but if they constantly *interfere* with phone calls or complaints, they may poison the student–teacher relationship. The student may lose respect for the teacher, and in turn the teacher may no longer want to instruct the student because he or she doesn't want to put up with the demands of the parent. Surprisingly, this happens more often than you might think.

Nonschool Choral Groups

If private voice lessons aren't for you, perhaps you should look at a nonschool choral group. There are many of them in major cities around the country. Examples are the Denver Children's Chorale, the Minnesota Children's Choir, and the American Boychoir. Smaller cities have these groups as well—for example, the Colorado Springs Children's Chorale and the Tucson Boys Choir. They can be a rewarding experience for the youngster who wants to sing for fun, as well as for the one who wants a professional singing career. Even if you decide on private voice lessons for the young singer, choral singing can complement them well. Let's turn to a discussion of the pros and cons of choral groups.

Understanding the Basics Whether a children's chorale is in a big city or a small town, there are common attributes as well as differences. Some are for-profit, while others are nonprofit. Some involve a board of directors made up of prominent individuals from the community, while others have boards made up of parents of the participating children. Some have both kinds of boards. Some organizations have as many as five groups, for kids of the ages 8 to 18, while others have only one group encompassing all age ranges. One chorale may have different directors or conductors for each group, while another may share the same director for all of them. Accompanists are usually available for rehearsals, while if dancing is involved, choreographers may or may not be on staff. The type of music sung can range from classical to Broadway to pop. And costs vary from $35 a year to $100 a month. Finally, most choirs require auditions before children are allowed to participate.

It is important for parents to ask the following questions before their child joins such a choral group:

* What is the monthly tuition?
* Who is on the staff?
* When are rehearsals?
* Does the new member need previous choral experience or voice lessons prior to auditioning?
* What are the parents' responsibilities? What are the children's?
* Will it be necessary to purchase a performance outfit?
* What are the consequences of a missed performance?
* What is an acceptable excused absence, and what is not?
* Are there activities that may conflict with school time?
* Will the chorus be the sole activity members can participate in, or are outside activities encouraged (are they allowed to participate in school sports activities, for example)?
* Are the singers required to participate in any fundraising events? Are parents obligated to make up monetary differences if a sales quota is not met?
* How many tickets are parents required to sell for special performances?
* Are there other financial obligations that parents should be aware of?
* What commitments must parents make as volunteers?

If parents don't ask these questions, they won't know exactly what kinds of demands being part of the choral group will place on both themselves and their kids, and this could cause unanticipated problems. Make the effort to find out the answers and protect yourself from those problems.

Some parents would like to see their kids involved in choral activities, yet don't want much involvement themselves. Others may want to participate to the fullest extent possible—for example, helping out by taking kids from visiting choirs as overnight guests, acting as counselors at choral camps, serving as monitors at rehearsals, distributing newsletters, or doing general office work for the organization. There are countless ways parents can help the choruses. Hopefully, these activities will be spelled out by the organizations in written form. Yet they aren't always, so the bottom line is . . . *ask.*

Breakdown of Children's Chorales A children's chorale may be divided into as many as four groups. The first one, for beginners, teaches young people to sing in tune and how to hold on to a part. They begin by singing in unison, and by the middle of the year progress to two-part music. Singing two-part can be difficult and confusing for young beginners, so be aware that they will progress at their own speed.

Members of the second group will have better music reading skills. The singers will be able to hold a part better and the group will always sing two-part. The director will be able to specify any given starting point in the music, and the singers will be able to find it. For example, they will be able to follow instructions like "You are on page five, first measure, first quarter note" without difficulty.

The third, or "concert" group, will be able to sing in three and four parts, using mixed meters and advanced harmonic structure. Their repertoire will include everything from classical to popular to show music, as well as choreography. They will continue to work on vocal production, with minimal emphasis on making a "full sound" (i.e., a sound that can fill an auditorium or concert hall), and will focus on being a polished children's choir.

The fourth group will sing in three and four parts and concentrate on making a full sound. This group will work with symphonies and operas, and appear at other high profile events. It comprises the recording group and touring choir.

What to Expect from the Director A choral director's primary responsibility is to ensure the vocal health of the members of the choir. He (or she) must encourage good singing habits, teaching proper voice production so that each student learns how to achieve the right vocal sound. The director also must work at instilling feelings of solidarity and teamwork in the members of the chorus. This is a good lesson for kids to learn and will benefit them throughout their professional lives.

Being in a choral group teaches young singers skills not addressed in private voice lessons. Among the most important of these is singing harmony, which is very important in developing versatility. In musical shows, performers don't always sing the melodic line. They need to know how to sing harmony, independent of what the other cast members are singing. Choral singing helps develop this skill.

Other skills *can* be taught in private lessons but can just as easily be addressed in a choral setting, including ear training, basic sight reading, music theory, rhythm, and understanding scale structure. All these are important ingredients for a successful career in musical theater.

It is vital that parents monitor their children's reactions to choral work. If young singers show signs of feeling discouraged, it may mean the group is too advanced for their age or abilities. Don't try rushing a kid to the top level; it may lead to him or her wanting to drop out of singing lessons altogether. Developing voice skills takes time.

Discipline Remember in the musical *Oliver* when the title character comes to the headmaster asking for more food, or in *A Christmas Carol* when Bob Cratchit asks Mr. Scrooge for Christmas off so he can be with his family? The icy stares of the headmaster and Scrooge let Oliver and Cratchit know they're in for trouble. You will find that, organizationally speaking, children's choral groups run the gamut from being headed by severe taskmasters who run their choirs with iron hands to being run in such a disorganized manner that virtually nothing gets done.

Parents must decide what level of discipline they want for their children. But discipline, tempered with encouragement and support, is a far more effective way of getting young people to do what is asked of them than either harsh discipline or no discipline at all. In choir directors, look for someone who knows how to offer a challenge. But also look for someone with a sense of humor and the ability to establish a comfortable, upbeat environment. Being positive is always more desirable and effective in teaching than being negative. Imagine rehearsing with a tyrant for two hours. The choir might get the desired sound eventually, but it will most likely lack any real enthusiasm or joy. How long before the young singer comes home, his or her spirit crushed?

Chorales are not the place for untested psychological experimentation. Avoid directors and instructors who see their students as test specimens for their pet theories about teaching or music. Children studying voice do not need "head trips" laid on them. Directors who show humor, flexibility, and honesty toward their students, and who allow occasional downtime during rehearsals, will produce young singers who look forward to rehearsals!

The American Boychoir, under the direction of James Litton, offers formal training in choral music. It is the country's premier children's chorale.

The Other Side of Choral Training I asked Irene Chapman, a prominent voice teacher: "If your child wanted a career in live stage, with the ultimate goal of being on Broadway, would you recommend they be in a choral group?" She answered as follows:

> *If children really show promise as soloists, they would do better if their parents put them in children's theater or in a musical theater group. They will be able to use their voices in a stronger way than if they were just in a chorale. Remember, in a chorale, they have to keep their voices blended. They are not going to utilize the strength of their voices or learn to lean on that strength.*
>
> *I am not against choral groups. I like to hear them if they are good. But if you are looking at being a soloist or a professional performer, that isn't the route to necessarily stay with.*

Opera singer Martille Rowland reflected on this question and told me:

> *If the student is really interested in a solo career as a performer, maybe chorale training isn't the right place to be. If you hide in a group, you can never get used to being in front of a group. Being in a group can be exciting and build confidence in your musical skills and all that, but you'll never get over the fear of performing until you are out on your own as a soloist.*
>
> *Group singing may be done in school programs, theater groups for children, and community theater, where there are parts for them. That, I think, strengthens the performer's confidence. I would never advise anyone to go to a choral setting for voice training. That's just not going to happen. The group is geared for the whole group sound, not the individual sound, and no performer is going to get vocally trained in a choral group. They can have fun, and they can have a great musical experience, but they won't receive vocal training. Often, they will receive vocal restriction, which itself is training in the negative sense.*

Finally, Jerry Teske commented on the differences in choral directors:

> *Some voice scholars think that choral directors have a direct effect on ruining solo voices, because they make certain demands on the singers that restrict them a bit. This is one of the things about choirs, I suppose, that poses some problems to solo singing. If you are a soloist, you stick out in a choir—so what do you wind up doing with that loud voice? You will always have to sing softly, and may feel repressed. The director says, "Softer, softer, blend, blend, blend, balance." So you have to pull back and not sing any louder than the person next to you. This can create bad habits. I think the way to ruin your voice is to develop restrictive habits that you cannot break.*
>
> *However, there are choral directors . . . who allow the singers to relax their voice production and sing with a natural vibrato [with] good vowel delineation, proper posture, and efficient breath management. Singing with this approach can enhance a singer's ability and allow for positive growth.*

As you can see, the choral experience can be a positive learning tool for kids, but it can inhibit the solo voice. The parent of a young singer should observe closely to ensure he or she isn't singing in an unhealthy way, and to find out what approach a prospective choir director has before the student joins the choir. As I said earlier, the student should be checked out every six months by a knowledgeable voice teacher, and if he or she is developing bad habits, choral training should be halted.

AGES 14 TO 18

If the young singer is beginning voice lessons at the age of 14 to 18, the material earlier in this chapter on finding a good teacher is just as relevant as it is for younger children. But for teens—even if they have gone through training at an earlier age—there are additional points to consider. And the most important of these have to do with the physical changes children go through during adolescence.

Around the age of 14, of course, boys enter puberty and their voices change dramatically, dropping at least an octave. This means they go from singing in a high register to a lower one. Before puberty, the voices of boys are alto or soprano, and they often sing confidently and well. During puberty, however, most boys lose control of their voices, which may crack and vary in pitch as their register changes. They may want to sing but, due to the loss of control over their voices, be afraid to.

If lessons are continued through this stage, the teacher must be careful not to require anything that causes tension or discomfort in the boy's throat. If the lessons are discontinued until the boy's voice has settled, on the other hand, the teacher will have to find the boy's new register when lessons resume. This will probably not be easy. Most boys will barely be able to match pitch, having only four or five notes they can sing. The teacher, and the student, will have to be patient, developing this new instrument slowly.

A girl's voice doesn't tend to fluctuate as much during puberty, but there are usually some changes. Between the ages of 12 and 16, young women add more substance to their tone, and develop a stronger and thicker sound. Girls' voices begin to mature during these years, but unlike the boys, girls can continue voice training without much of a problem.

Remember the goals of the voice lessons children take during the foundation years from ages 8 to 13? The idea was to be a kid, have fun, sing out, and feel free. The only real warning was to avoid developing bad vocal habits. Think of ages 14 to 18 as a period of "starting over." The adult voice is just being born, and training that instrument now begins in earnest.

Voices, like bodies, change very quickly between the ages of 14 and 18. A teacher needs patience during this period, knowing that this year will be better than the last and that next year will be better yet. Teachers must be able to encourage their students to look ahead, to visualize the results attainable in the long run.

Also during these years, the adolescent's voice begins to take on the individual characteristics that will get him or her noticed, vocally speaking, for better or worse. A child singer with a sensational voice can, because of the inevitable changes that come with puberty, become a has-been almost overnight if proper training is not applied. A good teacher will take the student back over the fundamentals of vocal training. If the student's earlier training has been good, the teacher might not have to go back very far, but the rapid physical changes every teenager goes through must be dealt with. If a solo career is the goal, now is the time to find a teacher aware of the demands of the teenage voice. The student must learn to look on her or his body as an instrument that must be lived with every day, aware of the changes it is undergoing.

Finally, no matter whether the adolescent wants to sing on Broadway, in opera, or in cabaret, it's good to remember that a thorough grounding in classical technique is the bedrock of versatility, helpful in taking one wherever one might want to go.

Weekly Practice

Unlike dancers, who are used to training in a studio every day of the week, singers must find their own personal time, space, and discipline to practice. Lesson time is not practice time. Teachers provide information during lessons, but the student's progress in developing his or her voice largely depends on what the student does the rest of the time. Students must set their own practice schedules and provide their own discipline and focus.

Interpretation

With a good teacher and enough practice the student's voice should develop steadily during the teen years. With a solid foundation in vocal training to build on, the teacher at this point should introduce the student to vocal interpretation.

Interpretation is not an easy concept to teach. In fact, many instructors and performers maintain that it is a gift that some singers have and others don't. Nevertheless, a good teacher will be able to walk all their students through it. If the teacher can't, or won't, find another teacher. As in any field, there will be some incredibly talented children, "naturals" who will learn interpretation with ease. However, that does not justify a teacher avoiding or ignoring a student who may be having trouble with it.

Interpretation means bringing a song to life, taking the lyrics and conveying their meaning to the audience through clear diction, word meaning, musical phrasing, and vocal dynamics.

Singers ask themselves questions such as: Who am I? How do I relate to the others in this song? What am I singing about? Where am I and what am I trying to accomplish through the song? In essence, singers are creating characters and emotional lives for themselves through their songs.

When they do this successfully, their performances take on a life of their own and their audiences truly become involved with the characters and lives created. If all a singer does is sing words with a blank expression, suggestive of nothing behind them, he or she is merely giving a vocalization performance. It shows a lack of dramatic understanding, and there is not a musical theater director alive who will hand a principal role to someone who lacks dramatic understanding.

At this point we see that acting and singing are beginning to merge. A good acting class (see Chapter 6) is vital in creating the total singer. Remember, an expressive voice not only stems from good singing technique, but from the willingness and ability of the singer to provide emotional content. A good teacher will introduce this concept. If the student can't quite pull it off to start with, at least the notion is beginning to be addressed. It's not easy for everyone to tap into their emotional depths, but the freer singers are with their feelings, the more expressive their singing will be. And as noted earlier about developing good vocal technique, relaxation here also holds the key.

One big advantage students have today, which didn't exist for students fifty years ago, is the ability to listen to many different performers singing the same songs the students are working on during their lessons. No matter the type of music the student wants to perform—jazz, opera, popular—he or she can listen to all the professionals on recordings, picking up vocal tricks and interpretations to incorporate into his or her own style.

And this advantage stays with singers throughout their professional lives. Say a singer is waiting for that big Broadway break and finds herself singing in nightclubs and cabarets. She'll need to know the vocal demands of those venues, in which interpretation plays a big part. She might want to steep herself in the work of artists like Ella Fitzgerald or Carmen Macrae—even someone famous from the movies or stage like Barbra Streisand can teach one a lot about phrasing. In this way, the singer will extend her interpretive skills.

Singers never really know what they'll be called on to do. In order to cover all the bases, I suggest they constantly learn to expand their versatility. I also think they should learn to sing in different languages. This trains the ear to hear vowel sounds in different ways, and trains the mouth and tongue to find the right positions for producing those sounds. Training in dialects is also important. Along with acting lessons, all this makes a singer more valuable to directors everywhere.

Dangers to the Voice

Yelling and Screaming When we're young, we think of ourselves as indestructible. We're not, and neither are our voices. They can be damaged more easily than you might think. One of the biggest dangers to the vocal chords is yelling or screaming; overdoing it can result in permanent harm. Cheerleading is a prime example. So many teenagers can't wait to tell everyone they made the squad, but they don't consider the damage their voices may suffer. Other examples are music camps and overnight school functions, where you are out in the cold air, and carrying on in ways guaranteed to harm the voice.

Material Inappropriate to the Vocal Range Another danger is musical or choral works that are demanding and possibly out of the student's vocal range. This type of singing should only be done in short increments. The student should be taught to stop vocalizing and just mouth the words when she or he feels her or his voice getting tired. Let the musical director sing for the student instead.

Singing When Ill Another danger to the voice is singing when sick. Unfortunately, kids do it all the time, their attitude being: "I have a cold, but I can still sing." Depending on how sick they really are, the voice teacher may have them come to their lessons or rehearsals anyway. Through warmup exercises, teachers can work them through such periods and help them learn how to handle the situation. This is important as it may happen to them later on as professionals, while they're actually in a show. But if an illness is too severe, parents and teachers should not allow young singers to sing until they are well. Forcing a voice to sing with swollen vocal chords can cause permanent damage. Overtaxing a voice can produce polyps and nodules on the vocal chords. If these develop, rest or even surgery will be needed to undo the damage, if it can be undone at all.

Belting Belting is controlled yelling. The standard example is in *Annie*, when the title character sits with her dog Sandy, belting out the word "Tomorrow" over and over again. Voice teachers have to deal with the reality that a lot of singers are going to belt, and a lot of them will sing rock, pop, and Broadway belting types of songs. The instructor can't pretend it doesn't happen or say it isn't important. Kids are going to want to belt.

In fact, it's part of what they'll need to know to sing on Broadway, so they'll have to learn how to use their belting register. While the young voice is in an unsettled state, undeveloped and as yet lacking control, the instructor's goal should be to teach belting in a healthy way. Kids should learn to produce the sound in a stable manner, without producing hoarseness, huskiness, vocal fatigue, or neck muscle problems. Find an instructor who will address belting objectively, and who actually knows how to teach it. Determined Broadway belters of the future will need someone able to help them combine the ability to belt with the solid technique of classical singing. The strength of a classically trained voice is that it allows a singer to belt without hurting him- or herself.

Smoking and Drinking In a business where a large percentage of people smoke, drink, or do both, a few words on this topic are in order. Cigarettes are addictive. They are expensive. They are hard to quit. They deplete your lungs, your voice, and your energy. Have you ever seen a smoker rehearse a song and dance number? It's not a pretty sight, gasping for air, the body struggling to meet the demands being asked of it. After suffering through this ordeal, such individuals need a break and head outside for a smoke. It would be comical if it weren't so sad.

Similar warnings apply to alcohol. The consequences of drinking are destructive to both the body and the psyche, leading to high blood pressure, diminished energy, and apathy. Alcohol dehydrates the body, and dehydration depletes the body of nutrients, sapping it of the energy it needs to perform.

Simply put, stay away from these two drugs. Students, learn this truth—and if you're already an adult, teach it to young people and keep it in mind yourself!

THE JOB OF THE VOCAL COACH

Having spent several pages discussing issues related mostly to the training of child and adolescent voices, let's now move on to some topics important to singers of all ages.

The first has to do with the role of vocal coaches. A voice teacher works with a singer on vocal technique, correct breathing, phrasing, and learning to sing properly. A vocal coach, on the other hand, works with the artist on developing material for college and professional auditions, concerts, or shows. The coach's job is to put songs together for you, the singer, in your own key, and guide you through your vocal interpretation of each piece. The aim is helping you display your vocal assets effectively and memorably.

Most voice teachers in smaller towns also act as vocal coaches. This is acceptable, as long as the teacher really understands how to prepare the student for auditions. But how many times have I watched young vocal students audition by performing a piece out of their range? Stretching for notes they can't hit, they show themselves in the worst possible light. To land performing jobs, you have to sing well at auditions—better than well. The songs have to be in your range and appropriate to your voice. Determining the songs that are right for you takes time and patience, and that's why you need the guidance of a good vocal coach. You'll be trying lots of songs before finding the ones that are perfect for your voice. A coach should take the time to help you patiently explore for the right songs. He or she should make sure that you're well rehearsed and ready for auditions. A good coach should never let you go in unprepared, with a song you learned the night before the audition. This is a business and should be treated that way, so that you are able to land yourself a job.

I should mention that a bad vocal coach can do as much damage as a bad vocal teacher, so choose one with care. Vocal coaches charge anywhere from $50 to $250 an hour. The better known, the more expensive, and part of what you'll pay for is the name. At the same time, the best known vocal coach may not necessarily be the best coach you can find.

PIANO LESSONS

Everyone loves to play "Heart and Soul." "Chopsticks," too. Surprisingly, singers and voice teachers alike say that, regarding a solo singing career, playing piano is the most important element of all. In fact, it might be wise to study piano before starting voice lessons. Performing on piano conveys a complete musical foundation, providing melody, harmony, and rhythm, a foundation that stays with you forever, especially if you learn to play while young. The ideal age for young performers to start piano lessons is 8 or 9. However, if a student shows an interest in piano even earlier, say at age 4 or 5, his or her parents should go ahead and start lessons then. For one thing, piano lessons are very good for mental development, positively affecting math, reading, and learning abilities in general. They might even lead to perfect pitch, which is very useful in this profession.

Everything I said earlier about finding a good vocal teacher applies to studying piano as well. As with voice, anyone with even a minimum of piano training can claim to be a piano teacher. So ask others for opinions and recommendations, and apply the same guidelines for interviewing piano teachers as you would for interviewing voice instructors. Once you've found a good teacher, put your trust in him or her to establish a program that's right for the student. There are special piano methods that can inspire kids, exploring areas of theory and technique and involving music spanning the range from pop to Christmas music to classical masterworks.

The skills to be gained from studying piano involve dynamics, phrasing, and articulation. Students learn note identification, and key identification through five-finger patterns in single and multiple keys. They develop a basic sense of rhythm, including the meaning of whole notes, half notes, quarter notes, and eighth notes. They learn how to sense a basic beat and subdivision of a beat, as well as direction in note reading—that is, whether a note is up or down on the staff. They develop the ability to recognize intervals, whether they're skips or a step. Eventually, after moving out of the five-finger pattern, and learning to shift hands on the keyboard, they can start playing more advanced pieces from their song books. At that point they can be, if they want, on their way to becoming terrific pianists!

Learning piano is hard work for adults or children, and parents must do their part to keep their children's interest level high. Nevertheless, learning to play the piano at a young age instills a discipline that will carry over into other areas and ensure that the concept of training becomes second nature. Later on, the skills acquired in studying piano become tools that provide an edge in finding jobs. Audition callbacks provide a good example: A lot of singers today can't read music and consequently have to be taught everything they perform. What if you're called back to sing a portion of a song from the show you're auditioning for? If you've learned to sight-read from your piano lessons, and are able to sing the lyrics without extensive preparations ahead of time, you'll have an edge over a singer who can't sight-read and needs all those preparations.

A WORD TO DANCERS

The breathing technique needed for professional singing is quite different from that needed for professional dancing, and so it may seem to be a mysterious process to dancers. Because of their strong muscular torsos and the onstage demands put on their bodies, dancers are "shallow breathers." They have a tendency to resist dropping their diaphragms to acquire the deep breath required to support a tone. Yet dancers in musical theater who are also called on to sing have to know when to change the way they breathe. They must know when to let themselves go and assume a singer's breathing pattern so they can maintain good vocal technique and not strain their vocal chords.

Ken Prescott, who has played Billy Lawlor in *42nd Street* and was seen in the original cast of *The Tap Dance Kid*, notes the following:

> As a dancer, you're pulled up through your stomach and held tightly around the midriff. This is your center, holding you up so that your weight appears lighter when you dance. When singing, you have to take a low breath, so you need to let your rib cage expand. Your diaphragm will then descend or flatten, and your lungs will fill with air. You can't keep your stomach pressed in since that won't give you the proper breath support needed for healthy vocal production.

Keep in mind that these days, in a business of singers/dancers/actors, you can't sustain a career by merely being a one-technique performer. The days of George Abbott musicals, with their chorus of singers, corps of dancers, and group of lead performers, are long gone. Productions are expensive to put on, and everyone involved with the money side of the theater business wants to hire individuals with multiple talents. Competition is fierce, and only those who can handle all three demands of singing, dancing, and acting have a chance at success.

Dancers in musical theater have to learn how to sing, period. Often, they don't want to do this. Yet they have to be open-minded enough to know that they must develop the skill. Once they realize and accept that fact, a knowledgeable voice teacher can help them learn how to adapt to the needs of singing.

A WORD ABOUT MICROPHONES

A word about the quality of microphone systems in today's theaters is necessary. Years ago, when actors or singers auditioned for a Broadway show, they would do so in the theater where it would actually "play": The director, producer, and others involved in the show would sit in the rear of the house, and each performer then had to project his or her voice loudly enough to be heard clearly all the way in the back. Performers who couldn't do this were cut immediately, and the next performer's audition would begin.

Today, with the extensive use of microphones, that situation has changed drastically. Voices that carry are no longer so important, so auditions are usually held in dance studios or other locations smaller than the theaters in which the productions will appear. In such locations everyone can be heard fairly easily, and the ability to project just doesn't matter. With the amplification that body microphones provide, even singers with small voices can perform heroic vocal feats.

With the body microphone being such a great equalizer, of course, the nature of auditions and the type of performers sought by producers and casting directors have changed. You just have to be able to sing. This has opened the door to a lot more competition among those seeking work on the musical stage. As a result, your singing has to be that much better.

Of course, despite the increased competition, many of today's singers are glad to have microphones. They consider them life savers, protecting the voice from strain and injury and helping to extend the length of a singer's career. The current generation of singers use microphones extensively and wouldn't perform without them.

A SINGER'S PASSION

If you really love to sing and want to perform as a professional, there's no better way to make a living. To achieve this, however, there has to be dedication, focus, and a willingness to pursue the goal of being a complete musician.

A beautiful voice is a gift. Yet, as we've seen, it requires proper care. A voice changes daily, weekly, and yearly throughout a singer's life. It cannot be taken for granted. Learning to sing is a lifelong process that ends professionally only when a singer decides no longer to perform. Consequently, singers must vocalize every day. Even when performing in a show, they must find the time to practice. They can't become complacent, thinking that now they've made it in musical theater and will never again be without work.

Remember that you never really hear your own voice objectively. You hear it from the inside, and you need someone who can hear it from the outside to help you evaluate its needs. This means a teacher is an extremely important continuing tool for a singer throughout his or her professional life. Continued training with solid instruction will ensure the continuing health of the vocal instrument.

3

Finding the Perfect Dance Studio

Milton Berle has joked: "I'd be a great dancer, if it wasn't for two things—my feet." There is nothing better than finding some humor in what you do. But if you want a career in musical theater, dancing is no laughing matter. Throughout my years as a performing arts consultant, I have seen dancers make the same mistakes over and over again in how they approach their careers. And the main mistake is specializing in dance or in certain types of dancing instead of becoming qualified for virtually all the dance work available. This specialization mentality means they are limiting their job opportunities. Instead of being able to market themselves broadly, they are reduced to looking for specific types of work, which usually means they can only work on a part-time basis. Do you fit into this category?

I'm talking about dancers who refuse to study singing, or jazz dancers who may also be able to do hip-hop and funk but little else. I'm talking about dancers who attended college for musical theater training, but because of the school's limited dance curriculum studied only ballet and modern dance. This list could go on and on, almost forever, but I'm sure you get the point. You can't specialize. Not if you're interested in musical theater, anyway. You might get lucky and land a job or two, but your chances of long-term success will be seriously diminished. Ballet, modern, jazz, tap, ballroom, musical theater style, acrobatics, and specialty dances such as flamenco and Spanish—you have to learn them all!

Vickie Sheer, Executive Director, Dance Educators of America, makes the following observation: "When I think of show business, as a dancer, I think of hard work, training, discipline, dedication, and the resultant joy of accomplishment. Entering the twenty-first century, the accomplished dancer must be knowledgeable in acting, singing, costuming, staging, and lighting. Know your craft and show business is ready for you."

To survive professionally, and have a real career in this business, be prepared: The more you know and the better prepared you are, the better your chances. You just can't predict what style will be called for in that new musical coming along. You have to be ready if you want the job. You have to be proficient in whatever dance styles will be requested at the audition. You can be sure others trying out for the part you want will be prepared.

SPORTS AND DANCE

So many times I've heard dancers and teachers compare dance to sports like ice skating or gymnastics. But I think dance and sports are really two entirely different things. First of all, dancers are artists, not athletes. Ice skating and gymnastics are beautiful to watch, even thrilling at times, and take a considerable amount of training to do well. But while there is some artistry involved, that's not really the goal. Points in competitions are awarded based on the level of difficulty of the feats being performed. That means the emphasis for athletes is on mechanical competence and technical proficiency.

There is plenty of competition in the dance world. It has become far too cutthroat these days, with dance competitions and many other events that pit dancers against each other. But turning the art of dance into a contest is wrong. Dancers are different from ice skaters. They are artists first. If they develop some secondary technical wizardry, that's fine. But their technique had better say something artistic, and not be merely athletic prowess alone.

As artists and communicators, dancers should express something in their movements. Too many young dancers today seem only concerned with doing tricks. But while that kind of dancing may be exciting to watch for a while, dancers who never make any kind of artistic statement through their dancing are no better than singers who stand there bellowing out a bunch of notes with no musical interpretation. What's the point of doing that?

People become dancers to feel the joy of movement, to express themselves through physical movement. To succeed in that, it's important to learn the fundamentals of dance. And to learn those fundamentals, the beginning dancer must have the best training available from the most qualified teacher. There are a lot of *bad* dance teachers out there—people without the proper background, training, or experience to teach who nevertheless open studios. Not only are they not qualified to train people to become professional dancers, but they can do a great deal of harm, teaching bad dance habits that may take other teachers years to undo. Those long-term problems can be avoided, and this chapter and the next on types of dance will help you do just that.

This chapter tries to answer the questions that may cross the minds of those in search of a qualified dance teacher or dance studio. It is aimed at dance students, and, since dancers must start training young, it is aimed at the parents of young people interested in dance. Finding a good teacher or studio is crucial to laying the foundations of a successful dance career. As already noted, making a wrong choice can cause great harm. By understanding what is involved early on, you can avoid disaster later on, so take the information in this chapter very seriously. It will help you make the proper decisions that will make, and not break, a career in dance.

ENCOURAGING THE YOUNG DANCER

If you're a parent looking for a dance teacher or studio for your child, the very first issue needing clarification is: Whose idea is it to start dancing lessons? Is it yours or your child's? Research has consistently shown that a child "forced" by parents into an activity will usually not engage in that activity with interest or enthusiasm. He or she might even resist it outright. On the other hand, kids who have their own ideas about what interests them and are excited about doing something should be supported and encouraged to pursue those interests. This doesn't mean a child will stick with each new activity. Few do. But parents should allow their children to explore, to determine for themselves what best suits their talents and personalities.

Parents should also avoid pushing conformist standards of behavior on their children. They might say something like, "Son, you don't really want to be a tap dancer. How about going outside and playing some football instead?" But this second-guessing what a child wants to do merely gives the child negative messages. Of course, there is nothing wrong with football for someone who wants to play football, but if your child is truly motivated and wants to study dance, or any of the performing arts, he or she should be given the chance to do so.

Some kids take a long time to discover an activity or goal that truly interests them. That's why it's part of a parent's job to encourage them to try doing different things, to allow them to experience a variety of activities. At the same time, this can also be carried to an extreme. Some parents have their kids doing far too much, taking too many lessons, being members of too many groups. If a child's schedule involves activities virtually every night of the week, he or she may not have time to enjoy the other aspects of life—family fun, peer relationships, school studies, the exuberance of childhood in general.

While children need structure in their lives, the job of childhood is still childhood. Young people need to go to school, build relationships with family and friends, and learn to relate to other people in the world at large. As they become adolescents, their job is to learn who they are and what they want to be when they grow up. In essence, they need to establish their unique identities. By living a balanced life, they also learn to make healthy choices later on, especially when they're out on their own.

Everybody has talent, something they can excel in. The trick is determining what that something is. Many people never actualize their potential, and I strongly suspect it has everything to do with the lack of encouragement they themselves received as children. So by all means encourage a kid who wants to study dance. Just be sure it's he or she who wants to study dance, and keep in mind that children have other needs too if they are to grow into a happy adulthood.

STARTING OUT

Every child who indicates an interest in dance deserves the very best training.

Where do you start? How do you find the right teacher or studio? What should you look for—and look *out* for? In the rest of this chapter, I will take you through the process, step by step. With the homework done properly, both the parent and the young dancer can experience, and enjoy, the most exciting adventure possible.

Sources of Information

When searching for a dance teacher or studio, the first source most parents use is the Yellow Pages. Although Yellow Pages ads won't supply detailed information, they can provide a general overview of the training available. They'll list the names of the studios and the studio directors, and give the studio locations.

When looking at an ad, notice the dance styles taught, such as ballet, tap, jazz, hip-hop, and so forth. Usually the one listed first is the studio's strongest suit, and the one listed last its weakest. If the ad says something to the effect of "National Award Winning Ensembles" or "Award Winning Performance Group," the studio is telling you its students attend dance competitions, and have won medals, trophies, or cash awards at such events. This can be good or bad, depending on how much technique time students are being denied in order to rehearse the dance numbers specifically geared toward competition dancing.

Some ads may indicate that a studio has its students perform an annual recital, even listing the theater where it is put on. Don't be thrown off by this. Just because an ad names one of the more impressive theaters in town doesn't mean the studio will offer the best training. Other, smaller studios may not be able to afford this kind of theater space, because they don't have as many students. And the ad won't tell you how long the students work on this recital. Recitals are one-time performances, and you need to know this kind of information—again—in order to know how much technique time is being sacrificed in the classroom.

Ads sometimes describe the studio's flooring. This is important information. You have to make sure your young dancer trains on a raised, wood floor, anything from masonite to oak. Remember, "raised" is the key word. A dance floor that's flat on concrete will be hard on students' knees and shins.

Finally, an ad should indicate whether the studio offers group classes or private lessons, and should include the studio's phone number as well as its address. Often it will include a simplified map showing its location.

Remember, a Yellow Pages ad is a marketing tool for the studio, a device to get you interested in what it has to offer. However, the biggest ad may not correlate with the best studio. The young dance student may be best off attending a small studio— one with a single-line ad in the Yellow Pages listing only its name and phone number. You have to go beyond the phone book in deciding on the right studio or teacher.

Studios Close to Home A studio located near where you live may be the best one, but picking a studio only on this basis is a bad idea. You can't just walk down the block and enroll a kid at a dance school without checking it out. Whether he or she will be taking lessons for recreation or to lay the foundations for a dance career, hunt around for the best teachers, the best flooring, the best approach. In regard to a dance career, I can't stress enough that a bad choice of studio and teacher at the start will only lead to trouble. Learning bad technique means locking that technique into the muscle memory associated with dance. At best this means valuable time lost later on, finding a good studio or teacher who can help the dancer unlearn all those bad habits. Young people in this predicament have to rebuild themselves as dancers in order to have any chance at successful careers, and there's no guarantee they can ever recover. Avoid this pitfall in the first place by spending the time and research needed to find the right studio.

Word of Mouth Most people choose a dance studio based on word of mouth. This, too, can be good or bad. Say, for example, the student has a friend attending a specific studio and wants to attend it, too. If the studio offers the right kind of training, this might be perfect. But what if the training is inadequate for his or her needs? Be wary. No car pooling, or peer socializing, is worth the risk of injury or inadequate training that may result from poor preplanning on your part.

While getting basic word-of-mouth information is certainly helpful, it's just a small part of the parent's fact-gathering job. Without actually attending recitals, watching classes in session, or asking questions that relate specifically to the young dancer, the parent may wind up placing him or her in a strange environment based merely on hearsay. I don't recommend doing it.

Making the Initial Phone Call

After looking over the ads, learning about the studios located near your home, and listening to the recommendations of friends, it's time for more serious research. I recommend calling as many studios as possible, gathering as much information as you can from each studio. In this way, your chances of making an intelligent decision will be dramatically enhanced.

First off, when you call a studio and someone answers the phone, make sure you're talking to either the studio owner or the office manager. If you're not and they aren't available, call back another time. In preparing for the calls, you'll want specific, detailed information and you'll ask some important questions, so list them for yourself in writing, leaving enough space on the piece of paper to jot down the answers. Inquire about things such as:

* What dance styles do you teach?
* What other kinds of services do you offer your students?
* IIow long has your studio been in business?
* Who are your teachers?
* What are their dance backgrounds?

A studio is only as good as its teachers, so you have to learn everything you can about the staff. If the student is interested in a professional career, ask about the employment track record of the studio's graduates. You want to find out if any of them have gone on to the pro ranks, and, if so, where they have performed.

Ask about the expenses involved up front. Be very thorough about this. You don't want any hidden charges sneaking in later on. (I discuss costs below.) Ask what types of recitals and performance opportunities the studio offers. Request any brochures or other literature the studio has had printed up about itself. Finally, ask if it's possible for a prospective student to come in and take a single class, to see how he or she fits in and responds to the teaching. A reputable studio will always let you watch a class for free, or let a potential enrollee participate in a class at nominal cost, to allow you to make an informed decision. If the owner or office manager hesitates or says it's against policy, take the answer as a red flag warning. The studio may be in it just for the money, and not for the sake of their students' artistic development.

Investigating Studios and Observing Classes

When investigating a studio, take time to observe its training methods. Attend not just the class your young dancer will be going to, but a more advanced one as well. If a professional career is at stake, you'll need to know how far a studio can take its students. If the advanced ones are performing the same kind of material as the beginners, stay away!

Make sure the teachers stress dance technique as well as the routines needed for recitals and performances. Again, you don't want a studio that gets carried away with preparing its students for dance competitions, shortchanging the time required for them to learn good technique.

Dance training is different from other lessons kids take. It's such a one-on-one experience that the teacher and the student have to connect. If their personalities don't mesh, or if any sort of animosity exists between them, the training will be doomed to failure. Observing a few classes will help you determine if an instructor's teaching style is right for a child. Will he or she like spending time with this teacher? Does the teacher yell and intimidate students? Does he or she care about technical sophistication? Does the instructor see the lessons as just a chance for children to have fun, as if the studio were a playground, or is there an effort to pass along a lot of information about being a dancer? Is the teaching done patiently and with care? The right atmosphere can be wondrous for a child, the wrong one devastating. Is the teacher capable of expanding the student's repertoire once the basics have been learned?

Pay attention to the general etiquette of the class. What are the students wearing? What is the teacher wearing, and how does she or he present herself or himself? Sloppy dancewear, or a lazy demeanor, may indicate a lack of discipline at a studio. Notice the class size, whether the teacher has an assistant. What is the assistant's age (see below)? Scrutinize the class carefully. This is the time to take it all in so you know what's necessary to make an informed decision.

Red Flags Waving

Some dance studios may not like the following observation, but I'm going to make it anyway. I believe anyone under age 20 isn't fit to teach. Why? Because it takes a psychological, as well as a physiological grounding, for a teacher to deal effectively with young students—and their parents. Young instructors lack the kinesthetic knowledge to work with young bodies properly. This can lead to many unnecessary injuries. Therefore, watch out for the studio that has 12- or 16-year-olds conducting classes. Teaching is a learned skill, and people at that age do not know how to go about it.

Also, there should be some distance in age between a teacher and a student. Without it, students won't accord the respect necessary to teachers who correct their errors. A 14-year-old, perhaps the owner's overly indulged child, can't possibly have the same authority as someone who's 30. A good teacher with a few years of living under his or her belt is able to operate at an emotional level beyond that of an adolescent, and has the experience necessary to enter the professional work force. So let me emphasize the point: *A child should never teach a dance class to other children.*

Another red flag is a teacher who yells at the students. This is totally unacceptable. Because of the pressures that kids already go through—in school, at home, or with members of their peer groups—they need dance teachers who create a fun, relaxed atmosphere. A good teacher, with sound training skills, can build healthy self-esteem and produce beautiful dancers without resorting to abusive behavior. If the teacher screams, throws things, or exhibits any other kind of similar conduct, the students, seeing this person as a role model, might come to see this as appropriate behavior and emulate it. Just what you don't need.

Another warning has to do with class size. For a healthy learning experience, a studio should limit class sizes to ten or twelve students. When classes are too small, say six students or fewer, the kids may become rowdy and feel overindulged because of all the personal attention. With more than twelve students, they may get rowdy for another reason: feeling they have to "act out" in order to get any attention at all. In my experience, ten or twelve students is optimal because it seems to promote a group cohesiveness, a feeling of solidarity that helps avoid all the nonsense that can occur when children feel a lack of attention, or are receiving too much of it.

Be aware that some studios are so large they must play the money game. With high rents and high utility and upkeep expenses, they have to sign up as many paying customers as possible.

Perhaps the biggest red flag warning against a particular studio or teacher, as far as I'm concerned, is hearing a dance teacher speak badly of others in the area, just to get you to sign with his or her studio. When he or she behaves in this manner, know that the student will invariably be exposed to it. Few parents want this kind of behavior passed on to their kids.

Costs

Most parents pick a dance school for their child without thinking about the total cost this will involve. To illustrate, let's say the cost of one class is $35 a month. Over a year, that comes to $420. Now add in the fee for one recital, the cost of the costume for that performance along with the costs of the shoes and tights needed to match the costume, the cost for hair styling or a wig, and the price of the ten tickets you'll be obligated to sell to yourself if you can't sell them to anyone else. That one-year cost has now ballooned from $420 to more than $600. Now add in the costs of entering your child into a full-blown dance competition—the entry fee per dance to be performed, and the costs of transportation, food, and lodging if the competition isn't held near your hometown, as well as the money that will be spent at the recital store and on incidentals. All this could bring the total to more than $800, or nearly $70 a month for your child to take that one class. It could be even more.

If the student is taking unlimited classes at the studio, five days a week, and winds up performing in five or seven recital dances, watch out for sticker shock. If you planned your budget for a family vacation in Hawaii, you may have to stay home. If the student trains at a large studio, where recitals are expected, limit his or her participation to no more than two or three dances. Quality is the key here. If you don't see any improvement in technique after those two or three performances, what can you really expect after seven?

Ask about *all* the expenses connected with dance lessons, and do it at the outset. And learn to budget carefully.

Loyalty to One Studio

The most successful dancers in the musical theater world are the most versatile, and the only way to achieve that kind of versatility is to study with good teachers of as many dancing styles as possible. Unless you live in one of the major dance markets like New York, Los Angeles, or Chicago, it's unlikely that you'll find one studio able to teach a kid everything necessary from the age of 3 until he or she is ready to enter college or embark on a professional dance career. Your chances of winning the lottery are probably better. So achieving versatility often means changing studios in the course of a dance education.

Studios in smaller towns have a tendency to tell new students or their parents that they expect loyalty. They claim they offer students everything they will ever need in terms of dance. Some studios even draft contracts spelling out the kind of loyalty they expect, demanding that students or parents sign them. Don't ever sign a contract like that.

As a student, you have the right to say, "I'm here to learn ballet because I understand you have the best ballet teacher to teach me what I need to learn at this point in my life as a dancer. However, I will be taking jazz and tap at another studio, because I feel it offers the best training in those specialties." Parents have the same right to say this for their children. If a studio balks, move on. You don't want to feel trapped in one studio, and there's no reason to be.

Training at different studios simultaneously can sometimes cause problems for students. For example, I once had a student attending my studio and another one concurrently. The other studio was participating in a competition, so I taught the student, an 8-year-old girl, a dance to go with "Rock Around the Clock." Her mother told me that the only way the other studio would let her perform the dance at the event was if, when registering for the competition, she made no mention of me. Silly, isn't it? Why do studios engage in this kind of nonsense? Who does it hurt? Not the studio owners or the teachers. It only hurts the students. The basic point is that dance students who want to become professional performers have to get extensive performing experience under their belts, tempered with sufficient technical training. It's the right balance that counts. If they need to go to more than one studio for it all, and doing so doesn't conflict with any other commitments, they should go ahead.

It's the job of dancers to grow and improve, to reach their maximum potential. That means studying with as many people as required to learn different styles and gain the skills they need. If you're a dance student, do the best to ensure that you're a versatile performer. If you're the parent of a child studying dance, do the same for him or her. A performer can't be successful in musical theater without versatility, and that often just isn't possible by sticking with one studio. Don't feel bad about going elsewhere. Don't allow the staff at the studio to make you feel guilty about your decision. Your only obligation is to obtain a good and complete education.

TYPES OF STUDIOS

Biggest Isn't Always Best

The biggest studio in town may have as many as eight hundred students. Usually such studios have the largest facilities, hold their recitals in the biggest theaters, attract some of the better teachers as faculty members, and participate in scores of competitions. These studios can also be very expensive.

On the positive side, you can expect big studios to have the best flooring, making injuries less likely. They will have more instructors and teach more styles of dancing than small studios can. The students will develop great discipline, and will learn to dress and act appropriately both in the studio and in public. They will also develop great studio loyalty.

On the downside, sometimes, depending on the faculty, technique is lost in a large studio. Sixty percent or more of class time may be spent on preparing for dance competitions or recital routines. Consequently, the students don't really get a dance education, as the studio is geared toward performance. This isn't always the case, but remember to watch for the red warning flags discussed earlier. If you find that a studio concentrates more on performance than on teaching the student who wants a dance career the mechanics of being a dancer, pick another studio.

Competitions have their value. They're a wonderful method of getting students into a performing environment. Used for the right purpose they can teach kids a lot about the business of professional dancing. Winning competitions may validate the winning student's abilities, and the worth of the studios who produce the winning students. To see how important many studios find those events, all you have to do is walk through their front doors and see the trophies lined up for display. It's like a proud mother bragging about her kids. But also keep in mind that a studio which spends an entire year concentrating on choreography cheats its students of learning dance technique in the process, and—as I've emphasized—that's not a way to train a kid for a professional musical theater career.

Large studios tend to be impersonal and to encourage favoritism. Sometimes the owners and teachers don't know the students by name, or how they're progressing in their dance education. These problems can be avoided if the studio is well managed, and if members of the staff work together, holding weekly meetings to discuss the progress of the students and how to move each of them along to the next level of her or his development. For example: Ashley might be doing well in ballet. How is she progressing in jazz? One teacher talks to another. The members of a good staff are serious about how their students are advancing as dancers, where they are currently and where they're going.

The attitudes and skills of students at any studio largely reflect the philosophy of the owner of that studio, with all the limitations that may entail. If the studio just wants the kids to have a good time, the kids will. But don't expect a professional career to come out of this. On the other hand, if the stated goal of the studio is to prepare students to train with any teacher, anywhere, to help them reach their own desired levels of proficiency, or to train them for a professional dance career, a professional career is more likely to be achievable.

Choosing a good studio is like choosing a good college. You must do your homework properly, and not just buy into how big or glitzy a studio is, or how many trophies from competitions it displays. Listen beyond all the sales talk, and determine if the training, in and of itself, is sufficient. If everything doesn't mesh, it's not the right studio for you.

Smaller Studios

Smaller studios usually have between 50 and 150 students. You're likely to find these studios make a better use of class time, with more quality learning coming out of each lesson. The classes themselves will be smaller than at the largest studios, with teachers having more control over what is happening and really getting to know their students. The teachers will be aware of what each child can do technically, and where he or she is heading. They will know and respect each child's dreams and goals, and treat each one as an individual.

Smaller studios also tend toward specialties, or teaching just those styles they are the most proficient at, although they may also have a few instructors teaching other dance forms. They will have fewer teachers than the larger studios, but because they are small will admit their limitations and even send students to other studios if necessary, something the bigger studios rarely, if ever, do.

Small studios usually have recitals, but keep the costs for costumes and other expenses at a much more reasonable level than the larger studios. And while the recitals are not full-blown extravaganzas, they do show the progress of the students in nice, intimate settings. However, some of these studios have gotten to the point where they hold recitals only once every two years, which can conflict with the need parents feel for a big-time venue where their kids can show off regularly for family and friends.

In the smaller studios, training for dance competitions may not be part of the instruction process, but attending workshops, conventions, and master classes, and going on trips to see professional performances are greatly encouraged. Learning from a variety of teachers and growing to become the performer you set out to be are the motivational tools at these studios.

Specialty Studios

I like the idea of a specialty studio. I run one myself, and I think the training is very focused and effective. Think for a moment: What kind of person would open a studio and just teach ballet if they weren't good at it? They'd be out of work in no time if they couldn't deliver the goods. A specialty studio does what it says, focusing on one dance form, be it ballet, jazz, tap, or flamenco. The teachers are usually experts in their field, at the top of their profession. Because no nonsense or bad training goes on in these studios, students really learn. Specialty studios promote a serious, conservatory type of attitude that stresses training and accomplishment. If you're not serious about your craft, don't bother knocking on the door.

Whether you're a beginning student or advanced, technical brilliance is what specialty studios strive to teach. A specialty studio may not hold recitals, but instead put on a full-blown show. You can expect to pay a little more than market price for studying at them, but you or your child will learn at a much faster rate, progressing quickly.

Waste of Time Studios

As in any other profession, there are people who claim to be dance teachers but aren't. They open up a studio with little idea of what they're doing, attempting to teach students whatever they have learned themselves along the way. They might well ask students to dance on concrete floors and hold poorly produced recitals. My only advice about these kinds of studios is to pay attention to all the warning signals when you run across one and don't get involved.

"Competition" studios don't train dancers at the beginner level, so they tend to attract students from other studios, who are already at the intermediate or advanced stages of training. They concentrate all their lesson time on performance techniques, giving no time at all to dance technique. The only reason they exist is to win trophies and awards, at all costs. No one interested in a professional career should waste his or her time in this kind of stunted environment. Avoid such studios like the plague.

SMALL-TOWN STUDIOS

There's not much you can do if you live in a small town that has just one dance studio. You'll have to settle for what's available, and hope that the owner is bright and interested enough in the students' welfare to hire competent teachers (if the studio is large enough to have more than the owner teaching) and to be on the lookout for new information useful to the students. Teachers can improve their teaching skills through attending workshops, visiting dance centers in major cities like New York or Chicago, or studying dance videos. But like anyone else, teachers can also become complacent, content with what they have and with the fact that they're making a living. Remaining ambitious, for their students' sake as well as their own, can be a constant battle.

A lot of small-town studios aren't well enough equipped to gear their program toward the young person who wants to be a professional. They're mostly "good time" facilities, and as long as they teach the kids a little dance here and there, and offer recitals, most parents are happy and the teacher can coast along for another year.

If your town is near a large city, you have more choices. And during the summer months studios in most large cities host some kind of dance camp.

A Word to Parents

Now that I've offered up the preceding information, I just have to say: In selecting a studio for a young dancer, do your best. You might make mistakes, perhaps even picking the wrong studio initially. But you can try not to by asking, observing, and learning. Do your homework, think it all through, and don't rush into anything.

As a parent, you have to understand that bad training is permanently ingrained in a child's neurological muscular system. It's actually worse than no training at all. You might think, "Well what's a little bad training? It can be corrected later on." The truth is, it can't really be corrected. It's like writing on a blackboard. You may erase what's on the board, but there's always a trace of what was written there before. So it's vitally important to avoid having bad training ingrained in the body in the first place. If you're not sure which studio to choose, hold off deciding until you are sure. Two months of caution is better than two years of bad training.

STUDIO EQUIPMENT

What differentiates a professional dance studio from an unprofessional one is not only the quality of the teachers, but having the equipment and tools a kid needs to learn dance properly. Let's run through some specifics.

Studio Size

The size of the studio should be appropriate to what is being learned there. The main thing to look out for are columns stuck in the middle of a room. Columns are a disaster, since they hinder fluid movement as the dancer keeps dodging the poles. You also need to be sure that there is enough ceiling height to allow good jumps and lifts, and if tumbling is taught, to allow students to throw front handsprings.

Proper Flooring

Don't enroll at a studio that has concrete floors, even if there is tile or carpet over the concrete. It's irresponsible of the owner to have a concrete floor, and dangerous for the students. Concrete promotes bad knees, shin splints, ankle fractures, and lower back injuries. It will shorten the performing life of any dancer and even keep students from becoming professionals. *Never, ever allow a dancer to perform on concrete.*

A good dance floor has to be raised, but the surface shouldn't be tile. Not only is tile too high in pitch for good tap instruction, it's too slippery for other styles of dance. The best surface for dance floors should be some kind of wood.

For the studios that roll out a Marley floor—which is a generic term for any non-slippery type of dance floor—make sure it's not rolled out over concrete but over a raised wood floor. Remember, Marley is not a substitution for a floor, but is used instead for texture's sake; it provides a consistency to the surface, neither too slippery nor too sticky. In doing ballet on it, you don't need rosin, and there is also better friction for ballet, jazz, and modern. New Marley floors are also compatible for tap. While there are a lot of different companies that sell these types of floors, Harlequin is the most popular brand.

Of course performers working on cruise ships, in a theme park, or even on Broadway will find themselves dancing on a variety of surfaces. So the use of Marley is not all that important in training dancers who plan to work in musical theater. It's basically a material often used in classroom settings and by dance companies in their performances. In regard to dance studios, the most important concern is making sure the floors are made of wood and are raised.

Mirrors

It may be hard to believe, but studios without mirrors exist even though they shouldn't. There is no single tool more valuable to dancers than mirrors. They allow students to learn more quickly by clearly seeing what their teacher is showing them and then applying those examples to how they move their own bodies. Mirrors promote corps work, helping dancers match the movements of the people next to them. Mirrors also allow dancers to see the entire class simultaneously. If a student just can't seem to get a step right, he or she can watch others do it in the mirror and ultimately learn how to do it correctly.

Mirrors are a must for any serious studio.

Ballet Barres

If a studio teaches ballet or jazz, then ballet barres attached to the walls are also a must. I would avoid portable barres, unless they are very sturdy. Supported barres are needed for certain types of technical work, so if a studio only has portables, it can be a problem. Also, look to see whether the barres are attached too close to the walls. They need to be suspended anywhere from eight to fifteen inches away from the room's walls.

Dressing Rooms and Water Fountains

Nice dressing areas are always ideal, one for boys and one for girls. But as long as the studio has a bathroom, it can take the place of a dressing room, if it's fully equipped.

Because studios are getting away from having drinking fountains, students should carry water bottles in their dance bags, for two reasons. First, they won't have to leave class to get a drink and, second, they won't have to share a fountain with others, thereby cutting down on the possibility of their picking up germs.

I should add that if the student is a child, he or she should also stay away from soda pop and other carbonated beverages. The phosphates used in the carbonation actually deplete the bones of calcium. This is bad for anyone, but particularly bad for growing children who need to develop good bones as dancers. Juice and water are far healthier choices.

A Good Sound System

A good sound system will fill a whole room with undistorted music, yet it won't be too loud. The teacher has to be able to talk to the students and note corrections when needed without needing to shout. A variable-speed record player or CD player is a good tool to have, so the teacher can make slight adjustments in the music's speed when necessary.

FINDING THE RIGHT DANCE TEACHER

Whether you're a student yourself looking for a good teacher or a parent looking for a dance teacher for your child, try to find someone who is genuine. By that I mean look for someone with self-confidence, a real mastery of teaching dance skills, and proficiency at dancing themselves. Of course, good teachers tend to be upbeat and positive, encouraging their students with high expectations. They are also very direct and honest. They may encourage students to practice by saying something like "You're coming along, and you're making good progress. Keep it up!" A good teacher will break down a dance step the student may be having trouble with, and make it understandable. Even if a student has trouble practicing, or doesn't meet the teacher's expectations, it's most important that the teacher not be psychologically damaging by inducing feelings of guilt or shame. Good teachers never call a student lazy, or say a student's doomed to be one of life's failures, especially in the presence of others!

A good teacher also knows when to put a dancer on stage or when to wait until he or she is both technically proficient and emotionally ready. Encouragement is critical, as are high expectations that students be on time, practice, and be responsible in how they approach their studies.

The ideal teacher has had some professional performing experience. This provides a particular kind of perception about performing and a deeper breadth of knowledge for the teacher to pass on to students. However, watch out for teachers who aren't really finished with dancing themselves, who are still performing. Their minds won't be focused on their students' needs. They will still be in a performance mode, with a corresponding mind-set. So look for teachers with some stage experience, but ones who have now turned their minds more to teaching and passing along the knowledge they've acquired along the way.

Also keep in mind that the best performers, the very best professional dancers, do not always make the best teachers. A person may have many years under his or her belt performing with a variety of companies or in Broadway shows, but that doesn't always ensure good teaching ability. Sometimes you'll even find a superb teacher who hasn't had any actual performing experience.

Make sure the teacher is using the proper French terminology for each step in ballet classes. Instructors should have a fairly good French accent, pronouncing the words properly.

Most important, look for an instructor who teaches students how to have fun dancing. A teacher with enthusiasm and energy will actually cause students to feel the some way. If an instructor walks into the room and says, "I had a lousy day—my car was stolen, and my dog was run over," the students' mood will bottom out. But teachers who stride into the classroom smiling and genuinely happy to see their students are laying the foundation for a good student–teacher relationship. Look for a teacher who is a coach, a teacher, a cheerleader, and a disciplinarian, someone who builds up students' spirits instead of tearing them down.

Planting Seeds

A good teacher plants seeds. Some of those will sprout and grow right away, some will germinate, sprout, and grow later, and some will never grow. However it goes, it is the responsibility of the teacher to plant the seeds, tend the soil, and encourage growth. In any learning situation, there seem to be three types of students. Members of the first type come to the situation highly motivated, knowing they like the activity right from the start. Members of the second type come into the situation and are exposed to the activity, but show no interest in it and stop participating. However, members of the third group, if the right seeds are planted initially, will return to the activity later on, no matter what their initial reaction, and eventually come to excel at it.

Practice and Time to Develop

Whether people want to be good at baseball, roller blading, or tap dancing, they have to put in the time and practice, and commit to the activity for at least one year. In the last decade, there has been a debate over quantity time versus quality time. In regard to children, some parents seem to have taken the tack that if you spend sufficient quality time with them, it can make up for a lack of quantity, or amount of actual time. I disagree; in terms of developing talent and skill, real time, duration of time, is more important.

What if a man thought that in order to become a professional golfer all he had to do was to put in some "quality" practice time? What if he believed that instead of playing eighteen holes of golf all he had to do was to go out and practice playing at one hole, but a really good hole? Of course, that's an extreme example of quality versus quantity time, but I consider the whole notion to be laughable. In order to do anything well, you have to devote actual, clock time to learning how to do it. You also need to develop good practice habits you can apply to learning situations throughout your life.

If students don't devote the required quantities of time to their art, they won't ever make the mistakes that are so vital in learning. It takes time to achieve mastery, to do things right and, yes, to do things wrong. It also takes time to make an informed decision about whether or not to continue an activity or pursue an interest.

Another problem that frequently arises is parents being anxious for their kids to move ahead in their studies to a higher level despite whether the kids themselves are ready to move on or not. Progressing from one level to another takes time and practice, and unless a young dancer has mastered the level she or he has currently achieved, it is not wise go to the next level.

Good teachers understand this natural progression in students and don't push them beyond their level of development. Avoid teachers who automatically advance students regardless of talent or ability. Remember that time is one of our most valuable resources, especially in regard to developing talent. You can't hurry it along.

CHOOSING THE RIGHT DANCE STYLE FOR YOU

You've read and absorbed the information in Chapter 3 about locating the right dance studio. The time has come to sign up for dance lessons. But how do you go about that? As I've said, if the goal is a career in musical theater, the aspiring performer ultimately needs to study all the styles of dancing. And I mean *all* the styles. Whether the student is male or female, we are talking about the disciplines of ballet, tap, jazz, ballroom, and ethnic dance. We're also talking about tumbling and anything else that trains the feet and body to move in the ways performing in musical theater requires. Remember, the more versatile performers are, the more marketable.

But with so many styles of dance, where do you start? Does it matter in which order the styles are studied? In this chapter I discuss that issue. I also cover the different dance styles to be studied, giving brief overviews of each in terms of what students can expect to learn, what they can expect from their teachers, and the clothing and dance studio equipment involved.

Since dance training should begin as early as possible, the parents of small children interested in musical theater will be making the decisions early on. But nearly all of the information applies to older students, too, who are making their own decisions, perhaps in consultation with their parents.

So, where do you start with dance studies? I recommend ballet. It's the oldest of the theatrical dance forms, going back more than four hundred years. And studying ballet builds the body into a strong dance instrument. Once dancers have developed a strong ballet technique, most of them find it easy to learn the techniques associated with all the other forms of dance. You should also keep in mind that many auditions for dance parts in musical theater start with ballet, even for the shows on the stages in Las Vegas. If a dancer can't get past the ballet combination, he or she won't be asked to stay to do the jazz combination.

PREBALLET CLASSES

What the Student Will Learn

Preballet training can begin as early as age 3 and continue until age 8, at which point professional training can begin. Preballet classes should be fun for kids; they should be protected from any pressure that might be created by preconceived expectations on the part of teachers or parents. The exercises should be very basic, taught slowly, and repeated. The classtime should be divided between working at the barre, going to the center of the room, doing exercises on the floor, and traveling across the room. There should be frequent variations in activity because at this age students don't have long attention spans. Creative movement should be a major element of what is taught, along with very elementary ballet exercises. Kids at this stage of physical development don't have very good motor skills. If the teacher is too focused on technique, it may lead to burnout and the kids rejecting dance altogether. Therefore, to repeat myself, any class has to be creative and fun.

In preballet classes, children work on improving their coordination through a variety of movements, perhaps using props such as scarves, hats, and balls they can toss to each other. At this point, imagery (story-telling) will be an important part of the class. They learn basic foot positionings like right from left, point from flex, as well as the basics of dancing with partners. They find out about dance configurations like "circle and line" and going "under the bridge." They play games on different levels and explore directions which can be introduced into dance movement.

The classes are also an important way of helping the kids expand their social skills as they get to know each other, have fun, and learn how to cooperate with each other and the teacher. There are a lot of kids who grow up without playmates, always watching TV or sitting in front of a computer. Some are even home-schooled, which tends to be socially isolating. Preballet classes increase the students' personal contacts, and help them learn how to make friends with others they can look forward to seeing every week.

Kids should also begin to explore the differences between musical forms like waltzes and marches. Preballet class doesn't have to be restricted to learning just ballet movements. Incorporating some basic tap instruction is ideal, because kids this age love making sounds with their feet. Introducing some basic tumbling moves like front rolls, back rolls, and cartwheels can also be fun. However, there should be no serious backflip–type work at this stage. These classes should be nothing more than a fun time for kids to learn how to use their bodies.

There is no right or wrong at this stage when young dancers are learning basic coordination. But there still must be some discipline. The classes shouldn't be free for alls, where the kids are out of control and running around the room pretending to be butterflies or Indians. A good teacher who knows how to work with young people will come up with creative, imaginative, and fun exercises and still know how to instill a sense of discipline and control in the students. Even young children need to be taught what is proper, and not proper, in a ballet or dance setting.

I think of preballet as a kind of head start program. Once the students reach the age where they begin their serious dance studies, those who have had these kinds of classes will start out ahead of the students who have not had them, and will learn the lessons more quickly. They will know something about dance already, and will associate dance classes with having fun experiences.

What to Look for in Preballet Teachers

Good teachers of advanced ballet are not likely to be good at teaching preballet. The teaching skills needed and the procedures of teaching are too different. Good preballet teachers know how to work with kids. They have a creative fluidity that allows them to assess the class situation moment by moment and a flexibility that allows them to change lesson plans on the fly. They know how to work with 3- to 7-year-olds on a creative movement level, how to keep the children motivated and the classes interesting.

Preballet Clothes and Shoes

Kids love wearing the basic leotard and tights used for ballet classes. These allow them to say, "I wear something special for dance, and I act special and learn special things." But good teachers are flexible about the kinds of dance outfits they allow their students to wear. For example, little girls love wearing tutus, just like grown-up ballerinas. There's no reason they can't wear one for part of the class.

In regard to shoes, some teachers don't even want ballet slippers worn to this type of class. Instead, they want the kids to work barefoot and barelegged, so their feet develop naturally, without the confines of slippers or shoes. In this way, the kids get the feel of the surface they're working and moving on, and the teacher gets a chance to see how their feet and legs are developing. With shoes, a teacher can't tell if the students are pulling their toes up or if their feet are relaxed or not.

BALLET, THE KEY TRAINING

If you want a career in musical theater, learning ballet is key, because in the Western dance tradition, ballet is the foundation. You can't fake knowing it, and knowing it prepares you to learn all the other kinds of dance styles. If kids don't learn to love ballet at an early age, chances are that they'll fight studying it and will continue fighting until they're allowed to discontinue studying it altogether. But keep in mind that aspiring dancers in musical theater who haven't studied ballet are not properly prepared as dancers and won't be able to market themselves. They might as well plan to spend the rest of their lives dancing in their living rooms for family and friends and not even bother to pursue a professional career.

Clothes

The standard ballet class clothing for both male and female dancers is pretty much leotards, tights, and ballet slippers. Hair that is long must be pinned up (and no gum chewing is allowed!). Students studying other types of dance can get away with wearing clothes that obscure the body and detract from its movements, but to study ballet seriously, they must have the proper clothing. The teacher must be able to see all parts of the body in order to make corrections to movements, and flowing or loose-fitting clothes make that impossible. Sometimes boys at the beginning of their ballet studies will feel uncomfortable about wearing tights because of peer pressure. So, for a short time, most ballet teachers will allow them to wear a looser type of outfit. Usually within a month or two they become more comfortable with the idea and switch over.

Many ballet students and dancers feel they can't begin class without warmup clothes. To my mind, clothing designed for warmup exercises is more about making a fashion statement than for filling any dancer's real need. Many years ago such attire was used in Europe because studios were unheated, and on cold days you could actually see your breath as you took class. Dancers had to wear ankle warmers and other such items to stay warm; there was a legitimate need for this type of apparel then.

Dance studios today are always heated in cold weather. The only purpose warmup clothes serve now is allowing dancers to dress in designer togs—and the makers of those togs to rake in millions every year from the dancers who buy them. Unless you practice in a meat locker, chances are you won't need them. (The need for warmup exercises is something else, and I'll discuss this in a minute.)

Finding a Good Ballet Teacher

Ballet is serious work, and, as I say numerous times in this book, aspiring performers deserve to study with the very best. If you're a parent looking for a ballet teacher, your child deserves the very best. We discussed some of the qualifications of good teachers in Chapter 3, and to maximize your chances of finding good instruction, I discuss a few more here.

Knowledge relating to the world of dance has made great advances in the last twenty to thirty years. Good ballet teachers keep abreast of the new research and discoveries in fields like anatomy and kinesiology (the study of movement), and are open to incorporating the new information into the way they teach dance. Years ago, people didn't know what was hard on the body, especially when it's cold. Through the years, dance instructors have learned that warming up the body is better done slowly and gently, to gradually work in more complex stretching exercises. They also know a lot more about foot and leg placement. At one time, teachers used to force students' feet into turnout position. As a result, students' feet and ankles were torqued, which probably increased the number of orthopedic doctors. The young dancer's turnout comes from the thigh and the hips, and if the foot won't turn any further at this point, the good teacher will "let it be." That is, teachers with a thorough knowledge of anatomy will know when they can ask a child for more turnout-and what it means to ask for a certain height of the leg or a certain placement in the hip structure, and so on.

Every person's body is different, and a good ballet teacher will work with students to maximize the potential each body allows. If you're having trouble with turnout but work on the problem slowly, say over a two-year period, it will improve. Eventually you'll be able to open up your legs and feet and turn out more, although it won't happen overnight. And be on the lookout for those teachers from the old school. Forcing turnout causes the feet to roll over so that all the dancer's weight is on the big toe, which is not good. Forcing the feet into the desired position can cause the knees and ankles to become so badly torqued that the dancer will eventually suffer injury. You need a ballet teacher who is aware of body placement, and if yours is not, it's time to find a new teacher.

Good teachers also understand when private lessons are useful and when they're not. Beware of those who want to give private lessons to a child who is just beginning in ballet. Private lessons are only needed for students at the intermediate or advanced stage who could use some special coaching on techniques they may be having difficulty with. Beginners need time to digest what they're learning. Private lessons are fine *if* they are separated by enough time to let the student work on all the theory the teacher presented during a lesson. Let the dancer continue in regular classes with the other students for a few weeks. Then perhaps another private lesson can be scheduled. Good ballet teachers will not try to milk parents for money by suggesting private lessons. Most of the time it's unnecessary at the early stage of dance training.

The Barre

Beginning ballet classes usually start at the barre. When children come to a ballet class, they go to the barre and pick out a spot for that day's session. Standing at the barre provides a moment of meditation, allowing each student to leave the busy outside world behind, change focus, collect energy, and center on what he or she is about to do.

The exercises performed at the barre are relative to the type of ballet being studied, but will usually consist of movements such as plié, tendu, dégagé, rond-de-jambe, fondu, frappé, échappé, jump work, relevé, grand battement, and stretches. (Many of the terms come from the French, who developed classical ballet.) It usually takes students about three years of class study to fully understand the techniques involved in his type of extended ballet barre. But dancers will continue to build on this foundation throughout their careers.

The barre is used for warmup. It is used for exercises that teach dance technique even while building strength. The exercises done at the barre help dancers avoid injury, improper alignment, and bad working habits, such as doing a plié without knees properly positioned over toes. They help students learn correct technique to extend their lives as dancers. Barre exercises strengthen the different muscle groups a dancer needs to be flexible. And the barre serves to support students as they lightly hang onto it while working on specific dance steps. Everything done at the barre is repeated in the center work in one way or another. If a teacher doesn't have the students start with the barre, it's akin to putting the cart before the horse.

The Center

Next, all the dancers move back from the barre and begin the center work, which is designed to bring the alignment and centering techniques away from the barre to a unsupported position. In other words, the center is where students really learn how to dance, where they gain musicality in their movements. It's not that dance skills aren't learned at the barre, but that full-body musicality can be learned only at the center, where the students have to stand and move on their own with no support. When students have no barre to support them, they begin to open up to other parts of dance, such as weight changes. They begin to do center steps like glissades and jetés among others that move both right and left, and front and back. They become aware of the placement of the body, such as the épaulement, which is the relationship of the shoulders to the audience or the mirror and involves the height of the arms. They begin to become more aware of the alignment of their bodies, and begin to do bigger, more athletic steps than are possible at the barre.

Students are now focused on everyone else in the room. Because of the studio mirrors, students can make more visual comparisons between the teacher and the other dancers. They also start using space differently, making sure they're not too close or too far away from their fellow dancers (a skill they'll use later on at auditions). Most importantly, this is the time in class where the teacher will be implementing combinations, which is when two or more steps are put together. The more advanced the students are, the longer the combinations the teacher will give them, which will challenge their memory development.

Pointe Class

In musical theater, pointe work isn't something dancers use much. In fact, they may never be asked to do it onstage. But for the sake of being employable, and because every once in a while some show may want performers who have the ability, it should be learned.

Just be aware that pointe work is serious business, and learning it requires a good teacher. Did I say "good?" Sorry, I mean the most qualified instructor at the best ballet academy in your area. Understand that, basically, pointe means putting the entire weight of the body on three toes. If done incorrectly, dancers can damage ankles, feet, and knees.

Barbara Early, in her book *Finding the Best Dance Instructor*, has this to say about girls learning pointe: "What they fail to realize, however, is that it takes an incredible amount of training, strength, and dedication to even begin dancing on toe. It's not a right, but a privilege, that should not be granted to the amateur dancer." Some parents don't understand this, and consequently try to rush their kids into pointe shoes by rationalizing that their children are exceptional, the best in their class, and deserve to be *en pointe*. Even worse are teachers who give in to this demand, and let a student into pointe class even though they know good and well that premature pointe work can only damage someone who is quite young or not advanced enough in ballet for this type of high-level, intensive work.

I list here for adults some specific criteria to adhere to when making this all-important decision for young dancers:

* No one should ever go en pointe unless they are taking two or three regular ballet classes a week, and have done so over a period of three to six months.
* Pointe work usually begins at age 12. To start at age 11, the student should be an exceptionally strong dancer.
* Students shouldn't go en pointe until their ankles and feet are strong enough to support their weight when standing on their toes, and they have acquired the degree of hip socket turnout required for pointe work. Hip socket turnout can be checked by an orthopedic surgeon to make sure everything is fine physically. But remember that orthopedic surgeons are not dancers or performers. Not all of them know what dancers do in toe shoes once they begin to move, so you may have to explain the importance of what they're checking out to them ahead of time.
* Dancers must be placed, and strong and competent enough, to have strong centers before they go en pointe. Ballet teachers should check this by determining if a student considering pointe work can balance in a stretched manner, without wiggling on the floor.
* Weight is also an important factor in deciding whether to start pointe work or not. Even if the student is a fine technician, excess weight interferes with the proper placement of the bones and can endanger the dancer's health and safety.

Remember, pointe work isn't for everyone. If you decide against it, it won't be a disaster. A dancer can still have a full career without acquiring the skill. But for those who have the right body type, and meet the other physical requirements that serious pointe work demands, it can help. Just have a competent ballet teacher check the student's balance and placement off point, and have an orthopedic surgeon who understands what dancing en pointe means check the degree of hip socket turnout, before any decision is made to go ahead.

MODERN DANCE

A lot of dancers make excuses for not studying modern dance, but the fact remains that in this day and age if you want a career in musical theater, you need it as an integral part of your training. It's different from ballet or other kinds of stage dancing, and you might not "get it" for awhile, but it has to be part of your repertoire.

Modern dance opens the dancer up to story-telling through the body. Innovative dancers and choreographers earlier in the twentieth century, like Martha Graham and Ruth St. Denis, used the body and its movements to create incredible stories of pathos. Not only were the "plots" interesting, they were free of the constraints that rigid costumes and strict technical steps imposed on the stories enacted through other styles of dance. Unlike ballet, modern dance offers a real freedom of expression through movement.

Musical theater shares some of the elements of modern dance. It also tells stories and makes demands on the imaginations of dancers. How often does a dancer in a musical just go onstage and dance? These days dancers are involved in each moment of the story the musical is telling, creating elements of time, space, and energy. Dancers must be able to use their bodies freely—to be trees, to hold themselves in different shapes, to change directions quickly and improvise a moment expressively. In short, they must be able to use dance to become and portray characters. Studying modern dance offers them that ability.

Finding Modern Dance Training

In small towns, you will have a difficult time finding modern dance training. In fact, it may be next to impossible. If a local studio does offer it, it's apt to be at the bottom of the list, and you'll have to check out the teacher to make sure she or he really knows how to teach this style. You might check with local colleges to see if they offer modern dance lessons to nonstudent members of the community.

If none of this pans out, you have two options. The first is the dance program of a college or university that does teach modern dance. Second, you can take a trip to New York during your summer or Christmas vacation, and study modern dance in one of the major modern dance studios, such as the Martha Graham School of Contemporary Dance, the Merce Cunningham Dance Studio, the Alvin Ailey American Dance Center, the Isadora Duncan Foundation for Contemporary Dance, or the José Limon Dance Foundation. Even a short immersion in one of these programs—which of course can be repeated over different summer or holiday periods—will give dance students a whole new perspective on dance that will show up in their performing.

In your research to find a studio, you will find that there are two schools of thought regarding the study of modern dance. One is that students should not train in a non–technique based form of dance training—like that taught by many modern dance studios—until they have some kind of technique-based studies under their belt. "Technique-based" means learning the proper body placements and movements needed for interpretation, communication, and maintaining the health of the dancer's body. Some teachers of modern dance invented their own techniques, including Doris Humphrey, Charles Weidman, and Martha Graham, and these are still used by teachers and studios espousing their methods. The studios you investigate will tell you which, if any, technique they use.

The second school of thought concerns the mixture of techniques that many students will be exposed to. In most small cities, you won't be able to find technique-based classes. Instead, you'll be exposed to a variety of techniques. But because modern dance has come a long way, this blending of styles can be healthy for the dancer.

When researching specific studios or teachers, start by asking questions about their philosophy of modern dance and their approach to teaching it. Read the teacher's resume. Attend one of the more advanced classes to observe what goes on, because this will tell you what will ultimately be learned at the studio. If observing a class doesn't show you anything, if you come away questioning the level of accomplishment of the staff and the students, that's a warning sign that the studio or teacher may not be for you.

Look for class discipline. No matter what technique or style of dance is being taught, discipline should be apparent. A class needs structure. If what you see amounts, in effect, to a free-for-all, you had best look for another teacher or studio. The class should be sixty to ninety minutes in length, depending on the level being taught. If it's too short in length, the students probably aren't learning much.

What Modern Dance Students Can Expect

A modern dance class usually starts with students on the floor. The particular technique base used will determine what the instructor teaches at any particular moment. No matter how the teacher starts warmups, whether at the barre, on the floor, or at the center, warming up always needs to proceed gradually, to avoid injury to the students' bodies.

In most classes, students spend time learning to breathe properly while dancing. They concentrate on studying body contractions and releases. The teacher will emphasize awareness of torsos and focusing on the difference between turnout and parallel positions. Sometimes the teacher will have the students travel across the room, performing a variety of basic steps at different tempos and elevations. Creative movements, rhythmic games, and improvisation will also be part of the class. The teacher will list certain parameters and ask a group of students to create something within them, then perform what they have created for the rest of the class. Implicit in these exercises is fostering a sense of connectedness between the students as they dance.

One of the best things about studying modern dance is that it teaches students how to work with other dancers as part of a group. Modern dance is really the only dance form that aims at connecting bodies so they interact together in an organic way. It allows dancers to explore using their bodies freely to express emotion, create characters, or do whatever else is called for at a particular moment in a performance. And because modern dance doesn't stress turnout, it's a safer form of movement for kids to study, as well as being a wonderful introduction to dance in general.

Modern Dance Class Clothing

Female students can wear a dark leotard; black, footless tights are optional. Male students can wear black, footless tights, and either no top or a T-shirt. No shoes are required. At some studios, it is acceptable for male students to wear loose fitting pants.

Music Used in Modern Dance

The music used for modern dance is very specific, and related to the technique base used. Tempo and rhythm are usually important, so it might involve a drum, a piano, or just about anything that can make a beat.

TAP DANCE

Tap dancing is an important skill in the musical theater performer's repertoire. Many musicals such as *42nd Street, George M, Crazy for You,* or *Bring in Da Noise, Bring in Da Funk* are full of tap numbers. Others like *Big* and *A Chorus Line* only showcase tap in a single number. But performers trying out for a show that includes even just one tap number will be cut from the auditions if they don't know tap.

Tap has a great history, and it's a shame that most kids studying dance today are unaware of its great legacy. With the amount of tap preserved by Hollywood's movie musicals, parents and dance teachers could do more to pass the information on to the younger generation. Everyone should know where this wonderful art form came from. For young male dancers, what could be a greater introduction to dance than learning that most of the great tap artists of the past were men—dance legends such as Peg Leg Bates, the Four Step Brothers, the Nicholas Brothers, the Berry Brothers, Fred Astaire, and Gene Kelly? Great female tap stars have included Ruby Keeler, Eleanor Powell, and Ann Miller. It's unfortunate that the technique and style of these great dancers, who delighted audiences for decades, is almost unknown today. Thank goodness for the efforts of the few who try to keep it alive.

Tap teaches dancers a great deal. While ballet provides a great sense of turning and a total understanding of center, tap gives them a sense of rhythmic stylization and musicality, along with a confidence in performing they'll need when performing all the other styles of dance. It's an important art form that must be taken seriously, and only the best instructor will do.

Beginning Tap Lessons

Frequently, kids show up in my studio ten years after they began training with another instructor, knowing virtually nothing. Ten years, and they're still at a beginner's level. Having been taught by unqualified instructors, they've often been taught advanced steps even before learning the fundamentals. They tend to produce sloppy tap sounds and show no sense of musicality. And, unfortunately, no one seems to have noticed these problems. Standards have dropped. What would have been shouted off the stage only a generation ago is now applauded.

This kind of mislearning is a shame, and a waste of hard-earned money spent on the classes. You must always strive to find the best teacher and the best studio to study tap dancing. Like any other dance form, the teacher has to build a solid foundation first. If he or she doesn't teach steps in the proper sequence, then when the student has to put those steps together at an audition later on, it just isn't going to happen. The learning process must itself go a step at a time. Teachers shouldn't try to fudge progress. If they do, the students lose.

If you're the parent of a kid studying tap, you have to make sure he or she gets the proper training at the beginners' level. In order to lay the proper foundation for solid tap training, young students, from age 8 up, have to learn the basic steps. These include:

Basic sounds: Hit, dig, hop, jump, leap, stamp, stomp, scuff, toe
Front steps: Flap, flap heel, flap heel heel, flap ball change, shuffle, shuffle hop step, hop shuffle step, cramproll
Back steps: Back flap, back flap heel, back flap heel heel, shuffle hop step, hop shuffle step, drawbacks

Tap students have to be taught how to rock back when traveling backward, right from the first lesson, to make clear and clean sounds, to stay on their toes, and to know when to be flat-footed.

From this stage on, anything goes. A class or lesson may or may not start with a tap barre. After the barre, if it's used, the student or students will go center and do a variety of exercises. From these exercises, the students, if it is a group class, may travel across the room in twos, and at the end of the class do a little combination. Nothing needs to be remembered for the next class. It's up to each student to practice what he or she wants to practice.

Private Versus Group Classes

Taking private or group lessons is the student's call—or an adult's call in the case of very young dancers. I personally have taken terrific group classes from high-caliber teachers like Danny Daniels, Al Gilbert, Jerry Ames, and Betty Morrow. But tap is one of the few dance forms where I would recommend taking private lessons, with a thoroughly knowledgeable and professional instructor. If you can't find one available in your town or nearby, then take a group class. However, keep in mind that private lessons advance taps students at a much greater pace. One year of private lessons is equivalent to three years of group class training. Why? Because in a group class, there might be twenty students tapping away at the same time. No one can possibly hear exactly what's going on in the tapping of each individual student. Students can be faking, and the teacher may never catch it. But with private lessons the teacher concentrates on one student only and his or her needs. It's clear who is making mistakes when they are being made, and every mistake gets corrected. If the student's dancing is sloppy, the teacher hears it immediately and can teach the student how to recognize it too. Private tap lessons provide a concentrated study of rhythm and sound, and in my opinion are the only way to go.

In private lessons, a good teacher instructs students through routines, each routine building on the steps learned in previous routines while introducing new ones. The repetition helps the students remember all the steps learned from the first lesson on. Teachers also work with students on fast pickup and improvisation. It amounts to building dance technique, style, and showmanship through routines that can be useful to know later on in the course of one's career. This is how the old timers taught tap, and a great way to improve very quickly.

So many young dancers today can do wonderful trick steps such as pullbacks, wings, toe stands, over-the-tops, and knee work. Yet it's clear from dance competitions that they don't have a clue about how really to tap dance. A good teacher builds from the bottom up, not the top down, making sure the students have a good foundation in the basics of tap.

Tap Class Shoes

Whether you take private tap lessons, or participate in a group class, the studio's policy will dictate what you can and cannot wear to class. Some studios are very strict about this, others let you wear what you like.

Have you gone into a dance store to buy a pair of tap shoes lately? A good pair of leather tap shoes, with the taps already on, will set you back at least $75. That is a lot of money, especially if you're paying for something a kid may grow out of in three or four months. Also, the price is the same, whether you buy a size 1 or a size 10. Personally, I wouldn't spend that much on shoes for a beginning student unless I absolutely had to. What if he or she doesn't like tap after taking a few lessons? There are many options in buying tap shoes, but remember these two important points:

1. If you're a parent buying tap shoes for a young person, whether it's for a boy or a girl, make sure you buy the shoes a little large to allow for foot growth.
2. Realize that price doesn't always coincide with quality. Tap shoes that cost $75 to $150 dollars usually have an endorsement name attached. Don't buy into a name. Instead, buy shoes that fit well and are comfortable, that don't hurt, and that the person studying tap will enjoy wearing.

Tap Shoes for Girls When a girl is just starting out in tap, my advice is to buy inexpensive, patent leather shoes, which you can pick up at department stores for less than $20. Also, make sure her first shoes are flat, with no heels, regardless of how much she might protest. The one drawback of patent leather shoes is that the generic tap that is put on them requires a lot of work by the dancer to make a good, clear sound. On the other hand, once a student learns how to make a good sound in those shoes, it will be that much easier when she steps up to higher-quality shoes. If the store doesn't carry the necessary size in patent leather, or if the young dancer refuses to wear them, you can check the dance studio for a good pair of used leather shoes. Studios always have them and do their best to recycle them. You can find great deals this way, usually costing half the price of when the shoes were new, and the shoes are usually in good condition.

Again, girls should start their training wearing flat shoes. Tap shoes with heels will follow as they advance in their studies. Eventually when they are older and advanced enough for auditions, they will need two-inch heel shoes. Producers and directors like the leggy look, and women dancers can't achieve it wearing flat shoes.

A lot of young women today who are quite advanced in their tap studies don't like to take classes in heels. You'll find many of them at the intermediate and advanced levels wearing men's flat tap shoes, claiming they feel more comfortable and can do dance tricks more easily in them. They know that somewhere along the way they'll have to audition in heels, but figure they can just train in these boys flats and make the transition to heels with no problem later on. That's simply not true. To tap dance properly with heel shoes, students have to study in heels for a period. It's a distinct technique, just as dancing in pointe shoes is in ballet. Therefore, when a young woman gets to the intermediate/advanced level of her tap studies, do her a favor. Buy her a new pair of heel shoes and throw out the old flat ones. She'll thank you later on in her career.

Tap Shoes for Boys You might be able to find a cheap pair of boys' patent leather tap shoes if you buy them used from a dance studio. Also check out dancewear catalogues and dance clothing stores. Another option is to buy a pair of regular shoes and convert them to tap shoes by having leather heels and soles put on and metal taps attached. A good shoemaker or shoe repair shop will know how to do this, but doing this may cost you the $75 you would pay for an expensive pair of new tap shoes.

A lot of tap shoes come with the taps already attached, but if the ones you buy don't, heed this advice: *Do not buy jingle taps!* These taps aren't good for anyone, at least anyone who wants to be a professional tap dancer. They are occasionally used in clogging, but I find them noisy and obnoxious. There's another important reason not to buy them. A tap dancer's job is to make a clear, clean sound, something that just cannot be done with jingle taps. If a teacher insists the students wear them, find another teacher.

Also, if you purchase taps separately, make sure they fit the entire heel and toe area of the shoe. If they don't, the shoes will feel awkward and the person wearing them won't like the fit.

When you go to a shoemaker to have the taps attached to the shoes, make sure to show the shoemaker the placement of the taps. I have actually seen shoemakers put the taps in the middle of the shoe. It might sound ridiculous, but it happens. Also, the screws that are included with the taps are usually too short. Go to a hardware store and pick up some that are a little longer. They will stay in your shoe for a longer time and generally be less of a hassle than the original, shorter screws, which tend to gradually work their way out of the shoe toward the dancing floor.

Finally, don't try to attach the taps yourself, unless you absolutely know how to do so. You could ruin the new shoes before they're laced up for their first use.

Although I can't think of another dance style that is as much fun to study and from which students can derive as much pleasure, it's important to remember that tap dancing is still dancing. It takes practice and dedication to achieve style, technique, and true showmanship. It's not just a question of personality. And it doesn't happen overnight.

JAZZ DANCE

There are a number of jazz dance styles, including classical, lyrical, musical theater, hip-hop, and funk. Classical is the foundation, and a good studio will always teach its jazz classes with that underpinning. Just what else you'll learn in the class will depend on whether it's based on the style of Matt Maddox, Luigi Giordano, or Jack Cole. Funk is different from hip-hop in that it's a looser style of jazz. Hip-hop is cutting-edge, right from the street, with no rules or set technique.

As with all dance lessons, the earlier the training begins, the better. But it's best if students start jazz dance lessons with a solid background in ballet and tap dance training, preferably three years or so of each. Jazz dance requires the basic training in dance technique that ballet gives, and the sense of rhythm and musicality that comes from tap. Studies can start as early as age 8 as long as the student has acquired the necessary foundation in ballet and tap, although age 12 isn't too late. When the student does start jazz dance training, he or she should still continue with one or two ballet classes a week, along with regular tap lessons.

A few things to remember: Even though this society is competition-driven, jazz class is not about competing with other students. Kids should have this understanding instilled in them, and their dance teacher should keep it in mind, too. Parents who are always comparing their child's dancing with the dancing of other children, dance students who are always jockeying for attention and position in the classroom, and teachers who are always promoting their students as winners of dance competitions do a disservice to the education needed for a professional career in musical theater.

Look at the student–teacher ratio of the class. One teacher for twenty kids might not be able to give enough individual attention to each student, or enough time to correcting mistakes.

Also, be clear about the goals of the class and dance studio. Are the lessons focused on improving student technique, or is most of the time spent on preparing for recitals or competitions? How many shows does the studio do a year, and how long is the rehearsal period for each? Does the class combine dance styles—say forty-five minutes spent on jazz and forty-five minutes on ballet? A student past the age of 8 probably needs more concentrated training in the particular style he or she is studying.

Hip-Hop and Funk

If one class a week is all you can afford, it's best that it be technically based. Yet if a young person wants to start with a hip-hop or funk class, fine. It doesn't really matter where he or she starts, because other doors can open down the road. The student may attend a convention or workshop and see the incredibly talented kids that can do it all—musical theater, classical jazz, and lyrical jazz as well as hip-hop and funk. Soon he or she will want to be able to do it all, too. Once students start, if they're serious about being dancers, they'll branch out by themselves into many areas.

What does really matter, though, is that the student actually branch out. Hip-hop and funk are all the rage these days among young people, but it's important for dance students to realize that they aren't the only jazz styles they'll have to learn to become professional dancers. Also, while funk and hip-hop have their place, they don't train dancers for anything else. Students who study only these styles don't receive the technical training required to perform other styles like classical and lyrical jazz. I don't want to generalize and say that someone who studies only hip-hop and funk will be unable to do anything else. But I will say that without classical jazz training, the student won't become the proficient dancer he or she should be. Ultimately, this could mean losing out on work.

Aside from music videos, there aren't many other venues that use hip-hop or funk. The Broadway production *Footloose* uses these styles, as do a few shows in Las Vegas and on some cruises. But if hip-hop and funk are all a dancer knows, he or she isn't well rounded enough to be very marketable professionally.

Moreover, hip-hop and street jazz styles promote knee and lower back injuries, not good for the longevity of a dance career. Dancers who do hip-hop in music videos especially have to be careful about who they work for, as this type of job is frequently under no union jurisdiction of any kind. Salaries are usually whatever the producer, director, or choreographer decides to pay, and the work conditions may be impossible. Dancers offered this sort of work should read the contract carefully. Ask about the flooring, the shoot location, and the kinds of movements that will be expected of you. One job is not worth the cost of acquiring a permanent injury.

Jazz Class Clothes and Shoes

What students wear depends on the style being taught. In a classical jazz setting, leotards and tights are best. If they choose, both female and male students can wear jazz pants that are fitted to the knee. Whatever they wear, it has to hug the body closely so the teacher can see body alignment, placement, and posture to make the necessary corrections.

As far as shoes go, it's really up to the instructor. A jazz oxford, a sandal type of shoe, or even bare feet may be what the teacher decides on. Ballet slippers should not be an option. As dance teacher and author Barbara Early says, "They don't provide the right 'feel' for this type of class. Nor do they have the traction of jazz shoes; dancers might find themselves slipping and sliding through each session."

Funk and hip-hop are a different kind of jazz dancing, with clothing needs all their own. It's OK for students to wear something they find comfortable, very loose, along with tennis shoes or boots. It's important for a dancer to adopt the attitude and clothing required by any given style to exemplify its look. Funk and hip-hop require a street look. But keep in mind that these styles are where the most dance injuries occur. Rubber-soled tennis shoes stick to the floor and inhibit the movements required for turning. It's easy to twist knees and ankles and hurt one's body in other ways when dancing in this style, so dancers should pick the clothes they wear with great care.

Finding a Good Jazz Dance Teacher

During the early stages of jazz training, students need a knowledgable teacher, someone who focuses on good warmup technique and body alignment to avoid injury. When investigating studios, especially those in small towns, check out the beginners class carefully to see just who's teaching it. What often happens in studios in smaller areas, as compared to the studios found in the major dance markets like New York, Los Angeles, and Chicago, is that beginners are often taught by novice or student teachers. This is a huge mistake. I think the more experienced instructors should be teaching at the beginners level, to help the students build a solid foundation. Less experienced teachers might be able to handle the more advanced students, who already have a good idea of what they're doing. Inexperienced instructors teaching beginners just cause trouble. Sometimes they're not very emotionally mature themselves. They're not good at instilling discipline, and they may lack knowledge regarding proper body alignment, posture, and placement.

You need to know something about the background of the teachers. Where did they themselves go to school to learn what they're now teaching? What are their attitudes about themselves and their abilities? Do they think of themselves as powerhouse divas who have something to prove, so that they spend all their time dancing for their students instead of teaching? Do they introduce steps that are too hard for the kids—steps at their own level of dance and not at the students' level? That alone will cause big problems. The students will just get confused, and even if they move to other studios the new instructors will need to educate them out of that confusion, causing them to start all over again.

Jazz dancers typically have short career spans, and that's because injuries are more common in jazz dancing than in other dance styles. For one thing, the most important movement is the plié, where the dancer hugs the ground and puts far more strain on the back and knees than in any other dance form. And jazz dancing is power dancing—driving into the floor with quick changes in direction and unbelievable focus on your center. With their knees and lower back taking so much punishment, dancers are likely to injure themselves. This means it's particularly important that beginners have the best teachers possible, who know just how to guide students in their training, allowing them to learn steps and movements only when they're ready.

What Students Can Expect to Learn

The Basic Warmup No matter what the style of jazz they are studying, students must know how to do a proper warmup. Jazz dancers find themselves moving up and down quickly on the floor, and changing directions instantaneously. To do this without being properly warmed up can risk injury. Warmup is the first thing they need to learn.

There was a time when teachers didn't know much about the body. Grand battements (big kick steps) were done at the beginning of class, and splits were done ten minutes into the warmup. Today, teachers realize the importance of running body-safe classes. Many of them have connections to the fitness industry and know what works and what doesn't in keeping bodies healthy. Others work with doctors to properly formulate stretching routines and warmup sessions in the ways least likely to cause injury.

Different instructors use different warmup techniques. Some start with a jazz barre, while others begin with five to seven minutes of aerobic work, which allows the body gradually to warm up to 101 degrees Fahrenheit. At this point, the body is ready to stretch. Whatever the variations, the most important aspect of warmup is starting slow and gradually warming all the joints in the body. This allows the dancer to move freely throughout the class exercises, and helps prevents injury.

One common way jazz classes begin is for everyone to face the mirror and spread out on the floor. The teacher puts on the music, and the warmup begins. It consists of many elements, including torso stretches, arm reaches, side stretches, flat backs, back stretches, rolldowns, rollups, lunges, contractions, and swings. With beginners, the instructor will explain each of these stretches and have students do them separately. As the class progresses, the teacher will put them together in combinations, such as four-arm reaches, rolldown, and rollup, correcting the students as they do them. A good center warmup always ends with a good plié, tendu, dégagé, rond-de-jambe, and perhaps a full adagio combination.

Remember, warmups are done to protect the body, and beginning students have to learn good warmup techniques. If a beginners' class has a New York–style set warmup, with the teacher giving no corrections, find another class. This is a technique reserved for advanced students, and its use with beginners is a red flag to move on.

Isolations After learning how to warm up properly, students next learn how to do isolations, which is moving one part of the body without moving other parts. This includes learning how to move the head, shoulders, rib cage, hips, and feet.

Depending on the dancer, and the level of the class, the body parts can be moved in sequence. Students also learn how to do isolations not just while standing still but while doing foot work, keeping the heart rate up.

Floor Stretching Learning how to do stretches sitting on the floor will be next. The kind of stretches taught will be the kind of stretches that the instructor does best and is most comfortable teaching.

Across the Floor Next the students will be taught the technique of doing dance steps while traveling across the floor. The instructor will line them up in groups of two, and teach them how to travel from stage right to stage left, then back again. The steps taught will be basic ones, such as pas de bourrée front and back, chassé, step ball change, passé, and a variety of jazz walks. At some point in the training, the teacher may add an arm movement or two, so the students will learn how to work in opposition.

After these basic steps of traveling across the room are mastered, the teacher will link them together. There will be combinations such as pas de bourrée and chassé, or pas de bourrée walk. The teacher might allow battements across the floor, but only at a 45-degree angle. Later, the intermediate class teacher will not only link more elements together, but will begin to add turn and jump combinations. Battements will be at 90 degrees. Students will move into pirouettes and more technically difficult steps, and will start to add speed to their moves.

Combinations "Combinations" means putting together the individual moves learned into a larger whole. In a dance class, this is done by the instructor having the students face the mirror as he or she teaches them the steps in combination. This is similar to how an audition is conducted, but here the teacher goes slowly, breaking it all down into the separate movements and the count that accompanies each. No matter how long it takes, teachers usually wait until almost everyone has it all down before dividing the class members into smaller performance groups. Whether four or eight counts are involved, the combination should match the skill level of the class members so that they find it challenging yet attainable. If a kid becomes discouraged, it's a sign that he or she is in the wrong class in terms of ability or that the instructor needs better teaching skills.

Some teachers may leave out the across-the-room steps at this point, but students who find themselves attending a school where this final dance combination is being left out should look for a new studio. Beginning jazz dance students always look forward to performing the end combination, because it's a chance to really dance and to show their abilities in terms of what's they've learned. Not being able to do this is akin to taking acting lessons while never actually performing a scene.

TUMBLING

How many audition notices in the trade papers add at the end of their breakdowns of the characters being cast that "tumbling is a plus"? I have seen performers lose jobs because they couldn't tumble. Tumbling skills can give dancers an edge in looking for work even if they never actually have to use those skills in a show. They help a dancer's pliability and flexibility, and teach the dancer how to properly use her or his back. Tumbling is an important skill dance students should learn early on.

Finding a Good Tumbling Studio

A lot of today's dance studios include tumbling as part of their curriculum. Some of them have rooms of the right size and the equipment needed to teach students all the tumbling skills they'll ever need to know as dancers. Others, usually smaller studios, teach students what they can at the studio, and then refer them to a gymnastics coach, where they can learn the power tricks in a safer environment and in rooms with greater space and more height than the dance studio itself can provide.

Parents whose children will be studying tumbling should sit in on a class and observe how the students and teacher work together. Does the teacher relate well to the students and make it a fun atmosphere? Is the class loose and chaotic, or are the students taught tumbling skills and tricks in some kind of logical progression? Are the students doing tricks with tightly stretched legs, or is their technique sloppy and out of control? In order to pick a good tumbling studio, you need to know something about the basics of teaching tumbling. So we'll discuss that next.

A good studio will teach tumbling through a progression of tricks, and will never teach students out of that order. The reason this is necessary is that each trick teaches, or prepares, the student's body to progress to the next one. Teaching these skills out of order can discourage students and possibly set them up for failure or even injury. You may not know tumbling terminology or the tricks the terms refer to, but I list a good tumbling progression here so you'll have a checklist as you research studios:

> *Basic tricks* Bridge • Bridge and walking down the mat • Front roll • Back roll • Headstand • Cartwheel
>
> *Limbers and walkovers* Front limber • Front Arabian • Back Arabian • Back walkover (both sides) • Back walkover (alternates) • Front walkover (both sides) • Front walkover (alternates)
>
> *Power tricks* Running cartwheel • Round-off • Front handspring • Back handspring or flip-flops • Aerial • Round-off back handspring
>
> *Miscellaneous tricks* Kip-up • Valdez • Walking on your hands • Mule kick
>
> *Tricks that may or may not be used onstage* Backward somersault from a pike • Layout or tuck position • Frontward somersault • Twisting tricks

Spotting

There are two types of spotting techniques used in tumbling. The first is *belt spotting,* where the student is actually strapped into a belt attached to ropes. Robert Ito and Bill Roetzheim, in their book *Tumbling,* explain:

> *There are three general classifications of belts. Hand belts which are useful in spotting tricks, where the coach must stay close to the tumbler. Overhead spotting rigs are used when the tumbler is doing high tricks beyond the reach of the coach, and twisting belts are used whenever the student is learning a trick that requires twisting and flipping at the same time.*

Even though belt spotting is said to be the safest technique for spotting, I prefer *hand spotting,* where the coach actually follows the student with his or her hand, from the beginning of the trick to the end. This type of spotting should only be done by an experienced coach or teacher, but when done properly will speed up the learning process by placing the tumbler in the correct position every time the trick is performed. It also lengthens the amount of time students can spend actually tumbling at each lesson since there's no waiting time as different students are attached to and detached from the belt. They can line up and do their tricks down the mat in an orderly, time-efficient manner. Also, when a belt is used, students have to make an adjustment for its weight, and this can sometimes throw them out of balance. With hand spotting, the coach progressively eases up on the student, making it easier in the end for the student to make the transition to doing the tricks on his or her own.

Spotting is a very important skill, and you should always make sure that the teacher is good at it. Just one wrong tumbling move can cause major injury, so you can't trust just anyone with the job. If anyone does get hurt in a tumbling class, it should be the spotter. The safety of the students should be the number one concern. When researching studios always find out whether any major injuries have occurred in tumbling classes because of faulty spotting techniques. On your initial visit to observe a tumbling class, watch very carefully how the spotting is done.

Men Spotters Hand spotting is a very "hands on" activity. It has to be to ensure the safety of the students. But with the exaggerated caution of today's world, where teachers can be accused of unnecessarily touching or even molesting their students, coaches and teachers are taking extra precautions about touching them physically. If you're a parent looking for a good tumbling class but the idea of a male coach hand spotting your daughter bothers you, then by all means try to find a female coach. Observe several classes to satisfy yourself that everything is within your comfort zone. If it isn't, then do everyone a favor and leave the studio. Coaches and teachers love their jobs, and they don't need parents implying that bad motives are behind the physical contact that is necessary in tumbling or suggesting that something has happened when it hasn't. This kind of paranoid behavior isn't good for anyone—the parents, the kids, and especially the teachers, who can have their careers threatened by reckless accusations.

Tumbling Equipment

Whether you attend a full-fledged gymnastics studio or learn your tumbling at a dance studio, the tricks should be taught on mats. I think you should look for a minimum of two or three landing mats, each four inches thick, and at least one crash pad that is eight inches thick. A crash pad is used when a tumbler is trying a trick for the first time without spotting, and will protect the student against most of the injuries that can occur.

Of course the most important piece of "equipment" is an instructor or coach who knows how to teach tumbling in a safe way. I've seen studios with only two landing mats, and gyms filled with as much equipment as you could wish for. But in the end the quality of the teacher is paramount.

A Final Word on Tumbling

Many young performers start tumbling lessons, only to tell their parents a month or two later that they're bored. "We're doing the same thing, over and over again" is a common complaint. Everyone needs to realize that there are a finite number of tumbling tricks to master. However, acquiring this mastery requires repetition. Parents should encourage kids to stay the course. If a career in the performing arts is the goal, quitting tumbling will not serve a student well.

5
Avoiding the Dance Hype

D ance competitions. Dance conventions. Master classes. Together, they account for one of the biggest booms in the entertainment industry today. Targeting dance studios by mass mailings and magazine advertising, and offering some of the best names in the business as teachers and judges, these events in the United States alone attract over ten thousand dance studios and their students as participants every year.

But what purpose do they serve? How important are they for training to be a dancer? Are they useful learning experiences for dancers and their parents, or just another scheme to take their hard-earned dollars? Can they have harmful effects?

Because these events have become such big business, they deserve a chapter all to themselves. In the following pages, we'll explore the questions just asked about them and reach some conclusions. Before we start, just let me say that insofar as kids are concerned, they need time to develop, both as dancers and as people—time to be silly and unstructured, to explore their young lives at their own pace. Parents and teachers should respect this and allow the downtime from studies and goal-oriented activities all kids need. Immersion into competitions needs to be handled gradually and in an unhurried manner. Avoid stress and it can be fun for everyone.

DANCE COMPETITIONS

A dance competition is an event where dance students in a given geographic region perform routines prepared for them by the studios they attend. Each studio submits an entry form listing the students and the categories they will be competing in. The studio owner collects the entry fees from each student and mails a single check to the company sponsoring the event. (Keep in mind that there is a separate fee for each category the student competes in.) The parent or legal guardian of every child who enters must sign a form releasing the competition's owner from any liability for personal injury or loss of property.

The standard dance categories are ballet, pointe, jazz, tap, song and dance, and production; there are also usually specialty categories like drill teams, clogging, pompom, and gymnastics. The categories are divided by group—solo, duet, trio, and small- or large-group performances—and entrants compete against others of their own age.

The entry fees vary from competition to competition, running anywhere from $50 for a solo performance, to $60 or $70 per performance for duets or trios, to $18 or $20 per person per performance for small or large groups. There will always be a minimum number of performers required to compete in the small- or large-group categories, stipulated ahead of time. Some competitions are affiliated with beauty pageants, which have their own additional fees.

Every competition has its own judging system, but there are usually three or four judges who assess contestants in each category in five different areas: technique, showmanship, costume, choreography, and execution. And the contestants aren't just competing against each other at these events. They're competing for the studios they attend, which means the studio whose students accumulate the highest number of total points wins.

Positive Aspects of Dance Competitions

First off, let me say that dance competitions give their participants a chance to perform onstage, which is especially important for young people. Unfortunately, these days, there are too few opportunities for dancers at any level of training to do that. Performing before an audience helps a dancer develop the self-confidence and poise needed to perform successfully onstage. And performing as both a soloist and a group dancer promotes versatility, which is invaluable since each area involves different performance skills. Younger students particularly need to learn how to deal with the pressure of putting themselves on the line, something they will encounter later when auditioning and performing professionally. They need to learn if they have what it takes to be a performer, and if that's really the goal they want to pursue. Competitions are good teachers.

Kids participating in these events also learn about living with the feelings connected to competition. If they don't win first place, they learn the valuable lesson of handling defeat gracefully. The participation of parents is important here, pointing out that you don't always get what you want in life, and that the most important thing is knowing you've done your best. The young performer who learns this lesson will have taken a big step toward handling the disappointments that will inevitably crop up in pursuing a career in musical theater.

Competitions teach kids how to work with others, how to be part of an ensemble and not think of themselves as the "star" of the group. If you're a dancer, always thinking you're the star will make you stick out like a sore thumb. You need to learn how to work with partners or within groups, how to be part of a team effort.

The best thing about dance competitions is that you meet people from other studios, see how they're being taught to dance, and how your skills compare to theirs. Maybe you need to improve your skills. That's valuable to know, and dance competitions can be a healthy way to gain that knowledge.

Honestly, it doesn't matter who wins at these events. What matters is having the courage to get on the stage and perform. In that way, everyone's a winner. Remember, it's just a competition, and who wins is based on the opinion of just a few judges. Whether you and the other students from your studio are the best ones there, or competing reveals that you all need to work more on your technical dance skills, with the right attitude you gain something just from participating.

Some Negatives

In the opinion of Vickie Sheer of Dance Educators of America, the word "competition" is wrong for describing these events—wrong in the sense of the performance skills they should be fostering and wrong especially for the young people who participate in them. I agree with that opinion. I think "showcase" describes such events better— or at least describes such events as they ought to be run It's not as if participants have to "beat" each other, as if the events were duels to the death, so to speak. These events should showcase talent. Period.

Think about it. Most performers don't compare their own abilities to those of other performers as much as to the level they think they themselves should be performing at. They ask, "Could I have done this better? How can I improve?" An emotionally sound, healthy dancer doesn't compete against someone else, but against himself or herself, always striving to dance better. I think that attitude is the essence of what a performer, an artist, and a dancer should be. Unfortunately, I'm not convinced that competitions as they are run these days really foster that attitude.

If you sit through a dance competition, you'll notice that the numbers performed by different individuals and groups in each category all look the same. Most studios tend to rely on formulas, something they think the judges want to see. This results in a predictable conformity. Studios also seem to have the mind-set that the bigger a production is, the better. Elegance and simplicity seem to have fallen by the wayside.

Formula dancing is particularly irritating in that it makes choreographers lazy and uncreative. The creative spark seems to be sacrificed to playing it safe to win the trophy. So much for advancing the art.

Another problem with dance competitions relates to cost. They are getting expensive. The average fee to perform a three-minute solo these days is $50. Depending on how many numbers the dancer is in and whether he or she wins in any category, you could easily empty your pockets of hundreds of dollars at a single event just paying the performing fees. Most competitions award cash prizes for the winning high-score performance in each category. Say you pay $50 to get a dancer into a solo competition, and he or she receives the high score. In that case you might well break even and get the entry fee back—if the prize is $50. But take the case of a winning nine-person small group, where each member has paid a $20 entry fee. Even if the cash prize is higher, say, $150, it has to be split nine ways, which means each participant receives around $17. You're losing money.

Many competitions don't even award cash prizes; instead they give students ribbons or medals, while the winning studios get the trophies.

Don't forget that the costs associated with competitions don't stop with entry fees. How much will you have to spend on the dancer's costume? Will you have to travel out of town and pay hotel expenses? Will you have to buy meals for two or three days? What about entertainment apart from the competition, like going to a movie, or the other little expenses that will inevitably pop up? Add it all up, and the costs can be quite significant. You have to decide if all the money spent on the event actually did the young dancer any good, or whether it could have been used in a more productive way. Likewise in regard to the time and pressures competitions involve.

The Role of Dance Studios and Teachers

As a dance teacher myself, what really gets me on my soapbox is the part dance studio owners and the teachers that work for them often play in all this. Dance competitions can be enjoyable and valuable experiences. But why do some studios and teachers set their students on the path of winning competitions at all costs, stripping away the fun? If students don't win a trophy, are they suddenly worthless? Should studios set these kinds of priorities? I believe that if they pursued the concept of pure performance instead of emphasizing the accumulation of trophies and medals, it would lead to dance competitions being much more positive experiences for everyone involved.

And what about professional etiquette? Studios and teachers who foster a "win at all costs" attitude also usually set a tone of meanness by criticizing students from other studios. This merely teaches habits of hate and jealousy. A good teacher knows how students learn by example and strives to set good examples for them. In my opinion, studios that teach bad professional etiquette are engaging in abusive and unhealthy methods of teaching young, impressionable minds, and parents should pull their kids out of such places.

Studios that focus on their students winning competitions also usually do so at the expense of teaching the very valuable things those students need to know about dance technique if they hope to have careers in musical theater. Do these studios produce first-rate dancers, or do they produce dancers who merely function in the competition mode? Are they teaching their students how to prepare for actual musical theater auditions and get through them technically? Remember, winning a competition is meaningless if no dance technique is being developed, at least in terms of working toward a professional career as a performer.

Other studios turn out topnotch dancers because they don't substitute the time needed to prepare competition dances for the valuable time needed to work on dance technique. They schedule competition training on separate days or at different hours so the two don't conflict.

The Role of Parents

A lot of what determines whether dance competitions have a positive or negative effect on kids has to do with parental attitudes and how children have been raised. Competitions approached in the right frame of mind can be educational and uplifting, allowing kids to improve themselves. Yet too often you see parents who are caught up in these events for themselves, feeding their egos through their performing sons and daughters. The parents want the trophies, they want the money, they want first place. Their children become reflections of themselves, not people with their own needs and feelings. If they come in second rather than first, the parents act as if the loss is a slap in the face. By vicariously living through their children, and insisting on victory at all costs, parents defeat the real purpose of studying dance and being in a competition—which is for children to enjoy developing their talents, and to have fun.

There are also parents who are nasty to kids from other studios, trying to "psych them out" with hateful glances or harsh words. I worry about such people, poisoned by jealousy. This is every bit as bad for the young performers as rivalry between studios. If parents are going to act so immaturely, better that they stay at home. It's ultimately they who are responsible for teaching their kids that what is most important is not winning a medal or trophy, but just doing your best. I think Richard DiSarno, National Director of Dance America, and the driving force behind Dance Olympus, puts it all into the proper perspective when he says:

> *I always talk about respect. It starts with yourself and must continue on to include every other being on the planet. It is easy to respect the things we share with others, but it becomes a little more difficult to embrace the differences that separate us. Nevertheless, while we do not have to like everything about one another, we must respect ourselves and every person with whom we come into contact.*

Another kind of problem is *lack* of involvement by parents in the dance class process until a competition nears. Too many parents these days just drop their kids off at the studio and pick them up later, showing little interest otherwise until they hear the word "competition." Suddenly they're involved. Here's a chance to win! Parents should show an interest in the entire dance class process, from the beginning of training to the competition itself. If their son or daughter wins a trophy, fine, but the parents shouldn't fixate on that goal to the exclusion of everything else. They need to be involved every step of the way, working with the studio, and seeing to it that their children enter only the right kinds of competitions. Parents need to be aware of what's valuable to a young person's development and ensure that the dance teachers reinforce those values. Without that kind of involvement, young performers will end up poorly adjusted to the demands of a show business career.

Sexuality and Competitions

I'm concerned about the increasing sleaziness of costumes and physical movements that some studios are pushing to give their students an edge in competitions. It seems there's at least one studio like this in every region that thinks sexual flash is the winning formula. Unfortunately, if it *is* rewarded with high scores, other studios start picking up on it.

If your kid's costume is too skimpy to wear at home, how can it be acceptable on a stage, in front of hundreds of people? Why is this kind of over-the-top sexuality encouraged? I recently saw a 5-year-old wearing a black leather bra. The dance was cute, but the costume was totally inappropriate for her age.

Having kids perform sexually loaded gestures in skimpy attire is the worst thing adults can do to them. It's not appropriate or warranted. It's actually a form of child abuse, and more and more competitions are establishing strict rules to curb the practice.

Judging of Competitions

All competitions require, in their rules and regulations, that only top-flight, qualified judges evaluate the contestants. They might be performers, choreographers, or dance professionals from nearby. They're introduced during the course of the competition, so contestants and their parents know who they are, and short bios are usually included in the program. The bios provide some insight into their backgrounds and what they may be looking for.

Once the competition is under way, the judges either use a score sheet on which they also write a critique of each dancer's or group's performance, or they supply a numerical score along with an audiotape critique, dictated during the performance. Most teachers and parents prefer the tape, because it means the judges aren't distracted while watching the performance by having to write something down simultaneously.

Competitors are judged on an adjudicated point system, where there's a predetermined amount of points to compete for. Typically, after a few of the categories have been completed the points are tallied and the emcee (usually the owner of that particular competition) announces the top scores within those categories.

Now, there are two kinds of judges. The first, the "feel good" judge, basically gives high scores to everyone and positive tape assessments. Such judges tend to say things like "Good job, you're great," "What a talent," or "I really liked your performance." This may be flattering, but unfortunately it offers nothing of real value to work with, either for students, parents, or teachers. Feeding the dancer's ego without any constructive criticism makes this type of judging an empty exercise.

The second type of judge is more objective and helpful. He or she is also positive and upbeat, but even if the student really *is* good points out things that need attention. For example, a judge like this might say, "That was a nice grand jeté, but your back foot wasn't pointed."

Sometimes I wonder how many judges of dance competitions are really qualified to be doing this. What's their background? Are they themselves dancers or just people with no idea of what they're looking for? I also have to question how long a judge can sit and remain objective before he or she needs a break. It's a tiring ordeal, usually ten hours a day, spread out over three days with almost no letup during the actual hours of competition. Personally, I don't think judges should work longer than four hours at a sitting before getting a breather. Also, a lot of the same people judge many of the competitions. The competition circuit should have more judges, rotating them more often to keep the pool fresh.

Judges are increasingly noticing a lack of technique onstage. I suspect it stems from a lack of basic preparation. Kids need to spend more time in dance technique classes. It amazes the judges how many dance teachers put kids in the back row at competitions, clueless about what they're supposed to be doing, in an attempt to hide their shortcomings. Instead of camouflaging them just to get the competition point numbers up, shouldn't the instructors be training them? A teacher's responsibility should be to get the students' technique up to the level required for the competition, or he or she shouldn't be competing.

Judges like to see presentations that are sincerely artistic, not just a smile plastered on some kid's face. They're looking for dancers that love to dance. By being well prepared with a good entrance and a nice clean exit, you will add to your professionalism and deliver on what the judges are looking for. Judges would like dance teachers to realize that most of the time competitions are not held in a theatrical setting with a stage proscenium and legs, so they must have their students practice in different sized rooms and a variety of spaces. In that way, the dancers can hit center and stay in any space they might be put into.

Judges *don't* like dancers that relate specifically to them as judges, staring them straight in the eye and gearing their dancing just to them. They want dancers who relate to the entire audience and show sincerity of movement. More than anything in dancers, they look for a sense of ease onstage, a sense that performers are comfortable with what they're doing. They also tend to score lower when a dancer tries to use every trick he or she knows in a two-and-a-half minute performance. It's overkill, and neither judges nor audiences like it.

More isn't always better. Dancers with less technical ability, who know how to present themselves well at their level of accomplishment, almost always score more points than those at a high level who look as if they're taking a physical fitness test. Judges look for dancers with a combination of strong technique, emotional quality, and presentational skills. They like to see choreography and costumes that are age appropriate. They like to see the dance you perform match your ability level.

Dance Competitions as Business

Every dance competition is someone's business. It's free enterprise, the American dream, and every business wants as many customers as possible. Now ask yourself how many third-place awards and honorable mentions are given out at these events. The answer is not many. Why? Because if a competition gives out too many low scores, teachers may not patronize that event in the future. Parents and studios don't want their kids to be rated as mediocrities. They'll seek out the competitions that give them high scores. So it's not very helpful from a business point of view to have scoring standards that are too strict. It will drive the clients away. On the other hand, handing out all first- and second-place awards makes everyone happy. Parents feel good about their kids. The competition owners can look forward to return customers, which means more money in the bank. And inflated scoring doesn't just make studio owners and teachers feel good; it helps their students become eligible for the national finals, which makes them look good in the eyes of their current students and the students' parents, and helps the studios attract new students.

So, knowing all this about dance competitions—that they're basically a business involving the compromises just described—how valuable are they really in helping students achieve a career in musical theater? As I said earlier, they can serve a real purpose if used the right way. They're not crucial to developing dance technique. But they can be helpful venues for kids to explore what it's like to be onstage, what it means to perform before an audience. As long as parents and teachers take these events for what they are and tell the kids simply to do their best and not worry about winning, the kids can learn something from them and have fun along the way.

Preparing for a Competition

Success at these events is not random. Preparation is necessary, from the things you have to bring with you, to getting where you have to be, to arriving on schedule for your events. To start with, prepare a checklist ahead of time that includes everything you need to take with you for the competition itself, such as costumes, makeup, wigs, accessories, and music tapes. Write out a schedule too, once you know the venues and the times of the competition events.

Perhaps the most preparation needs to go into the piece or pieces the dancer will be performing. He or she must be able to nail the performance every time. It has to be second nature, a part of the dancer, as automatic as breathing. Whether performing as a soloist or the member of a group, no one can just wait until arriving at the theater or performing venue to put it all together. You have to focus on it long before that, whether in a classroom, a rehearsal hall, or even in your bedroom. Performing isn't restricted to the time spent onstage. It's something you have to prepare for methodically and deliberately well before you're on the stage itself.

The Competition Store

Competitions always have "stores" at which they sell merchandise related to the event. Shopping at one of these is much like shopping on a cable TV channel. In fact, many people come to these events just for the sake of shopping. You can buy drinking mugs, dance clothes, sweatshirts, and trinkets of all sorts emblazoned with the name of the competition. If you're the parent of a contestant at the event, remember that he or she will be passing through this kitsch oasis every day, so it's best to set buying guidelines before you get there and stick to them.

Competition stores even offer parents the opportunity to buy their kids first-place trophies if they didn't earn one! But before you do that, think about the message you're sending your kid regarding the importance of winning.

Competition Classes

Some competitions are beginning to offer classes to the attendees. Students can take lessons in virtually any dance style, from tap to jazz to musical theater. This is a big plus, as it adds the notions of education and learning to the idea of performing and winning. Competitions that offer these classes have a higher level of prestige and respect than those that don't. They tend to attract people with a better grasp of what's important about attending such events, making for a much more well-rounded and healthy experience.

DANCE CONVENTIONS

Second in popularity to dance competitions are dance conventions. Here the main focus is classroom training. Some of the best teachers in the business attend conventions. Each convention also holds a competition. But the competitions are kept small and informal so as not to detract from the larger purpose, and the spotlight is always on learning.

Conventions are usually weekend events. The competition may be held on Friday night, with the classes scheduled for Saturday and Sunday. Classes go on throughout the day. There are three class levels: one for juniors (age 12 and under), one for seniors (age 13 and up), and one for teachers. This varies according to the particular convention you're attending. But flexibility is always a goal, so juniors who are proficient enough might end up studying with seniors.

Conventions limit how many students from each studio can enter their competitions, and some conventions do not allow solo, duet, or trio performances, preferring instead to focus on groups. The rules are pretty much the same as already described for the larger dance competitions, but the judging is usually better. If the competition is held after classes are under way, the judges have already had some interaction with the students, and know what they're capable of doing.

If you attend a dance convention for the workshops alone, the cost will range from $100 to $150 for two days. If you take part in the competitions, it will be a bit more expensive.

Benefits of Conventions

Attending a convention can really benefit students. But remember, you only get out of it what you put into it. If, as a student, you're not just running around and acting silly, but instead paying attention to what's going on around you, you'll get the opportunity to interact with some of the best teachers from this country's dance communities, especially those from New York and Los Angeles. You'll study their choreography, their music, and the various styles in which they are experts. You'll experience first hand how they teach. Remember, once a basic foundation of learning has been achieved, exposure to as many teachers as possible is absolutely necessary. The more you can absorb, stylistically, from different instructors, the better an all-round dancer you'll become. While a convention may run for only two days, you'll get a real taste of what's out there, you'll be networking, and you'll be seen by new people who could be important to you in your career.

Attending conventions also benefits dance studio teachers. It allow them to interact with other instructors during the classes. They learn new routines and combinations they can take back to their own studios. They learn what's going on elsewhere in the dance world, gain new perspectives and ideas, which is important if they teach in small towns. Also, they're able to sit back and observe how their students learn. Each one processes information differently. By studying their students as others teach, they can discover if they need to alter their teaching techniques.

One caution, though: Teachers should avoid sending youngsters with only a few years of training to a dance convention. They'll be so out of their element that they'll forget what a plié is. They may try to keep up without really knowing what they're doing. Emotionally, this is unsound, and could discourage them from pursuing dance further.

Scholarships to Attend Conventions

A lot of conventions offer scholarships that kids can take advantage of during the summer months. The auditions might be divided by age groups, such as age 11 and under, ages 12 to 15, and age 16 and up. They might also have strict rules. Some allow students to audition solely within their age group regardless of skill level, when competing in a higher age bracket and winning would mean a larger scholarship. But all this varies according to the convention you want to attend.

MASTER CLASSES

A master class occurs when a studio hires a dance teacher, usually from out of town, to come and teach for a day or two in his or her area of expertise. The kids have a great time, and it's much more personal than a convention. The only problem with master classes is that they tend to function at the beginner/intermediate level, which means students at every level of development, even advanced, get lumped together.

The guest teachers are able to give special exercises and teach combinations, and have the time to correct any basic flaws in technique they might see. This is something that can't be done in a convention setting, where classes are time driven. Caring guest teachers focus on correcting those flaws, giving students a helpful amount of personal attention. They may not get as far along in a class as originally planned, but the effects of what they *are* able to teach will be long lasting.

When studios schedule master classes, it's important they be open to the new dance knowledge and corrections to dance technique that these teachers offer their students. If the regular instructors contradict those efforts afterwards by saying the instruction or criticisms aren't really valid, the students can become confused and conflicted. If a studio or instructor has that kind of attitude about other teachers, perhaps it's best to avoid attending or allowing a child to attend master classes altogether.

THE BOTTOM LINE

As you can see, dance competitions and master classes are venues offering a good sense of the real-world demands made on a dancer without all the stresses of the real world. They offer different learning and maturational experiences, and can help a young dance student who has a desire to enter the dance profession but isn't quite sure about it to discover more about that profession. Dance conventions are for older, more advanced students, but they too have a great deal to offer.

The term "bottom line" usually refers to financial matters. The bottom line on whether to participate in the types of events discussed in this chapter certainly has a financial aspect. After all, it's your money that pays for the experience. But there's also another bottom line here: whether attending a competition, a convention, or a master class will contribute to the young performer's ability to move into a musical theater career. By avoiding the hype that can be associated with these events, by approaching them with the right attitude, and by picking and choosing wisely from what they have to offer, some of the knowledge, maturity, and self-confidence needed to achieve a career in the performing arts can be the best prize of all.

6
LEARNING TO ACT

nyone wanting a career in musical theater today needs to know that he or she will need to study acting. Singers and dancers tend to overlook the importance of acting skills because they're so caught up in the disciplines of the body and the voice. They get the idea that acting is like ice skating—you just go out there, do your turns, and put yourself on display, with nothing else really mattering. As a result, they don't realize how important interpretive work is. In today's musicals, however, even if your ambition is only to be in the chorus of a Broadway show, you have to be able to portray characters believably, honestly, and plausibly, in a way the audience can relate to.

Unfortunately, performers today tend to specialize. In school they're encouraged to specialize. What you end up with is performers who can act but not dance or sing and performers who can dance and/or sing but not act. This is certainly not good in terms of building a career in musical theater. Remember the notion of "triple threat"? Performers in musical theater need to be able to dance, sing, *and* act. And the sooner they start their acting training the better because everything they ever do onstage will build on that ability.

Because it's best if acting training starts at an early age, the bulk of this chapter is aimed at explaining the issues related to teaching young people to act. But the issues aren't that different for anyone else. Learning to act is learning to act. Much of the material discussed in this chapter is relevant to aspiring performers of any age. And adult performers interested in taking acting lessons have an even wider range of options than kids do. If you're an adult looking for acting classes, check into your local community or regional theater. Sometimes they have conservatory-type programs you can enroll in. Also see the Appendix at the end of this book, which lists publications on the subject as well as the universities, colleges, and conservatories across the country that have programs in acting.

ACTING AND KIDS
When it comes to acting, it's best if the young person initiates the interest. Most kids who are interested exhibit definite signs, actually telling their parents "I want to act." They ask if they can audition for this play or perform in that community show. They badger their parents to cart them around town in an attempt to get a part. When acting is clearly the kid's and not the adult's ambition, paying for acting classes for him or her is probably a good idea.

When acting classes are the parents' idea, however, it's another story. A kid might agree to attend the classes at first but will simply stop participating if his or her interest in performing isn't sparked fairly quickly. Putting kids in an acting classes is useless if they don't want to be there, a complete waste of everyone's time and the parents' money. This may not apply when the student is very young, say from age 4 to 7, when parents make most of the decisions for their kids anyway. But even then parents need to watch for signs revealing how much interest in acting their child is developing and allow him or her to drop the classes if that's what their child wants.

A Word to Parents

A few comments here, I think, will help parents stay centered during the course of their children's acting studies.

Why is it that when a child begins taking piano lessons, the expectations of most parents are reasonable? They'll tolerate two years of hearing Chopsticks played over and over and three years of listening to scales because they understand the difficulties associated with learning to play piano well. But learning to act often seems a bit more mysterious for parents. They watch their kids start attending drama classes with expectations out of all proportion to the progress they actually see. They seem to assume that anyone can act, so the patience they extend to learning how to play a musical instrument doesn't extend to learning this "easy" skill. They look on improvisational skills as "leading nowhere" and don't understand the importance of voice exercises and acting play. They don't realize that, while these studies may not culminate immediately in a stage show, they are aimed at helping kids become accustomed to the ways their voices and bodies—the instruments of the acting profession—work. They are aimed at helping students learn how to control those instruments and develop the conscious ability to make logical choices about how to use them when performing.

Parents sometimes also overlook the importance of technique and quality in their kids' studies, instead wanting the instant gratification of "showing off" their abilities to other family members or friends. I have seen this happen with young people studying singing and dancing, and it's no help to them. The learning process shouldn't be encumbered by an overreaching need to impress. Parents will see their kids achieve better results if they simply encourage an honest learning approach rather than "performance" as the goal.

Learning takes time, in acting as in anything else. And, again, patience. If you're looking at a ten- to sixteen-week course of classes, then perhaps a performance at the end of that period is feasible. However, in the short term, it's what the kid gets out of an acting class that matters, not some ego-driven pleasure felt by an audience of friends and family. Stressing performance so early on denies the importance of developing the skills vital to a performer's long-term career. Attending some matinee to see how cute the kids are, or to be entertained by watching them struggle through their memorized lines, has no value whatsoever. Theatrically or otherwise.

DRAMA CLASSES IN PUBLIC HIGH SCHOOLS

There's virtually no drama taught in public school below the high school level. So this isn't even an option for young children. But what about high school drama departments for aspiring teenage performers?

Public schools want to support the arts, but with funding in turmoil and over-crowding getting worse, school administrations are being forced to compromise. How many times have we heard the story of a 26-year-old with a degree in English literature getting her first teaching job? As she prepares to sign the contract she finds out that—surprise!—she's "also the school's drama teacher." Even if someone *wants* to teach drama full-time in the public schools, the current lack of financial support for performing arts programs in many public school systems means they are being cut back drastically or even abolished as separate departments and merged into the English department.

When drama isn't regarded as a full-time program, it's treated as a stepchild, a warehouse for dumping the troublemakers from other, more "important" classes. The underlying philosophy seems to be that anything goes in drama, it's not really an important subject, so let's just toss the losers in there. That way at least they'll be able to graduate. How can this kind of thinking benefit serious drama students? It can't. What does it tell them when half their classmates don't care about what they're studying? All it does is make theater seem irrelevant.

Yes, there's a certain amount of school pride associated with putting on a big play or musical, with students performing onstage and their peers watching in the audi-ence, perhaps attending a live production for the first time. There's always that sense of "Wow, we did it." The pride even extends to school administrators and parents. But it's a nebulous sense, and it doesn't last very long. What's the point? There's no commitment to anything ongoing. Kids serious about drama understand this. They're aware of the lack of support for the drama program, and know that aside from the excitement of an actual performance, studying acting is not treated with respect but almost with contempt. Often they want nothing to do with any of it.

High school musicals can sometimes even be painful for the students participating in them. Say a musical is allotted a meager $3000 budget. That's not enough to pay for real sets. With costumes stitched together at the last minute, choreography done by a twelfth grader who took a few classes at the corner dance academy, lighting strung haphazardly by self-appointed techies, and a cheap public address system on the scale of a karaoke bar, it's tough on the eyes and painful to the ears, just a sug-gestion of what a real musical should be. Is there any value in putting it on?

I don't see any. If lack of commitment by the school means a play must be done poorly, why do it at all? It's not a good learning experience for the kids on any level; it's just something that teachers have been forced to do as part of their contract. The end result is an embarrassment to theater in general.

There are also high school drama teachers who create more problems than solutions for students interested in studying acting. Some of them stage plays or musicals with an attitude of "Just learn your lines and don't bump into the furniture." Some are even worse. They nurture the "star" system by taking those few students who have more natural ability than the others and casting them as leads in play after play.

In riding a sure thing, these teachers make themselves look good to parents and administrators who see the plays and are impressed by the level of acting. But all they're doing for students is fostering an exaggerated sense of self-importance in some, and never giving others a chance to develop any feelings of self-worth as actors. The students the teachers favor think they already "have it," and don't learn one of the most important things an actor needs to know: how to be part of an ensemble cast that works together. What happens to these "stars" if they decide to enter the real world of professional acting later on and must endure rejection after rejection before at last landing one small part that has nothing to do with their internal definition of success? It will be a rude awakening. Meanwhile the students who are left out of playing the important parts usually lose interest and drop out. At best they must wait until college or until they can find some other type of training to explore and develop their skills.

Don't get me wrong. I realize that many high school drama teachers are unrecognized geniuses, who understand acting, put on great shows, and actually encourage students to pursue a performance career. Some school systems actively support the performing arts, supplying the funds needed to hire and keep good teachers who know how to motivate students and put on worthy productions. But by and large public high schools are not the place those wanting to acquire acting skills will be able to do so.

OTHER SOURCES OF ACTING CLASSES

If the public schools can't supply the type of training young people need to develop good acting fundamentals, where *can* they go for it? As already noted, some communities have theaters with conservatory-type programs attached to them that teach fundamental acting skills to adults. Those programs may also offer classes for kids, although not usually on a conservatory basis in the sense of being a comprehensive attempt to educate their young students for a professional career. The same is true of the acting schools or colleges and universities with drama departments that might be located near where you live. The classes are usually taught by knowledgeable professionals, and they can be a fun and positive experience. Just keep in mind it's important that the student be in classes geared toward her or his age group. A list of those schools is included in the Appendix.

WHAT ACTING CLASSES TEACH

Acting classes are only as good as the teachers giving them, and that's especially true for those aimed at teaching youngsters. The first task is to help them learn to free their imaginations and remove the mental barriers and restrictions that can paralyze aspiring performers with a sense of "I can't do that." Good teachers do this by helping their students learn how to think creatively, take risks, and go as far as they can in developing their talents. With young kids this is done through playing different types of theater games. Later they move into scene study, preparation of character, and the other elements of acting. There is a logical progression in all this, and I will describe each step, explaining its importance and what the student can be expected to learn.

A basic drama class can be a rewarding experience for young people, an environment where they can act out stories, portray characters, and stoke their imaginations.

The idea is not to teach young students theater skills, but instead how to participate in creating dramatic plays. For example, a class of 6-year-olds might be introduced to a story or poem like the tale of the "Three Billy Goats Gruff." The class members will collectively explore what they would do if they were the Big Billy Goat Gruff by stomping around the room, making plenty of noise, swinging their horned heads around, and in general acting like the character. Then the students would do the same for the other characters in the story. Eventually they would explore elements of the plot by acting out scenes from the story.

In this way the kids learn what it takes to create a dramatic work. The story is played out a piece at a time, before being pulled together at the end, and the performers have, in essence, done a little play. Acting it out takes only a few minutes, so the teacher can rotate the characters to allow all the kids the chance to play the main character, Big Billy Goat Gruff. It expands their imaginations, and they learn something about the basic life issues the story involves.

An exercise like this is not aimed at developing an audience presentation, but to teach the students the basic elements that make up a drama. For the kids, it's just the joy of the story that's involved, not the joy—or anxiety—of performance. It allows them to have a loose and free encounter with the feelings the story generates without any intrusion of the pressures that working on a performance can cause. At the same time, acting teachers who know how to work with kids are instilling in them a commitment to behaving truthfully in imaginary circumstances, just as they must do with older people in adult acting classes. For example, this story involves billy goats and trolls, so a teacher might have the class spend a little time discussing what trolls are. Some kids will have a better idea than others, describing trolls as mean and ugly, with funny walks or strange voices. The teacher would build on this, asking the students to act like trolls, hopping around the room with squinty eyes or exaggerated walks. At that moment, the students are absolutely committed to the circumstances of the moment and learning how to act. It's at a level that engages their interest and abilities. On the other hand, if they had been given lines to learn for roles created by someone else, they wouldn't have any way to connect. They'd probably stand there reciting lines as if they were multiplication tables, and become stressed out.

Young kids between the ages of 4 and 8 won't understand acting theory. But they *can* understand the truths of a story by being taught how to interpret what is being communicated to them through play.

Developing the Speaking Voice

When young kids finish their basic drama class, it may still be too early for them to move on to the more rigorous parts of the formal acting training such as scene study. But it may be the perfect time for them to begin learning how to use their speaking voices. Charles McGaw, in his book *Acting Is Believing*, says: "Anyone interested in achieving success in acting will seek instruction to improve his voice, and will regularly practice exercises in diction and voice production." The speaking voice can convey much in terms of musicality and character. Young students taking this kind of class learn how to create different characters through sounds created by different ways of breathing and the relaxation of their throat muscles. They usually find it fun to explore their speaking voices in an unstructured way.

For example, one exercise focuses on emphasizing different words in a phrase. Take the sentence "I want you to come over to the desk." Different speakers will say it in different ways:

"I *want* you to come over to the desk."
"I want *you* to come over to the desk."
"I want you to come over to the *desk*."

This shows the variations in what spoken words can mean. This in turn teaches how people make choices in how they tell stories, which is what acting is at one level. As Charles McGaw points out, such exercises teach aspiring performers about the importance of things like volume of sound, relaxation, quality of articulation and pronunciation, voice flexibility, and the ability to hear.

All this is more important than may be obvious. You should understand that young people, especially during elementary school, speak with a lot of inflection. But as they enter middle and high school, social pressures of moving toward adulthood begin to weigh heavily. One way they cope or protect themselves is to shut down the vocal apparatus. You may have noticed the way many high school boys speak in a low monotone, often limiting their comments to simple phrases like "What's up?" and "I dunno." The goal in doing this is to appear *not* excited or enthusiastic about anything. Falling into this vocal pattern makes it difficult to explore the varied uses of one's own voice—not good for aspiring performers. It can be corrected, however, by a good voice teacher.

Improvisation

Professional actors or performers in musical theater doing eight shows a week find out that anything can happen onstage, and that each performance in a play, while essentially the same as every other performance, is at the same time slightly different.

You need to know how to improvise if you're going to make your living performing onstage, which means you need to study improvisation. A good improvisation class teaches you to be flexible enough to handle anything that might come along. It teaches you how to surrender to the moment, an invaluable skill for any actor to learn, and one that kids can learn fairly easily with a good instructor.

Simply put, improvisation is exploration, and it is valuable to actors in two ways. It helps them build their imaginations, concentration, spontaneity, and listening skills. It also helps them develop the habit of thinking on their feet and rolling with the punches. Say their blocking is changed in some way at the last moment or another actor in a play says a line differently one evening. Performers must be able to adapt on the spot; they must know how to surrender their expectations of what *should* be happening in order to cope with whatever *is* happening.

Good acting involves appreciating the unknown. You never really know what's going to occur onstage, even in a standard like *Carousel*. You might forget your lines or blank on what you should do next. But that's exactly where an actor wants to be, in a place where you don't know everything that's going to happen. It's a difficult concept to get across to young kids, especially after the natural play stage of their lives. They start trying to figure out what society expects of them, particularly their parents, teachers, and classmates. To achieve a sense of security, they start looking for scripts to guide their lives and trying understand the expectations they should meet. But that's counterproductive to the direction they need to take to be good actors. Instead they need to keep feeling comfortable playing in the moment.

In rehearsal, improvisation is useful in exploring circumstances and relationships by establishing a bigger field to play on. For instance, suppose two people in a musical portray a brother and sister, and begin to discuss an incident in childhood when their father beat them. By playing out that moment in an "improv," the actors can explore what their characters experienced and how they felt. Then, by taking that improvisation and applying it to their choices in the actual scene, they make the play richer and give it more depth than before.

Improvisation is therefore a good classroom tool in helping acting students develop their performing skills and, perhaps even more importantly, an exploratory device professionals can use to help them in their theater work throughout their careers.

Scene Study

Scene study is the key to acting. Young performers can be taught how to use their voices effectively, how to work in the moment, and how to develop basic improvisational skills. But if they don't learn how to tie it all into developing the characters they will play in particular dramas or musicals, whose needs and passions are driven by the stories dealt with in the script, they won't be actors. They must learn how to apply the techniques we've just discussed to produce the character in the script as written by the playwright. And scene study gives them that ability.

Acting teachers approach scene study in different ways, but in the end they basically boil down to two: the right way and the wrong way. Take two teachers: Teacher A hands out a scene to her students, and as they progress through it, taking turns reading the parts out loud, she and the students discuss all the elements of the scene as they come up. Teacher B hands out the scene and lets his students perform it without any explanation or guidance. Clearly, Teacher A understands the fundamental need all actors have to connect with and listen to each other as they rehearse scenes and work on their characters. Equally clearly, Teacher B does not understand this, most likely because he was never taught these fundamentals of acting himself. Teacher A is approaching scene study correctly; Teacher B is not.

Good acting teachers are also like good sports coaches, helping each student discover in himself or herself what is needed to portray a character well. Too often in acting classes you'll hear comments like "Did you do the scene right?" "Who was the best in that scene?" "Who did the scene the best?" Young actors aren't well served with this kind of rigid outlook. They need to feel valued, liked, and accepted.

Acting Scenes in Musicals

Actors in musicals often find themselves with only three lines of dialog before a song starts. Within those three lines, they have to clearly establish what they're doing, what they want, and how they're going to get what they want. Simply put, they have to get to the truth of their characters very quickly and know how to convey it, which means they must have that essential grounding in themselves and their characters that allows them to "snap on" like a light bulb. Often they have only a small sliver of time to sell the moment and the scene to the audience.

In addition, musical theater is a medium that often requires transitions between scenes that are much more exaggerated and emotional than those required by straight drama. Many musicals have characters that are larger than life. They're written that way, and it dictates how the actors must sing, as well as how they must move during the dance numbers.

Under those circumstances, actors must know their characters very well before they walk onto the musical theater stage. They must also be careful about how they play them. Inexperienced actors have a tendency to play to the audience, forgetting about the relationship they have with the others on the stage. For example, an inexperienced actor playing Snoopy in *You're a Good Man, Charlie Brown* might not know the right times to turn out and work the audience and when to bring it back to stage reality. If he turns out too often, the believability of what was happening onstage will suffer.

Doubtless some directors would disagree with or place a low priority on what I've just said, and have no problem with actors who work the audience with a great deal of energy but no thought as to how this will affect the content of the musical. But I think they are wrong. Likewise I think dealing with the script in just a presentational way, making the material larger than life without any thought as to why you're doing that, is a mistake. It doesn't help a play, and may doom it to failure. Actors in musicals have to personalize the material and make it more than presentational, even when the play calls for this type of acting, as in *The Boyfriend* and *Little Mary Sunshine*.

Singing Songs in Musicals

The best parts of musicals are the songs. If you think about it, singing is a direct approach to conveying emotion. It allows a straightforward path to love, hate, or fear, making the human experience more intense. The songs sung by a character in a musical are very much a part of the character's line of action. They spring organically from where the character happens to be at a given moment and make objective sense, moving the story along.

All the singing and movement an actor does must come from the character he or she develops. Songs are not about the singers singing individual, isolated verses with melodies having nothing to do with the character or the plot of the story. Both character and story are developed through songs and movement throughout the entire play. And at least insofar as the songs are concerned, that is done through interpretation of the lyrics and melodies. A performer can't treat songs just like a series of notes, like a grocery list. He or she has to treat them as insights into the soul of the character. A song is music with meaning embedded in it, and you can't just open your mouth and sing without knowing what the meaning is.

Voice training is a separate matter from learning to act. But a good acting teacher will provide musical theater students with an appreciation of the importance of learning how to act and develop their characters through songs.

Researching Roles

Actors must research their roles, and good acting teachers help their students—even their young students—learn how to do that research. Say you're a young student and the teacher assigns you to research the musical *Good News*, set in the 1920s. Because the play is about college life, you want to learn about what being in college is like. And because it's set in the 1920s, you want to find out about life, and especially college life, in that period.

Your teacher might suggest you start your research with the other members of the cast, especially if they're in college or of high school age and plan to attend college. Get a feel for their hopes and anticipations, of their understanding about what it means to be in college.

Once the play has been personalized in terms of what students going to college feel like, the teacher may suggest you look into college life during the 1920s. So next you look through books, photographs, and films from and about the era, so that you understand what it meant to attend college in those times. Other things about the

1920s are important also. How did men and women flirt in the 1920s? How did flirting then differ from flirting during the Victorian era of the nineteenth century. How does it differ from flirting today?

Research is important because all the information actors find out about the times, geographical locations, and social conditions of the plays they are acting in feeds their imaginations in regard to portraying their characters. The more historical perspective they have, the better they'll be able to convey the daily realities of those characters.

Cross Training

When it comes to learning acting styles young performers interested in musical theater are often narrow-minded. Thinking they're going to pursue only musical theater, they turn up their noses at the drama classics. But acting specialization is a constricted way of looking at the profession, and as I've said before, it can be the kiss of death to a career in musical theater.

Cross training in different acting styles is an important part of a performer's education. Young students should be exposed to every aspect of acting possible. Not only will it broaden their acting skills, but it will help develop their professional vocabulary. They might find themselves working with directors who have no background in musicals, while they themselves have no background performing in straight plays. They will have to be able to communicate with those directors, and cross training will provide them with the common language they need.

Learning What Directors Expect

Good acting teachers help the student understand that when onstage an actor is working for the director. It is the director's vision that is being bankrolled by the producer or the boards of community theaters. Directors react to this fact in different ways. Some trust the actors they work with and allow them to offer ideas about a production, providing they follow its basic concept. Others in effect say, "It's my way or the highway."

Acting teachers should help students learn how to work through scenes, moment by moment, understanding that it's the director's job to make sure these moments come together and move to some kind of climax. In rehearsals actors must be willing to take suggestions and directions at a moment's notice. On the other hand the time of most directors is limited, and they offer their own input only when they think it necessary to do so. Most of the time they rely on their actors to be trained well enough to make the right choices.

Directors also expect actors to be prepared. They want them to have their lines memorized by the specified dates and to know who their characters are in terms of the whole production and be willing to share their work with the others on the stage. They want actors who understand what it is to be part of an ensemble, part of a group of people working toward the same goal. All this in turn should be part of what students learn in their acting classes.

A Word to Parents

We've discussed how good acting classes, beginning at an early age, will incorporate all the skills and techniques performers will need. If you're the parent of a child who wants to go onstage while still a child, however, you'll be the person ultimately responsible for seeing that he or she is able to do that. It can be a real challenge, even with the help of teachers. Check your local community theater, or even commercial theaters if you live in a large city that has them, for productions that will need young performers. If you're willing to travel, you can even check out auditions for children's parts being held in the large theater centers like New York or Chicago. In any event, it's important that the stage experience have value, and not be something that forces the young actor to compromise everything he or she has learned up to this point, simply in order to perform. That means picking a project that allows students to use the tools developed in class, instead of forcing them to toss everything they've learned out the window.

SPEECH AND DIALECT

Every actor needs to take speech classes. Often our diction is lazy or sloppy. We don't finish final consonants, we bunch words together, or we just don't articulate what we say. Basically, we don't use our vocal instrument fully. Most of the time that's not a big problem. Our family and friends still get the drift of what we're saying. Speaking from the stage of a theater, however, is another matter. It's not as if you were having a conversation with a friend at a snack bar. You have to be able to speak so that three hundred—sometimes more—people can hear you.

Serious theater should be thought of as words. That means the words have to be shaped so as to be understood and presented in a way that's clear and articulated, while at the same time sounding natural. A person can't just get up onstage and expect to do this. It takes considerable training, limbering up the vocal and facial muscles and getting them in shape. And just like any other kind of fitness endeavor, it has to be done regularly.

Good actors must have good diction, but they do not necessarily have to get down to a dialect-free Standard American English. It depends on the type of career you choose. Personally, I think having Standard American English in your repertory gives you more range. If you only speak in a Southern accent and sound like you've never left New Orleans, chances are you'll get only Southern-type roles. The more range you have, the more dialect-free you are and the more roles you'll be considered for. Standard American English is the common denominator.

The ability to do dialects is a specialized skill, but many people can learn how. Dialect coaches can be found in large and small cities that have performing arts centers. Tapes that teach dialects can be bought in bookstores or ordered by mail.

I think all actors should study dialects, to help them slip into the personas of a variety of characters. Nevertheless, it's a skill that must be built on the foundation of the actor's own vocal instrument. So even if they study dialect, they should continue to develop their individual voice through speech classes.

ACTING COACHES

If you're really serious about getting the young actor into a good performing arts high school, conservatory, or college drama department, or if you're interested in actual auditions for shows, the actor's work can't be average. It has to be far better. Think about going to a large-scale audition, where he or she will be compared to some very talented people. Going unprepared would not only mean losing the role, but would be embarrassing.

To avoid auditioning unprepared, you need to find a good acting coach. He or she will pick an appropriate scene, and work with whoever is auditioning on scene analysis, voice projection, and character interpretation. A good coach will also advise the students about wardrobe and grooming, and offer auditioning tips over three or four sessions, in order to prepare them fully before the audition takes place.

SENDING STUDENTS INTO THE PROFESSIONAL WORLD

It's important to realize that acting is a series of simple skills leading to more complex skills that, in turn, lead to the complex abilities of the true actor. If you, as a parent or a teacher, don't think of it that way, it's easy to set kids up for disappointment. Think of the talented kid from a small town who's been given all the high school or college leads without really understanding the mechanics of what it means to audition or act. Suddenly the youngster is out there in the real world where a director simply places a script in the kid's hand, names the character, and says, "Do it." That may well be all the help a fledgling actor receives in the professional world of theater, and he or she had better understand how to work through a scene. That's where the exercises and issues I've been discussing help, especially in musical theater, where the director seldom has the time to hold the hands of those in the cast. He or she might offer some suggestions, but the actor will be expected to know how to do most of the work.

Acting can't be faked in the real world of theater. Not even in the world of musical theater. Performers who shy away from learning acting skills because they think they'll never need them are making a big mistake. They're denying themselves some of the most important, and basic, components of the performing arts. Neglecting to acquire those skills will certainly delay their journey to the Broadway stage. Ultimately it may stop the journey cold.

7
COLLEGE OR NOT?

In this country, we don't seem to put a high priority on turning out well-rounded performers. I'm talking about individuals who are skilled and comfortable in virtually any area of performance, who are "triple threats" because they can sing, dance, *and* act onstage. From a purely commercial perspective, a triple threat is always more employable than performers who have only a single skill. The trend these days in educating performers, however, is increasingly toward specialization.

Many of our four-year college drama programs and drama conservatories also seem to have an antimusical bias in the training they offer for the Broadway stage. At many institutions acting majors are not given vocal or dance training, or dance majors find they must take private voice lessons and receive no acting training whatsoever. Yet, somehow, once they have their degrees they're supposed to be employable and successful in the musical theater world. It's a mistake of major proportions, and a great disservice to American performers, to have such one-sided college training programs. And the problem doesn't start just in college. It begins early on in the training of kids to become performers, when not a single teacher introduces the concept of the triple threat. The student, without even realizing what is happening, thus becomes specialized in abilities, ultimately steering him- or herself toward a dead end.

The point is, to be successful in musical theater, you have to be a triple threat. Period. I already said this in Chapter 1, and because it's so important I repeat it here. It must be kept in mind by any young person interested in a career in musical theater who is deciding whether to go to college or which school to attend.

SEEKING GUIDANCE AND SUPPORT
Any young person trying to decide on how to learn the skills needed to perform in musical theater is going to look for guidance and support. So we'll discuss these issues first.

High School Guidance Counselors
"Should I go to college or a conservatory, or get a job in theater?" When asking this question, one resource young people usually look to are their school guidance counselors. Unfortunately the vast majority of high school counselors simply don't have the knowledge or background needed to know the ins and outs of working toward a career in the performing arts. Consequently, there's little or no practical information they can offer.

Nevertheless, a good guidance counselor (1) will never discourage a young person's dream by offering up statistics to prove why she or he shouldn't be pursuing such a career, (2) will never pull out transcripts and use the student's "excellent" grades as a way to push the idea of going into a career that will put his or her abilities in math or geography to "good use," and (3) will *never* advise a student about what college to attend to study the performing arts if they lack experience in this area.

What a good guidance counselor *can* do is steer the student in the direction of a performing arts consultant who will be able to help or provide the names of organizations the student can contact for the necessary information.

One organization worth singling out is the National Association for College Admission Counseling. It can provide students with all the information they need about the colleges, universities, conservatories, and other educational institutions with programs dedicated to teaching music, dance, and drama. It also sponsors a Performing Arts College Fair each fall, for both graduate and undergraduate students. Just keep in mind that some schools or performing arts departments do not have access to such fairs. Some are small and understaffed, and don't have the personnel to assign to these events. In other cases, a program may not teach ballet or modern dance, but instead concentrate on musical theater, emphasizing the study of tap and jazz styles of dance. Thus it may not be recognized as a valid, alternative performing arts program or invited to participate in such fairs. You won't be able to find out about *all* the schools that have performing arts programs at college fairs, and the program you don't find out about may be just the one for you.

Guidance counselors can also steer students toward other sources of information about musical theater study programs. They can provide, or at least tell you where to find, copies of publications like the *Dance Magazine College Guide*, *Peterson's Professional Degree Programs in the Visual and Performing Arts*, or *Dance Spirit Magazine*, which lists the top twenty-five universities with dance programs. These publications list school after school with ballet or modern dance programs, but sooner or later, you'll run across information about the three or four schools that emphasize musical theater. Just remember that, even though many schools offer tap or jazz dance courses, this can be deceptive. If a school doesn't believe that these disciplines are important, it won't have leveled classes. That is, instead of providing classes that group students by level of expertise, it may just offer a single class containing students at all levels of development in their jazz or tap training. That isn't good for students, for all kinds of reasons.

Why any guidance counselor would give kids unsound information, which could damage their future, jeopardize their careers, and destroy their dreams, is beyond me. But some do, so be very careful from whom you seek advice.

A Word to Parents

To be honest, most parents aren't comfortable with the idea of their kids going into the performing arts. I think it's a prejudice passed down from generation to generation. It's not uncommon for parents who were once interested in a performing career to repeat to their kids the same condemnations of those ambitions they heard when they themselves were young.

Nevertheless, parents should realize that this is their child's dream, not their own. While they may be concerned about allowing him or her to go into musical theater, I think they also need to realize that one can make a very good, even a great, living as a performer. It certainly doesn't always mean starving to death or living on the financial edge, particularly if the child hones his or her talents as a triple threat. What children want to do with their lives is their individual choice. Parents who don't encourage them to achieve their ambitions risk alienating them from the family. And parents who manage to convince children to pursue careers they don't really want are most likely setting them up for a lifetime of regrets.

Besides, these days finding a job in any field isn't as easy as it used to be. Thirty or forty years ago, a college graduate was almost guaranteed a job no matter what he or she had studied. Not any more. How many people today receive their diplomas one month and wind up working in a fast food restaurant the next? There is a glut of people earning degrees in all fields now, including medicine and law. So the risks are no longer just in theater and dance, but in any career choice.

Don't put negative pressure on your aspiring performer. Instead, offer support by discussing his or her ambitions with an open mind. Be involved in the planning of your child's career. Support her or his dreams. It's the best thing you can do as parents.

One solid sign of support is taking the child to visit the school he or she wants to attend to check out the campus and the curriculum. Make sure to go at a time when the school is putting on a performance to see the quality of students it produces, and make sure it's a musical theater performance, not an opera or ballet. Go to several schools if necessary to find the right one. Remember, taking a flight to check out a school beforehand is much less expensive than paying four years of tuition to the wrong institution.

Finding a good school, and the right school for your child, is important in other ways too. Every year, scores of acting majors enroll at local colleges because they're so convenient to attend, then drop out because the programs are run by abusive teachers or by people who have virtually no knowledge of the performing arts business. If a student still wants a career as a performer, he or she often winds up working in a local theater. This may offer the hands-on training the student needs, but it doesn't offer the total educational experience a good college or university program can provide. Short-sighted decisions early on rarely lead to good consequences, in pursuing a musical theater career as well as any other.

Finally, it's all too true that most performers need second jobs to support themselves until they establish themselves professionally in the performing field. So you as a parent may feel you must tell your son or daughter to learn another skill to fall back on. But be fully aware of what you're saying. With the many hours of dance study, vocal training, and acting classes performing arts students are required to take, you can't expect them to take on another full load of courses leading toward a totally different career. Work with your kid to find something compatible with his or her needs and abilities. Jill Charles, talking to actors in the *Directory of Theater Training Programs*, says: "The challenge for you, as an actor, is to create a support job which will be gratifying, will use your skills and intelligence, will provide enough income for food, rent, etc., and still be flexible enough that you can continue to pursue your primary goal of becoming a working actor." What you, as a parent, have to understand is that the most compatible support job for a young performer may turn out to be anything from "temping" in offices at jobs requiring computer skills, to waiting on tables at a restaurant, to selling perfume in a department store. Beginning performers often need second *jobs* to support themselves, not full-blown second *careers*. Remember when helping your child to plan his or her life that the performing arts *is* the career—it's not just a hobby.

Above all, remember to be there for your child regardless of what happens in terms of her or his performing career. Most importantly, never say, "I told you so." Building a career in the performing arts takes years of commitment, and your son or daughter may need your support ten years down the road when he or she is still struggling to do so. Don't burden the child with shame or guilt. Remember, this year could be the year he or she succeeds.

Pros and Cons of Going to College

If you, the young performer just finishing high school, have done your "performing" homework properly by studying dancing, voice, and acting to become a triple threat, attending a magnet or residential high school specializing in the performing arts, finding a mentor who has educated you about the business side of performing, and you have the gut feeling that you're ready to make your move, you *might* be one of the rare individuals who is able to make the leap from high school directly to the stage. However, most young performers aren't ready for such a transition because it takes a level of maturity and self-confidence, along with a sense of independence, that most young people don't yet have. At such a young age it also takes the solid support of your family and friends, which can be hard to come by.

Many ambitious young adults have terrific talent. After all, that's the source from which every successful performer springs. However, deciding whether to pursue a career at the earliest possible moment, instead of seeking a higher education, rests not on the issue of talent, but on the performer's emotional maturity. Sure, young people can get jobs on cruise ships, but are they emotionally prepared to face the world of being a professional performer, with all its demands? Some people who have become very successful at too young an age, emotionally speaking, have flamed out too early on, trying everything from drugs to fast cars. And you don't want that to happen to you.

The Positive Aspects of Attending College

Upon leaving home for the first time, it's common for kids to go a little nuts. The newfound freedom from parental watchfulness, along with peer pressure, may drive them to do things they've never done before. Alcohol abuse is a frequent problem, because it's a legal substance and easy to come by even if you're under-age. If you're a college student and drinking too much, it's one thing. Students are often only an easy ride away from home, and many colleges have established their own procedures and support systems for dealing with the problem. If you're out in the real world earning your own living and holding down one or two jobs, however, the situation is completely different. Your jobs, your whole performing career, can be jeopardized by substance abuse. You may be living thousands of miles from your family and have no one to turn to for help. You need a sense of emotional maturity to cope with life's problems, which not every young person has.

Our culture seems to extend adolescence beyond the teenage years. It's common to encounter 25-year-olds still acting like they were 15. However, college for some people serves as a transition to adulthood, helping them learn how to take on adult responsibilities. And it does this, in my opinion, by breaking down child–parent dependence. If you're attending an out-of-town institution, you have to do things like get yourself out of bed, make your own breakfast, do your own laundry. At the same time, you must set your own schedule and learn how to follow it to attend classes, do homework, and meet all the other responsibilities of your student life. In the process, you're becoming an adult.

A college education can also be valuable to you as a performer. The best singers, dancers, and actors all have a depth to them, gained from knowing something about history, philosophy, art, music, and literature, as well as singing, dance, and acting. Without an exposure to that broad knowledge base, best gained through the college experience, a performer can only reach a certain, superficial level of performing ability.

In grade school, you probably only had one teacher each year teaching you in a single room, and your teacher only had one point of view. That expanded a bit in high school. But in college, the opportunity to interact with many teachers having diverse experiences and philosophies expands dramatically, as does the opportunity to interact with students from various backgrounds, cultures, and countries. This kind of exposure opens the mind to new ideas and possibilities.

College also gives you time to grow as a human being, providing a four-year outlet for you to explore your interests and passions. You gain personal skills such as working with others, thinking on your feet, meeting deadlines, and communicating better, through both the written and spoken word. As a performer, you need to keep in mind that show business is "business" first and "show" second, so by taking a business—or better yet a marketing—course, you'll reach your goals that much more easily. As a professional performer you'll have to write resumes and cover letters, attend job interviews, and market yourself. In preparing to be a self-employed, independent business person, which a performer really is, what you learn in college can be invaluable.

The Negative Aspects of Attending College

While there *are* colleges and universities with a lot of clout in the professional theater world, most have very little influence. For the most part, colleges don't cater to performers, nor do they pay much attention to their dreams and aspirations. Basically, they teach technique, with little or no underlying philosophy aimed at helping the performers they train reach their ultimate goals.

Most college dance programs train students how to teach dance, not perform. This may also be true of voice programs. You need to find a college that will prepare you to go onstage. Your goals have to coincide with those of the school where you're studying, so you need to attend one where the underlying philosophy, and the faculty, share your same focus. And producing graduates who can work and earn a living as performers doesn't just mean teaching them technical brilliance—it means imparting all the personal qualities and attitudes we discussed in Chapter 1 that contribute to success.

DECIDING ON A SCHOOL

You're age 17, a senior in high school. The time has come to start thinking about what you're going to do with your life, the choices you have, and what's best for you. You've decided to go to college. But where should you go? Let's discuss the possibilities.

Bachelor of Liberal Arts (B.A.) Programs

A Bachelor of Arts degree from a liberal arts program is ideal for students not quite sure of what they're after, and for those with diverse interests. In such a program, a wide variety of subjects is covered without focusing on anything specifically. But keep in mind that even though you're taking voice, dance, or acting lessons, much of your time will have to go toward your purely academic studies. Also keep in mind that when applying to enter a liberal arts program your academic scores from high school are just as important as your performing talent. So if you're serious about a career in musical theater, a liberal arts bachelor's degree program is not for you.

Bachelor of Fine Arts (B.F.A.) Programs

There isn't a great deal of difference between a college B.F.A. and the kind of conservatory program discussed below. In fact, B.F.A. programs are often set up in a conservatory style. In these programs, you concentrate more of your efforts within your area of performing interest, but you still take some academic classes. You'll be required to take fewer academic courses for a B.F.A. than for a B.A.

Conservatories

These specialized programs are ideal for studying the performing arts. They prepare students for careers in their chosen fields, such as musical theater, dance, or vocal performance, focusing totally on that discipline. Conservatory teaching seems to attract more industry experts than college B.F.A. programs because of the freedom and purity of expression they are perceived to offer. As many of the instructors are working professionals, they teach on a part-time basis; others are full-time professors. Admission is largely based on auditions, and not on academic records, as the focus is on the student's talent.

Keep in mind that, unlike B.A. and B.F.A. programs, not all conservatory programs offer degrees. Instead, at the end of your studies you may receive a "certificate of completion." You want to know what you're getting into, so be sure to ask about this up front.

One criticism of a conservatory education is that it's risky, like putting all your eggs in one basket. You won't be exposed to the type of business, education, or marketing courses you can get in a college or university setting. You also need to be aware that the washout rate at conservatories is high, because people don't always know what they're getting into. This quandary is best expressed by the show business saying "Do you want to be an actor, or do you want to do what actors do?" Well, it turns out that most 18-year-olds who think they want to be actors change their minds when they find out how difficult it actually is.

WHAT TO LOOK FOR IN
MUSICAL THEATER DEPARTMENTS

One of the first things you should do is to check out college placement records, to see how students do upon graduation and what kind of employment they secure. Are they performing on Broadway, in Las Vegas, or for Disney? Are they finding work at all in musical theater?

Next, you need to find out which colleges, universities, or conservatories provide four years of focused training in your chosen art form, not two years of academics and two years of actual performance training. If a school doesn't allow you to focus full time on the performing skills you need to develop, it won't be the right school for you.

The performing arts departments at schools such as Oklahoma City University, Point Park College in Pittsburgh, and the University of Cincinnati actively encourage their students to pursue their career goals, helping prepare them to succeed in the performance business and the world at large. They push students hard, developing their skills and self-confidence, so they won't wind up feeling like very small fish in a very big pond.

It's harder than ever these days to make it in this business, so you need to look for a school that offers master classes, lectures, and demonstrations, and that supports an artist-in-residence program. Ask about the school's performance venues as well as the number of performances you will be participating in as a student there. You need to know how much actual onstage experience you'll be getting. This means checking out whether the school puts students onstage, or faculty members. The point of education is to teach students how to do something, but surprisingly enough there are departments that seem to prefer the teachers to parade around as performers.

The School of American Dance and Arts Management at Oklahoma City University offers an excellent dance program, including degrees in tap, jazz, and ballet. Shown here is the school's American Spirit Dance Company, under the direction of Jo Rowan.

Teachers should not perform onstage in school productions. The major roles should always be given to students so they are exposed to the challenges of really perform-ing before audiences, like professionals do. You should also find out if the school schedules showcase productions for students just about to graduate. These are important since they allow students to perform a song, a dance, or a scene in front of agents and casting directors.

Also keep in mind that a good musical theater department will offer courses in the nuts-and-bolts business aspects of how show business operates, including classes in business law and finance.

In order to be employable in musical theater, you must become a triple threat, which means developing your skills in all three areas of acting, dancing, and singing, no matter where your greatest interest lies. That in turn means the school you attend has to offer you the diversity you need in your studies to make you marketable upon graduation, no matter what your major.

If you're an ***acting major,*** you need to take the following classes:

Acting • Speech • Ear training • Musical theater acting • Shakespeare • Stagecraft • Voice (private lessons) • Piano • Dance (ballet, jazz, and tap)

If you're a ***dance major,*** you need to take the following classes:

Classical ballet • Modern dance • Jazz dance • Tap dance • Musical theater style dance • Partnering • Acrobatics • Acting • Repertory • Voice (private lessons)

If you're a *voice major,* you need to take the following classes:

Voice (private lessons) • Techniques in singing • Sight singing and musicianship • Harmony and ear training • Piano • Acting • Dance (ballet, jazz, and tap)

Along with the required academic courses, the classes just listed would comprise the ideal college curriculum for anyone interested in pursuing a musical theater career. The trick is finding the school that offers all those courses. Your best bets are conservatories, or colleges and universities offering performance-based degrees.

ALTERNATIVE EDUCATION

Apprenticeship Programs

If you don't want to go to college or attend a conservatory, but you're not yet ready to leap onto the stage, there are number of alternative routes to entering musical theater as a career. One option is joining the apprenticeship programs offered by some acting and dance companies around the country. Information about these is available in libraries.

Dance Scholarships

An option for dancers that I'll go into more detail about here is the dance scholarship programs offered by some of the big dance companies around the country. These are available in the major dance markets (including New York, Los Angeles, Chicago, Dallas, among other American cities) for people just out of high school. If you're admitted to one of these programs, you'll be dancing every day and meeting people who might hire you later on. These programs not only offer broad and extensive dance training, but workshops to help you develop skills like finding an agent. It's like being in school, but with the added benefit of being "out there" in the real world. Just remember that, even with a dance scholarship, to become a triple threat you also need to study voice and acting. Most likely, you'll have to do that on your own. Also, unless the scholarship pays for more than just the dance lessons, you'll have to find some way to cover all your other expenses like rent, food, and daily transportation. If you're not very self-motivated, this kind of program may not be for you.

There are terrific dance scholarship programs in New York, the two biggest being the Steps Studio program and the Broadway Dance Center program. Each has a slightly different focus, as explained below.

Steps Studio Scholarships Program This program is designed to offer professional and aspiring professional dancers the opportunity to take unlimited classes with a diverse resident faculty. In exchange, each scholarship student performs ten hours of work per week at the Studio, assisting with its administration or maintenance. It is a great chance for talented, responsible dancers who have a positive work attitude to further develop their range as performers while at the same time opening other doors for themselves in the dance world.

The program is primarily for professional dancers. However, anyone with a strong dance background interested in pursuing advanced dance training is encouraged to audition. Foreign students are also welcome to audition for the program. However, scholarship students not fluent in English will be assigned to do work such as night-shift cleaning and maintenance rather than daytime jobs like answering phones or staffing the front desk.

Nonprofessional dancers who show potential, but have not yet achieved the level of skill required to participate in the full program, must enter it through the provisional scholarship program. This is the perfect avenue for aspiring performers who want to improve their dance technique and diversify their training in order to prepare for a professional dance career.

You must be age 16 or older to audition; those under 18 are required to have a parent's or guardian's consent to participate in the program.

Auditions for scholarships in ballet and jazz are scheduled the second week of every month. However, it is wise to call the organization ahead of time, or to check *Back Stage*, the New York trade paper, to confirm dates and times, as they are subject to change. Scholarship candidates may pick up an application at Steps's front desk. Applications are accepted up to thirty minutes before the start of an audition. Head-shots and a resume are strongly recommended. (For contact information about Steps Studio, see the Appendix.)

Auditions to join the Studio's ballet and jazz classes are conducted by selected members of the staff in a ninety-minute class format. Those auditioning are evaluated by the teacher and the scholarship director. Technique and potential are the primary criteria in the selection process, with resume information and professional experience also factored in. The name of the audition teacher is posted two weeks in advance, and it is recommended that dancers take classes with that instructor before the actual audition. Note: There's a fee for each audition class.

You might find seventy to eighty scholarship students in the Steps Studio program at any given time. Because the program is designed for professional-level and aspiring professional-level dancers actively seeking work, the dancer population taking lessons tends to be transient. That means students on the waiting list can expect to be offered a position within two to four weeks of acceptance. However, there's no guarantee.

Once you're offered a work study position, it's recommended that you remain there for at least eight weeks. The studio prefers two weeks' notice if you decide to leave or you land a job that will keep you from taking classes. Provisional scholarship students who leave must reaudition and be placed on the waiting list again if they wish to return. Full scholarship students may take a leave of absence and reenter the program at any time within two years of their giving written notice they intend to leave. Remember that no matter which scholarship program you're in, it's important to remain in good standing with the organization in order to regain your scholarship at a later date.

As noted earlier, scholarship students must work at the studio ten hours a week, doing jobs appropriate to their experience and skills. Positions include the following: front desk cashier and sign in, cafe cashier, phone receptionist, night shift maintenance and cleaning, front desk receptionist (greeter), front desk manager or assistant manager, and an assortment of miscellaneous positions.

Steps Studio sponsors several showcases each year, where many scholarship students participate as performers, choreographers, and technicians and work with some of the elite members of the New York dance community. Scholarship students have the privilege of being immersed in a circle of people consisting of the top professional dancers and choreographers in the world, with whom they have frequent, direct contact. For those who make the most of this situation, the opportunities are endless.

The Broadway Dance Center Scholarship Program The Broadway Dance Center, also in New York, offers over two hundred classes a week in ballet, jazz, tap, theater, ethnic, funk, and other styles of dance, at all levels from beginner to advanced. It also offers an internship work study program for dedicated students interested in continuing their dance training in New York City.

To participate, a minimum six-month commitment is required. Interns are expected to attend ten classes a week; classes beyond that are available at $3 per session. There's a $150 nonrefundable fee, due upon acceptance to the program. Interns are scheduled to work a total of ten to twelve hours per week, in two to four shifts, either at the front desk or in the cleaning program. A faculty or staff member is available to serve as a counselor or guide for each intern.

Be advised that the Broadway Dance Center is not responsible for providing housing. At your request, however, it will provide a list of available residential halls.

To apply, send for an application form. Fill it out fully, answering the two essay questions at the bottom of the application on a separate sheet of paper. When returning the application and answers to the essay questions, include your resume and letters of recommendation. (Contact information about the Center is provided in the Appendix.)

DECIDING IF COLLEGE IS RIGHT FOR YOU

Let's face it: Not everyone's going to succeed in musical theater. It's that rare individual, one with personal inspiration and a strong work ethic, who's willing to work through any hardships he or she encounters to reach the top, who usually succeeds. These people are the exceptions, not the rule. So if you're not one of the people who manages to make a living in musical theater, it's good to have a college degree to help you secure a regular job. You'll be more employable with a degree, not only as an actor, but in a job that has nothing to do with musical theater, one that requires college skills.

If you do decide on college, just remember to check out thoroughly the school that interests you, making sure it aims at training its students to become musical theater triple threats and avoids the pitfalls of specialization. Also make sure its teaching philosophy and curriculum fit your needs as a performer. Check out its track record in helping graduates enter the pro ranks. Contact people who have attended the institution. Do everything you can to make an intelligent, informed decision. If money constraints mean you have to attend a school close to home for the first couple of years, accept that fact and work hard to succeed in the classes you're able to take there. You can transfer to a more prestigious institution later, possibly on a scholarship earned as a result of the abilities you've shown in those first two years.

The bottom line for most people interested in becoming performers is that college provides a safety net, and is a wise precaution in case their dreams of performing don't pan out. But ultimately, attending college, or not, is an individual decision based on individual needs and abilities.

With all that said, I think one last point needs to be made. If after reading this chapter and thinking about all the issues it raises you still can't decide on the route you want to take, it might be best to take a year off. Graduate from high school. Take some dance, vocal, or acting lessons, and put the decision about going to college on the back burner for the time being. Having some time to reflect can actually help you make a more reasoned, and effective, decision.

8

Tools of the Trade

How many times do performers hear that their picture and resume make up their calling card? No doubt if your career is already on the move, you've heard the comment often enough. These two items, if done well, can get you in the door to being considered for many jobs. If done poorly, they demonstrate a lack of the knowledge and professionalism necessary to make it in the performing business. Performers of all stripes need a picture of themselves—called a headshot or a three-quarters shot, depending on how much of the performer it shows—and a resume that will hit home with agents, producers, directors, and casting directors. Whether you're a seasoned pro or just starting out, a high-quality picture and solid resume listing your performing skills will lead to greater opportunities and better pay.

The Picture
The picture I'm talking about here is not just a snapshot like you'd take at a picnic. It has to be of commercial quality. Because it advertises you, it has to reveal a certain amount of luster and self-confidence.

Choosing the Right Picture Style Professional pictures come in several styles: the headshot, which is exactly what it says, a picture of your head only; the three-quarters shot, which also shows your body down through the upper torso; and the composite, which consist of four shots, each of them offering a different look. Which is the right style for you? It depends. For a long time, a headshot was the preferred style; then it moved toward the three-quarters shot, in order to show more of what the performer looked like and whether he or she was in good physical condition. There's no hard and fast rule, and trends change. Just keep in mind that you want a photo which shows you off to your best advantage. Also keep in mind that composites are used for modeling and commercial work, not for theatrical work. If your focus is on musical theater exclusively, they're a waste of money.

Agents keep up with the changing trends, and they also have their own ideas of what will best serve the performers they represent. If you have an agent, let him or her make the decision.

Finding the Right Photographer Don't think that you can go to just any photographer and get a good professional picture. And don't, under any circumstances, go to a portrait studio. Portrait photos try for a romantic image, something "laid back." Usually they're shot with a soft focus and in color. The type of commercial pictures theatrical performers need are crisp and clean, always in black and white, and exude a high energy content. While this kind of shot may not be suitable for display on a

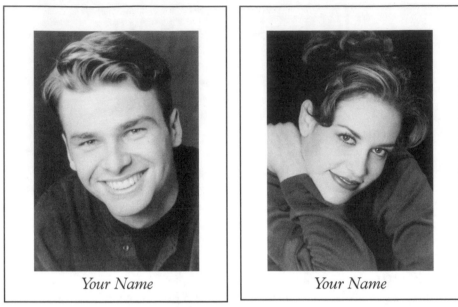

Two typical headshots, one male, one female—note their crisp and lively look.

living-room mantelpiece, it's what a performer needs to succeed in this industry. It has to shout: "Look at me! Hire me!"

If you live in one of the major cities, finding the right photographer won't be very difficult since they advertise in the trade papers. If you live in a smaller city or town, here are some tips for locating someone who can do the job properly:

Start by word-of-mouth recommendations from performers you meet at auditions, from your dance or vocal teacher, and from friends you might have who are in show business. Check out their pictures to see if you like them.

Once you have some recommendations from people whose judgment you trust and have seen some pictures you like, call the photographer whose work appeals to you the most for an appointment. The initial visit is not to have your pictures shot, but to look over the photographer's portfolio and assess your ability to work with this person. The portfolio will include pictures the photographer has taken throughout his or her career, including headshots. Right now the photographer is auditioning for you, letting you judge his or her work. Remember that the photographer will be working for you, not you for the photographer. If you don't like what you see, don't proceed any further, no matter what anyone else's opinion is about his or her abilities. If your personalities clash, or if for any reason you don't feel comfortable with the photographer, that's another warning signal not to go any further. In order to get good results, you have to be relaxed before the camera. Even the least bit of discomfort will show up in the shots, and you don't want that. So be certain you trust the photographer before signing on, and if you don't, look for another photographer.

Make sure to ask the photographer what his or her policy is if you don't like any of the shots.

About that last point, Eric Weber, a professional headshot photographer, has this to say:

> *If the photographer somehow messes up and the pictures are out of focus, the exposure is off, or something about you has really ruined the shot—a crooked tie or hair sticking up—the reshooting should be free of charge. But if you're not satisfied with the results for any other reason, you should pay for another session. You have to take responsibility for what you bring to the shoot, including expressions, attitude, and confidence. You can't lay everything on the photographer. Get enough sleep the night before and come in ready to do your share of the work.*

Photo Costs The price range of photos can run from $80 in small towns to $1500 in Los Angeles. The average price is $200 to $300. For that money, the photographer will shoot several rolls of film (there are usually thirty-six shots to the roll), and after developing the rolls will present you with contact sheets showing all the shots, from which you'll pick the best one or two. Those are then printed up as 8 by 10 photographs, in whatever quantities the two of you have agreed upon. Some photographers charge for the shoot itself, and then you pay an additional $15 to $20 for the copies of each picture you want. Since different photographers package their deals in different ways, be up front about asking them the costs and the type of package they offer, and pick the package that best suits your needs.

Your Name   *Your Name*

These examples of three-quarter shots add to the face the performer's upper-body dynamic.

Preparing for the Photo Shoot You want your face to be the brightest part of the picture, to stand out, so be careful what you wear. Your clothes should complement your features, not detract from them. Darker clothing is preferable, but not too dark. You should never wear a white top. Bring several changes of clothing so the photographer can pick the outfit that looks best on you—and always trust the photographer's judgment. Women should keep their jewelry small and tasteful so it doesn't overpower the picture.

At the shoot, women will need a hair and makeup person. The photographer always lines up this individual, who costs another $60 to $100 per shoot. Don't make the mistake of thinking you can get by without the service. It's money well spent. The hair and makeup person's job is to make sure that you look good at all times, that hair isn't sticking up, that no smudges mar your face, and that the makeup looks natural and flattering to you. Black and white photos require a certain style of makeup to look good, which means an expert should apply it. This is not the time for you to be attempting your own hand at it.

Men can get additional mileage from their photo shoots, if they want, by coming in wearing a beard or mustache. After being shot with facial hair, they can then shave and have another set of photos made. In this way, they can get two different looks. Men really shouldn't wear makeup at a shoot. But if they have uneven skin due to blemishes or any other skin problem, and they want their skin to look smooth for the shoot, they can use a minimal amount of makeup.

These pictures, which are aimed at selling you to all kinds of people in show business, shouldn't be faddish. You want to aim for a classic look, something that makes you appear natural, approachable, and friendly, not artificially glamorous. Women should be careful with how they wear their hair. It shouldn't be a drastic departure from their normal look. In fact, the most important rule about headshots or three-quarters shots can be stated as follows: The picture has to look like you—like the person walking through the door of the agent, the casting director, or the producer. Only it has to look like the best and most exciting you possible, so the people seeing it will want you to audition for their shows.

Contact Sheets When you receive your contact sheets, don't make the mistake of letting your family or someone close to you pick the shot. They will tend to pick something cute, not commercial. Get the photographer's opinion. If you have friends in the business, get theirs. Show the sheets to a casting director or an agent if you know one. Even if you don't have an agent, paying one for an hour of her or his time is money very well spent. Just be sure to get objective feedback and not rush into a decision. Choosing the right picture is critical. Make sure it says what it should. By that I mean look at the eyes, hair, teeth, and smile. You want your personality to shine through, saying, "Here I am. I'm the one."

After you select the one or two images you want, the photographer will print up one or two full-size photos for you, which you take for duplication. Make sure the photographer doesn't put a copyright stamp on the pictures. If he or she does, you won't be able to reproduce them without ordering from that photographer. This is something else to ask about up front, before agreeing to the shoot.

Duplicating the Picture As long as you don't plan on changing your look, it's fine to have the pictures reproduced in bulk. You do this by taking or sending them to a reproduction lab, where the lab technicians in effect take a picture of each of your pictures, creating a negative of it. From that negative the lab prints as many copies as you request, for which you pay a fee.

I offer a warning from my own personal experience: Be careful which lab you pick. If you send your picture to the wrong one, you'll wind up with the worst results imaginable. There is absolutely a difference between a first-rate duplication service and one that's bad or even middling. If a lab isn't careful about the quality of the negative it produces, the quality of the resulting picture will be poor—lighter or darker than the original photo. This in turn will affect how you look in it. The quality of reproduction at a topnotch lab, on the other hand, will result in photos that look virtually identical to the original picture. To be on the safe side, pay for a sample copy to examine. If it's not acceptable, you'll only be out only a few dollars, instead of hundreds.

Your name and contact information must appear at the bottom of the picture. Select a classic typeface for this. *Don't* choose something decorative or hard to read, like a Gothic style. If you have an agent, make sure the name of the agency, its address, and phone number are listed also. Some agencies have logos they supply their clients for this purpose.

Orders must usually be prepaid. If you will not be picking up the pictures in person, make sure the price includes shipping and handling charges. Your pictures should be ready in about a month.

Watching Out for Scams I wish I could tell you that everyone in this business is honest and aboveboard, but scams abound and you need to be aware of them. One of these involves agent–photographer deals. Performers and parents of young performers are sometimes so relieved to find an agent that they just go along with whatever the agency suggests about photos and resumes. Some agents then recommend a photographer or offer their own "in-house" photography services to their clients. What you may not know is that there are often kickback schemes between outside photographers and agencies, and, of course, if the agency itself does the photography it means the client is placing money directly into the agency's pockets. This can lead to bad results since the client has no control over how qualified the photographer is or the quality of the final results.

There are also plenty of unscrupulous people who label themselves talent agents and try to entice would-be clients into spending $700 or $800 on pictures. The performer winds up getting bad photos, along with a little printed-up card with his or her name on it, and the so-called agent winds up skipping town with the money.

Remember, don't be gullible or impulsive about all this. Every performer wants to be a star. But if our egos are out of control, we open ourselves up to being taken advantage of. It's nice to hear how beautiful and fantastically talented we are, but be careful about signing on the dotted line. Keep control over who takes your photos. Make sure you always have the final choice in the selection of the image that best represents you. If an agent *insists* you have your pictures taken in house or by the photographer he or she recommends, find another agent.

Resumes

As I said earlier, a performer's picture and resume together comprise her or his calling card. We've discussed the photo, so now we'll turn to the resume.

What purpose does the resume serve? Pat Criscito, author of *Designing the Perfect Resume*, states, "Your resume is an advertisement. It's a way to get your foot in the door for an interview or audition. It doesn't get you the job, just the opportunity to sell yourself, to get someone to call you back after reading it."

Most young performers tend to put too much information into a resume. They try to make it too complete when, in fact, it should leave something to the imagination. Also, many performers of all ages don't know how to lay out a resume in an easy-to-read format. A resume is not unlike a newspaper ad, which doesn't provide all the details about an item, just enough to entice buyers into the store, and which is designed to be reader friendly.

You can always have a resume prepared and printed professionally. But with the widespread availability of home computers, there's no longer any reason to go to that trouble and expense. You can do it on your own computer, or that of a friend. This also has distinct advantages. It allows you to update your resume quickly and conveniently as needed. It allows you to tailor it to specific job opportunities, so casting directors and others will see precisely the information about yourself you want them to see. It allows you to print out just the number of copies needed at a particular time.

If you're not great at grammar, layout, or spelling, you can ask a friend who has these skills to help. Make sure to use the spell-checker feature that is standard on most word processors. Study the sample resume shown in this chapter, which shows the kinds of information you need to include and a good layout.

How to Write a Resume To look professional, resumes should never be longer than one page. They should, however, always be eye-catching, and easy to read.

At the top of the page should go your name, centered. Under your name list your performing union affiliations, also centered. If you don't have any, simply type: Nonunion. Below that give your address and the phone number where you can be reached. Many people are uncomfortable about giving out their addresses, so don't

YOUR NAME
Union Affiliations
Address
City, State, Zip Code
Phone: (000) 123-4567
Contact: Name of Agent or Agency; Phone: (000) 987-6543

PERSONAL STATS
Height:
Eye Color:
Hair Color:
Vocal Range

THEATER EXPERIENCE

Name of Show	Part You Played	Name of Theater
Name of Show	Part You Played	Name of Theater
Name of Show	Part You Played	Name of Theater
Name of Show	Part You Played	Name of Theater

INDUSTRIALS

Name of Corporation, City, State	What You Did
Name of Corporation, City, State	What You Did
Name of Corporation, City, State	What You Did

FILM/TELEVISION

Name of Movie or Show	Character Played	Production Company
Name of Movie or Show	Character Played	Production Company
Name of Movie or Show	Character Played	Production Company

COMMERCIALS (tape available upon request)

Company Represented	Regional or National	Production Company
Company Represented	Regional or National	Production Company
Company Represented	Regional or National	Production Company

TRAINING

Acting:	Teacher or School, City, State	Years Studied
	Teacher or School, City, State	Years Studied
	Currently studying with [give name of Teacher or School, City, State]	

Dance:	Tap: Teacher or School, City, State, Years Studied
	Ballet: Teacher or School, City, State, Years Studied
	Jazz: Teacher or School, City, State, Years Studied
	Ballroom: Teacher or School, City, State, Years Studeid
	Tumbling: Teacher or School, City, State, Years Studied
	Currently studying [give dance style, Teacher or School, City, State]

Voice:	Teacher or School, City, State	Years Studied
	Currently studying with [give name of Teacher or School, City, State]	

SPECIAL SKILLS
Languages and dialects; professional trick roping, juggling, magic, or other variety act skills; sports.

This sample resume shows the kind of information you should include and the best layout.

include it if you don't want to; the phone number alone is enough. If you have an agent, list him or her as the person to contact, along with the agency's phone number.

Next come your vital statistics, often called "personal stats," which should not be centered but placed on the right and left as shown in the sample resume. Here you should list information like your height, hair color, and eye color. Singers should list their vocal range—for example, "E below mid C to high B"—or their vocal classification, such as soprano, alto, tenor, baritone, bass. Do *not* include your age and weight. Let those considering you for an audition determine that information by looking at your picture instead.

Below your personal stats, list your show credits. As musical theater is your primary goal, list theater credits first, giving the name of the production, the part you played, and the theater where it had its run. Experienced performers can break this down by subheadings into Broadway productions, national tours, summer stock, and dinner theater. Below the theater credits then come the lists of commercials and/or industrials, television shows, and movies you've appeared in, giving the information appropriate to each as shown in the sample resume.

Within each category, don't list your credits in chronological order. List the most important ones first to emphasize their importance and catch the eyes of the casting people. In regard to commercials, don't list more than the five most important you've appeared in.

Performers just starting out won't have all these kinds of credits, so go with what you have. You might have college theater, community theater, showcases, summer stock, theme park, or cruise ship credits, and those should be listed under the appropriate headings. If that is all you have, list those accomplishments and don't be embarrassed about them. As you begin to work semiprofessionally or professionally, you'll gain more extensive experience and credits that you can add to your resume, while you delete those that are less impressive.

Always tell the truth. *Never lie* on your resume! You don't want to list a show you didn't perform in, only to come face to face with the director of that show during an audition. It has happened. And people know each other in this business. Lies are easily detected.

After your show credits, list the information about your professional training, showing who you studied with and for how long. Use subheadings for acting, dance, and voice. If you're new to the business, it's especially important to show that you're continuing your training. Beginners don't have many professional performing credits to list, but they can let the casting people know they're serious about their careers by continuing to train with reputable instructors.

And again—as I've pointed out elsewhere in this book—don't limit your training to one or two areas, and don't fail to list the training you've had or are getting in every performing area. As Melba Huber, winner of the 1998 Savion Glover Award and a writer for various dance publications, notes, "For goodness sake, don't become so specialized that you can only do one thing. Dancers should study singing and acting and vice versa. List any skills that you have, no matter how insignificant you think they are. If you are good at many specialties, you have a better chance to work all the time. Continue studying and developing new interests that are related to your goals."

The final category on your resume should be "Special Skills." These include talents like the ability to do dialects or speak foreign languages; professional experience in variety-type acts such as magic, trick roping, juggling, and so forth; and sports you are good at. Never list anything that you're not reasonably competent at doing. But remember that if you fail to list something you know how to do, casting people and others who make the decisions about who to audition or hire for shows have no way of knowing about it.

When your resume is done, print it out on the same size paper as your picture. Get a spray adhesive, apply a thin layer to the back of the picture, and attach the resume to it. This way the two will be attached without the need to put staples through the photo. Your picture will probably have your name on it. But if it doesn't, as an added protection in case the resume comes off, before spraying on the adhesive write your name on the back of the photo. Do this with a felt tip marker, not a ball point pen that makes an indent which will be visible on the other side. Remember, neatness and attractiveness are as important for your "calling card" as they are for your personal appearance.

Cover Letters

When your send out your picture and resume, you'll need a cover letter to accompany them. As Pat Criscito says in *Designing the Perfect Resume*, the perfect cover letter should be short, sweet, and to the point. It needs to grab the reader's attention and entice her or him to want to learn more about you via the resume. The appearance of a cover letter is just as important as its contents. Remember to use your computer spell-check function. Often! This piece of paper represents you as much as your performing skills do.

According to Pat Criscito, the perfect cover letter has three parts:

1. An introductory paragraph, which usually runs about two or three sentences. Its content will vary, depending on the reason you're contacting the person. (a) If it's for a part in a musical, mention the part, where you heard about it, and why you want to work for that director or company. Do your homework here. Make sure you know something about the production and be sure to mention some of the details about it to show that you are knowledgeable. This is the point in the letter to drop names if you know someone personally who is involved in the production. (b) If you're seeking agent representation, mention how you heard about the agent and what you know about his or her reputation.
2. The second section is the "I'm super-great because. . ." paragraph (or two). Here, you summarize why you are absolutely perfect for the part, or why you

Date

Mr. Fred Will
The Will Agency
123 Park Avenue
New York, New York 12345

Dear Mr. Will:

Jimmy Smith, one of your long-time clients, recommended that I contact you about representation. He knows about my history of success in Off-Broadway shows and felt you would be interested in representing me.

As you will notice in my enclosed resume, I have performed in many regional theaters, summer stock companies, national tours, and one recent Off-Broadway production, *Nunsense*. I played the part of Mother Superior, in which I both acted and sang. I have also enclosed the reviews from the national tour of *Grease*, where I played the part of Rizzo.

My resume will give you more details of my experience and accomplishments. I have also enclosed a recent photograph for your consideration. Please feel free to contact me with any questions. I look forward to hearing from you soon.

Sincerely,

[Your signature goes here]

[Your typed name goes here]

Enclosures

Sample cover letter written to accompany the picture and resume.

think you are someone the agent should represent. Really sell yourself. Captivate the reader enough to want to find out more about you from your resume. Elaborate on the experience and training you have that specifically qualify you for this part or this agent. Just remember to make the section brief, so the reader won't lose interest.

3. The closing section should be short. Be sure that it conveys what you want (an interview, an audition, a callback). If you want the person to contact you, say so. If you are planning to call the person yourself, give the day and time and remember to follow through (but find out ahead of time through a secretary or mutual friend if the person minds such calls; don't phone if he or she doesn't like that approach). Remember to say something pleasant like "Thank you for your consideration" or "I look forward to hearing from you soon," but don't overdo it. Close by saying, "Sincerely," followed by your signature. You name should appear typed below your signature, and below that should appear the word "Enclosures" (which can be abbreviated "Encls.") to remind the person of your photo and resume.

Use the sample cover letter shown in this chapter as a guide. But be sure to personalize your letter not just with your own information, but with your own way of saying things. Make the letter yours, like your picture and resume. And mail it in a photo mailer with cardboard to protect the photo. You want your image to arrive looking its best.

TRADE PAPERS

Among the most important tools of the trade for performers are the trade papers, where you find out about auditions, agents, photographers, and a lot of other information vital to building and maintaining a career in musical theater.

If you're a young performer attending high school or college in a small town, your chances of finding trade papers at newspaper and magazine outlets are slim. Your school or public library may not even subscribe to them. I live in a city of 400,000 and can't find them locally. If that's the case with you, you'll have to subscribe. (A list of the trades, with their mailing addresses and phone numbers, is included in the Appendix.) Some of them let you subscribe on-line.

For performers just starting out in the business, the trade papers are a lifeline. They list what's happening where and when—auditions, new shows, other job opportunities. They provide articles on every aspect of show business, including writing resumes and having pictures shot. Reading the trades also helps stoke the inner fire that performers need to get out there to the auditions for the new jobs listed in them every week. They keep young performers revved up about the entertainment business they want to be part of.

There are often complaints about how few jobs there are for young performers in show business. But if you're serious about this business and training hard, you'll find an abundance of work. Not every job will be the one you find perfect, but you'll definitely find as much work as you can handle. If you're still in school and too young to travel to the big cities where most of the jobs are, read the trades with your parents and friends, paying special attention to the nonunion work available to see what might be right for you. This will help you learn to focus on planning your career and take control of it early on.

Let's discuss a couple of the trade papers in more detail: *Back Stage,* the performing arts weekly, and *Dirt Alert.*

Back Stage If you're in the theater industry and don't have a subscription to *Back Stage* (or, on the West Coast, *Back Stage West*), you're being left in the dark when it comes to getting work. As the Bible for theater professionals, there's no other publication that comes close to listing jobs in such a clear, concise format. You'll find auditions for singers, dancers, and actors in stage shows of all kinds, including Broadway, off-Broadway, touring productions, summer stock, cruise lines, and Las Vegas, as well as for voice-overs and other kinds of nonstage work. The ads cover both Equity and non-Equity jobs that are represented, and list shows from New York to Berlin to Moscow. The section "Auditions at a Glance" provides a convenient index to casting calls that might interest you, while the "Regional Roundup" provides in-depth coverage of productions in various regions of the country, updated weekly.

Not only does *Back Stage* keep novices up to date on auditions, but it tackles all the ins and outs of being a performer in longer articles, covering everything from photo shoots, to resumes, to financial planning for paying your taxes, to the hot spots to go to for the lessons you may need in preparing for a particular role or audition. At the back of each issue the paper has classified listings relating to health, beauty, and fitness products and services, as well as listings of professional services like studios where you can do voice-over demonstration tapes, people who do music copying, pianists you can rehearse with, voice mail services and companies that provide beepers. You can find ads by gyms and personal trainers if you need to get into physical shape, by vocal coaches if you need to work on your voice or a dialect, and by studio spaces if you need to rent a place for practice or rehearsals. There are ads for dance, voice, and acting studios and teachers, with the class schedules listed, as well as for photographers and photo services. And you'll find information about summer training programs in all aspects of theater.

The people at *Back Stage* realize that everyone will need a second job at one time or another to tide them over until that big break, so the paper also lists employment agencies that specialize in temporary work. This isn't limited to being a waiter, either. Employment agencies understand that actors have a wide variety of skills, and they're prepared to supply a wide variety of jobs. Some of the possibilities: domestic work (personal assistants, childcare), advertising agencies, Wall Street, computer information services. If you have a marketable skill, they'll be able to find you work with a schedule that allows you the time you need to actively pursue your entertainment career.

A regular feature in *Back Stage* is "Face to Face," which features interviews with some of the most prominent people in show business, who offer fascinating insights into their professional lives. These candid discussions tell you what it's like to be a singer, a dancer, or an actor. The people interviewed talk about coping with the demands of the business, how they prepare for their performances, and the satisfaction that comes from a job well done. The interviews provide humor, wisdom, and motivation, something you can draw on as you work to develop your own career.

I can't stress enough the importance of reading *Back Stage*. It's a lively publication, fun to read, and chock-full of indispensable information that you won't find anywhere else. About the only thing it won't provide is personal references, which you'll have to secure for yourself. In every other way it will give you a leg up in your career.

Dirt Alert The audition trade paper published in Las Vegas, *Dirt Alert* comes out twice a month, and lists audition opportunities for everyone, whether you're a total beginner or a seasoned pro.

With its extensive listings, *Dirt Alert* will keep you abreast of auditions as diverse as nonunion touring companies to replacement calls for Broadway shows. You'll learn what's current in Atlantic City, at overseas venues such as Guam and Japan, on cruise ships and at theme parks, and find detailed listings for all Las Vegas shows. Also, separating *Dirt Alert* from the rest of the trades are their audition notices for lookalike casting, trapeze and circus acts, variety acts, and other specialty skills.

Besides audition notices, there are articles and profiles on performers and how they got to where they are today. Young performers invariably find it motivating to read how others have achieved their goals.

Every spring, *Dirt Alert* publishes a directory for entertainers and entertainment-related businesses. Those who use it include directors, producers of larger shows, cruise lines, and entertainment buyers. In short, just about everybody.

Dirt Alert doesn't have as many acting and commercial listings as some of the other trades, but the singer–dancer who doesn't subscribe will be unaware of many venues listed nowhere else. There are 25 retail outlets in Las Vegas that carry *Dirt Alert*; the rest of the readers have subscriptions. See the Appendix for contact information.

TALENT DIRECTORIES

A talent directory is a book or catalogue containing pictures and resumes of available talent. A number of companies publish such directories, and you pay to be included. If you decide to go this route, be very careful about which directories you agree to be listed in, however—most of them are scams. One legitimate directory that has been around a long time is the *Academy Players Directory* (see the Appendix for contact information). Most performers have their pictures published in these directories because they have been promised that casting directors use them. The bottom line is that if a casting director is filling roles for a specific production and one of those directories—be it in book, CD-ROM, or Internet form—falls into his or her hands, the director might browse through it looking for new, interesting faces, or might pick one up if a trusted agent recommends that the director "look at page 56 of such-and-such guide."

But do casting directors shop for talent in such directories? As a rule, no. Here's why: Each production has very specific requirements, in terms of characters, production dates, rehearsal dates, and so forth. Casting directors do a call for each casting so they can define those terms and narrow their focus, considering only those actors who are both proper for each character and available for the job. Let's say a casting director actually goes shopping for an actor or actress in one of those books and finds someone with the perfect look for a particular character. What if that actor isn't available? What if he she looks great in the photo and the resume sounds good, but in reality the person can't act, sing, or dance well? What if the biggest gripe of casting directors comes true and the picture in the book bears little resemblance to the performer's current look? Casting directors don't see the point of using these catalogues. They would rather make a specific casting call with defined terms, and receive the picture and resume submissions of those interested in the role.

MAILINGS

Mailings are a great way of maintaining contact with people in the business. Many agents send these out when a performer they represent gets into a Broadway show. It's a smart thing to do.

A mailing usually consists of a postcard that you can mail out, telling people what's happening with your career. These are used to alert people like agents, producers, or casting directors that you're available for work or to let them know you're appearing in a show where they can see you perform. Maybe you want a choreographer to see you dance, or a director to see you act or sing. Postcards are worth sending to anybody in the business who might be helpful to your future career. Just don't waste anyone's time, or spend your own money on a ticket for them, if it's a bad show or one where your talents aren't showcased at their best. Instead, wait until you appear in something better for them to see. Agents, casting directors, and entertainment buyers will know something worthwhile when they see it and will appreciate the care you put into steering them toward something worth their time.

The format for such cards can vary. Here are a few tips on how to make your cards work for you effectively. On one side of the card put your headshot, or a picture of you in your current show. List your name in bold print, along with your union affiliations, if any, and the name of your agent with his or her phone number. If you're in a show, list the name of the character you're playing. If you're in the chorus, put "Chorus member." Beneath that list the name of the show, and under that the dates the show runs, the theater or venue where it's playing, and the address and phone number of the theater or venue. If you particularly want some of the recipients to attend a performance, wait a few days after mailing the card,

Your Name

Sample postcard mailing. Sending this type of card keeps performers in contact with agents, casting directors, and managers. It can let them know where you're currently performing, so they can come and see you, or simply reminds them you're still out there, available for work.

then call and offer to buy them tickets. It's a courteous gesture to busy people, and if they like what they see, they'll be more likely to help you.

The second side of the card is used for the name and address of the recipient. But like all postcards, that need only take up part of the space. You can use the rest of the second side for the information just discussed. Perhaps that's what the person did in the sample postcard shown in this chapter. Or perhaps he was not currently in a show, but wanted to remind an agent or casting director he had met on some social occasion that he was still out there and available for work.

THANK YOU CARDS

This is actually another type of mailing, a card that includes your image on one side. Instead of the message being printed as with the type of card I described above, you handwrite the message on the side with your picture if space allows or on the side with the address otherwise. Examples of the kinds of things you might say: "Thanks so much. I really enjoyed auditioning for you the other day. I look forward to the opportunity of signing a contract with you." Or "Thank you for the advice. I know that it will help in my career and I'll use it wisely. I enjoyed meeting you."

The thank you should be pleasant, without too much apple-polishing. It's a good business practice and helps people remember you as a professional. Most performers are self-absorbed; by sending this kind of card you indicate that you're thinking about people other than yourself.

WARDROBE

We often think of wardrobe just in terms of shows being produced. But having a good personal wardrobe is very important for performers because image is everything in this business. So set up your own working wardrobe. Determine the styles of clothing, jewelry, and shoes that work well for you, and keep those items separate from the items you wear every day. Have them at the ready, cleaned and pressed, for auditions, interviews, and special meetings. You have to be ready at a moment's notice. You never know when your agent might call with an appointment you need to get to within the hour, or when you might notice in one of the trades an audition you want to attend scheduled for later the same day. And make sure you have outfits suitable for all the different kinds of occasions that can come up—dance attire for dance auditions, clothes suitable for dramatic readings, or an outfit you can wear when meeting an agent or producer for the first time. In regard to auditions. remember this rule of thumb: If you get a callback, always wear the same thing you wore to the initial interview or audition. The callback obviously means they liked what they saw the first time around.

PROMOTIONAL TAPES

Promotional tapes are useful if you're looking for work in specific venues. They serve the same purpose as resumes and pictures: to get you in the door. Production companies hiring for theme parks, cruise ships, and a wide variety of entertainment events use them. They often want to see a tape before calling a performer in for a live audition, to make sure you offer exactly what they're looking for. That way, nobody's time is wasted. In some cases they hire from the tapes alone.

In the theater world, however, more than likely you won't need a tape. Casting people and producers prefer live auditions, and the ads in the trades bring in more than enough performers to make viewing tapes a waste of their time.

The bottom line is, if you're planning to do the type of work where tapes are required, get one made. Just be sure you know your market, and whether or not a promotional tape is something you should have. Also make sure it's professionally produced. If done poorly, it can cost you a great deal of time and money for nothing in return.

Most beginning performers are confused about the process of making a promotional tape. It frightens some of them to the point that they will put one together only if forced to. Well, don't be scared. Making a tape can be enjoyable, and the costs quite reasonable.

In this section, we'll focus on making videotapes, which is what musical theater performers need. However, audiotapes can also be handy tools to send to agents so they can hear your voice if you're interested in doing voice-overs or in singing jingles for TV or radio ads. Don't dismiss this kind of work. A lot of performers do it to support themselves while waiting for their theater break. It can help you survive financially in the early years of your career.

A bad promotional tape is every beginner's nightmare, and here's the perfect scenario for how to produce one: Imagine Uncle Festus and Aunt Bertha attending each of your performances, armed with their heavy, clunky 1985 camcorder. The sound is tinny and the lens doesn't quite focus, but there they are, being a nuisance to the rest of the audience so that they can capture those proud moments of their favorite niece or nephew. After following you for years, they have a trunkload of tapes showcasing your talent.

Now you need a promotional tape, and you want to avoid the anxiety of finding a good studio to produce it and paying out the large amount of money you think the studio will charge you. Gathering up everything Festus and Bertha shot over the years, you head down to your friend Billy Bob's garage where, with his cheap mixer and editing gear, you think he'll be able to create a work of art you can send to the Kennedy Center.

It's that simple, right? *Wrong!* In fact, you wouldn't even want to show this fuzzy artifact to your least favorite relative. Producing a good promotional tape takes professional expertise in both the shooting and editing phases. And it's cheaper than you might think to have this done. So read on as we discuss how to go about it.

Finding a Good Studio

Companies that make promotional tapes advertise in the Yellow Pages under the heading "Video Production Services." They also advertise in the trades. In the big cities there will likely be lots of them, so I recommend asking agents, professionals in the business, or other performers what facilities they've used or know to be good.

After compiling a list of possibilities, go to several studios and look at some of the tapes they've done for other performers. If possible, bring someone knowledgeable about promotional tapes with you. That person's opinion can be invaluable.

Watch a variety of tapes at a studio; if none of them grabs you in the first thirty seconds, move on to the next studio. The proof is in the product, not in slick sales talk or impressive looking equipment. The first step in choosing a studio is knowing you like the type of tapes they make.

Nevertheless, always check out the studio's equipment. Make sure it uses a high-quality camera and shoots the footage in Beta SP or a digital DVC pro format. You don't want the results to be fuzzy or grainy, where you don't look your best.

It might even be possible to salvage some of Festus' and Bertha's tapes. If the quality of the work is good enough, the studio may be able to incorporate it with the new footage. A reputable studio will be honest in its evaluation of any outside footage you have.

Length of the Tape

Keep the length down to about two to five minutes. Anything longer is too long. Keep in mind that agents, directors, and casting people don't have the time, or the inclination, to watch long tapes. What they respond to are tapes that overwhelm them in a positive way within the first minute—or better yet the first few seconds—of being viewed. They like seeing performers who bowl them over with enthusiasm, with intensity, with energy. If you don't do this quickly, your tape will either be filed away and most likely forgotten, or worse yet, thrown away and wind up as landfill. Those first few seconds count!

Studio Versus Live Performance

A lot of singer–dancers make what we call "their own little video" in a studio to show off their best performance attributes. Yet talent buyers tend to prefer seeing footage of live performances. That's because in a studio environment, conditions are perfect, and the performance can be shot as many times as needed to eliminate any problems. Live footage, however, shows whether performers have what it takes in real-life performing situations. A performer's interactions with the audience, and the audience's responses to the performance, give the tape a spontaneous air that helps agents, casting directors, and other talent buyers assess the performer's abilities better than they can with the tape of a canned, studio performance. These professionals know the difference. You want them to have the reaction: "This guy is fantastic! He doesn't miss a beat. The audience loves him." Still, if there are some things you feel should be shot in a studio, a good video editor can intercut both live and canned performances for a super finished product.

Costs

Of course, every video service will be a little different in their fee structure. But a good camera operator will usually cost about $100 to $150 an hour. Editing will run in the range of $80 to $250 an hour. Look to spend somewhere in the neighborhood of $750 to $1000 overall on production costs. Add $2 per tape for duplication, and you'll have a very nice video to send out as needed.

THE INTERNET

The Internet is the most recent tool available to performers, and if you're just getting started in your career, it offers a world of information at your fingertips. Sit down at your home computer, log on, and in just moments you can access many sites dedicated to the performing arts. The biggest problem, believe it or not, is the sheer amount of data available.

Finding the Information You Need

To search the World Wide Web for the information, you use what is known as a search engine—Yahoo, Infoseek, Lycos, AltaVista, and so on. You simply enter a word or phrase in a box on the computer screen and click on the button labeled "Search."

The problem, as I said, is the amount of information you're likely to find. Say you enter the word "acting," for example, and begin the search. In a matter of seconds you're told the search engine has located 1,228,876 sites related to the subject. That's an overwhelming number, more than you could check out in a lifetime. Moreover, not all of them will supply you with the information you want. Many of the hits will be small home pages created by other actors to promote themselves, each containing a picture or pictures along with a resume and other information the person considers important for those viewing the site to see. Some of these can be helpful to beginners wanting to jump-start their careers. However, they may not be helpful at all, and such small sites tend to come and go in a flash. Those aren't the kind we'll be discussing here.

Instead, we'll focus on the major sites relating to performing that are likely to be around for a while. To locate those, you can use tools such as online "yellow pages" and business directories, as well as books that list Websites by category, which are available in bookstores.

Websites That Are Proven Winners

If you're new to the Web, or just starting your career, here are some sites to get you going:
> www.backstage.com: At this address *Back Stage*, *Back Stage West*, and
> *Dramalogue* offer important information relating to musical theater, including
> articles on many subjects of interest to performers and casting notices.
> www.theatre-central.com: This address will link you to many theater sites.
> www.playbill.com: This address contains casting notices and lots of other
> valuable information.
> www.sag.com: This is the Screen Actors Guild site. You can get a list of fran-
> chised agents listed by city, plus any union information you may need.
> www.aftra.com: This is AFTRA's homepage.

There is also a Usenet newsgroup called "alt. acting" where many working actors gather to discuss their profession. The Internet's largest newsgroup directory, *Deja News*, is also excellent. Just type in the words "musical theater" and up will come loads of relevant information. Many online services, such as America Online (AOL), offer forums for various professionals. For example, there's one called "Casting Central," where actors, both novice and professional, can share information about their craft. This forum also has a headshot gallery, audition postings and tips, most frequently asked questions, and other features helpful to those seeking a performing career.

There are also dance sites on the Web where you can pick up new dance steps, whether jazz, tap, or ballet.

By working the Web, you can gain the information, insights, and practical advice that can make a major difference at the dawn of your career.

Message Boards

You'll find message boards attached to some of the above listings. These are locations where you can post (ask) questions about any number of topics, such as agents, pictures, resumes, auditioning, and schooling.

Because people with extensive knowledge of the entertainment business head up the message boards, you can get clear and concise answers in response to your questions. Unfortunately, the message boards have also become havens for teenage girls between the ages of 11 and 16 who, in their quest to find representation, often post information far too personal and revealing. At the least, doing this is naive. Even though message boards are a good tool for getting information, they aren't currently being used by any of the people who wield power in the business. No legitimate agent or producer uses the Internet to find talent. Conversely, legitimate performers should not try to market themselves by giving personally explicit information out over the Internet. Agents and casting directors aren't interested, and it can be dangerous for the young performer being so explicit in the public world of the Internet. I offer two examples of this kind of personal ad that have been brought to my attention:

> *Hi. My name is Ashley [not the person's real name]. I'm 13 years old, 5'8" tall, and weigh 125 pounds. I have layered brown hair, shoulder length, and beautiful long legs. I've wanted to be an actress since I was 3. If I sound like someone you want, please e-mail me at xxx.com. I'm willing to do just about anything to get my career going.*

> *Hot and sexy 13-year-old dancer looking for work in Oklahoma. Look older than I am. Please e-mail me if interested at xxx.com.*

Do the dangers of this kind of message need to be pointed out? Anyone, including someone dangerous, can sign onto a message board pretending to be a producer or agent. They can promise young people the world, ask for money to help them get started in their careers, ask to meet with them to discuss their future. Remember, scams are common in the performing world, and it's no different on the Internet. The problem can be even worse on-line, since these interactions with strangers often take place with no parental supervision.

Message boards should be places to get information, not to set up contacts with strangers. Parents should monitor what their kids post, as well as any feedback these postings get via e-mail. This is a case where passivity and lack of involvement could very well lead to trouble.

Even adults need to be careful when using message boards. As a safeguard, no one should give out his or her last name, address, or phone number over the Internet unless absolutely sure who he or she is dealing with. In most cases, an e-mail address will suffice, or the contact number of an agent if the performer has one. People should not describe their physical appearance or measurements. The Internet is a wide-open frontier where anything goes, so always proceed with caution.

In conclusion, performers, especially young ones, should remember the limits of the Internet. As Joshua Siegel, Assistant Forum Leader of AOL's Casting Central, says: "The Internet's like an infinitely huge library, full of information that's all at your fingertips. It's also a great means of communication, where you can meet and stay in contact with people who share your interests." But it's not a magic carpet that will instantly transport you to the Broadway stage.

9

THE PERFORMING UNIONS

The performing unions were created out of necessity. Before they existed, there was wholesale abuse of film, television, and stage performers, who were willing to give their all for any opportunity to work. Performers had virtually no control over their working conditions, travel time, or the amount of hours they were expected to put in. Often they had to endure more than the human body can reasonably be expected to endure.

Once the unions were formed, those problems ended. But as the years went by and the unions became more powerful, the pendulum began to swing and anti-union sentiment began to crop up. In fact, there is currently a pervasive attitude in the culture attacking union membership. Conversely, the number of high-quality nonunion job opportunities is increasing.

A young artist starting out in show business these days will not, most likely, find himself or herself performing as the member of a union. With all the nonunion venues available—"Guest Equity" theaters (where most of the cast is nonunion), cruise ships, theme parks, and Las Vegas shows—not only is union membership not necessary at the beginning, but joining a union could be the kiss of death for your career. For your performing career to blossom, you must be ready, professionally speaking, to join one of the unions—which means having the work experience and performing credentials needed to be hired for the name roles. And you're not likely to get that experience if you join a union early on. As Donald Oliver says in his book *How to Audition for the Musical Theater*, "Unless you are interested in being a chorus person for the rest of your life, you're better off getting roles under your belt in good non-Equity stock companies. Parts that you wouldn't get in Equity for years." It's also a good way to start making contacts and connections.

If you're thinking about joining the union, ask yourself the following questions:

* Do I work regularly as a performer?
* Am I competing for leading roles in musical theater or do I usually find myself in the chorus?
* Compared to others in my age range, how marketable are my skills?
* Do I live or perform in a location that supports union membership? (For example, having an Equity card is not encouraged in Oklahoma, whereas it's perfectly acceptable in the Texas market.)

Your talent and how well you've developed it is the key to any decision you make. If you have solid chorus dancing skills, but your voice is only so-so, on pitch and capable of sustaining harmony but not solid enough to carry lead or featured roles, you should probably hang back awhile and work on improving your singing. On the other hand, if you're getting leading vocal roles, or are being featured as a dancer and have solid dancing and/or acting abilities, you may want to think about joining the union. Remember, once you join Actors' Equity, or any other performers' union, you won't be able to test the waters in nonunion venues. And being a member of a union doesn't guarantee jobs. As Donald Oliver says, "I think you should always be functioning on the level where you're competitive. Those who attend nonunion open calls for Broadway shows and are not getting the jobs think 'All I have to do is get my card and then I'll work.' Do they really think if they go to the same call, and compete against Equity people, they are going to get cast?"

In the United States, three different unions represent those who work in the live stage performing industry: Actors' Equity Association (AEA, but usually known simply as Equity), the American Guild of Musical Artists (AGMA), and the American Guild of Variety Artists (AGVA). Each of these unions has different rules and represents different performing venues. In this chapter, we will discuss Equity and AGMA in detail. Unfortunately, AGVA refused to provide any information and declined my interview request. I'm sure it's a reputable union, but you'll have to do your own research in regard to its policies. (The addresses and phone numbers for all three unions are listed in this book's Appendix.)

ACTORS' EQUITY

The Actors' Equity Association represents many of the actors and stage managers who work in the legitimate theater in the United States. It negotiates minimum wages and working conditions, administers contracts, and enforces the provisions of its various agreements with theatrical employers. Currently its active membership is some 40,000.

Equity is a branch of the Associated Actors and Artists of America (called the Four A's), the umbrella organization for performing artists directly affiliated with the American Federation of Labor-Congress of Industrial Organizations (AFL-CIO), the American labor confederation headquartered in Washington, DC. Its contracts cover extensive theatrical venues, including Broadway; off-Broadway; national and bus and truck touring productions; many dramatic and musical stock theaters, dinner theaters, regional theaters (also known as League of Regional Theaters, or LORT), business theaters, theaters for young audiences, civic light operas, university theaters, cabarets, and developing theaters; many San Francisco, Chicago, and Hollywood area theaters; and Disney World theme parks. Equity contracts also govern guest artist and special appearances by Equity performers.

Background

Actors' Equity was established in New York City in 1913. Before that, exploitation was a permanent condition for actors. There were no basic agreements or contracts covering working conditions, no minimum wage, and no compensation for rehearsal time. Producers set their own rules and decided on the wages they paid. There were no time limits on rehearsals, and no guarantees on length of playing time. Frequently, actors in road shows that failed or folded prematurely found themselves stranded many miles from home with no way to get back. They had to furnish their own costumes and were often forced to perform holiday matinees without pay. If productions were closed down temporarily because of poor ticket sales, they were not paid, and they could be dismissed at any time without prior notice.

Attempts by individual actors and actor-managers to organize performers as a group and correct these abuses were unsuccessful until 1913. In that year a committee of actors drafted a constitution for Actors' Equity Association, and in 1919 the American Federation of Labor granted a charter to the Four A's with Equity being the largest component. The essential purpose of Equity to this day is, in the words of its charter, to "advance, promote, foster, and benefit all those connected with the art of the theater."

Let's take a look at what Equity does for its members.

Equity Contracts

First and foremost, Equity negotiates and administers national and regional contracts with theatrical employers covering minimum salaries, benefits, and basic working conditions. It also negotiates and/or administers letters of agreement, the Small Professional Theater contract, and theatrical codes such as showcase codes, which allow members under certain conditions to provide their professional services without Equity-approved compensation.

Benefits

Before a production is mounted, Equity generally requires employers to post a bond. This ensures that if the show closes and the employer becomes insolvent, the Equity members working in the show still receive their guaranteed minimum salaries for two weeks.

Other benefits include a pension fund, health insurance, unemployment insurance, and workers' compensation. Equity rules prohibit discrimination in hiring based on race, gender, age, national origin, or sexual preference. They also encourage nontraditional casting so as to expand opportunities for women, senior performers, actors of color, and performers with disabilities. Equity sends a newsletter regularly to all members in good standing, and also provides income tax assistance, which can be very useful for people whose income each year may come from a variety of sources.

Temporary Withdrawal from Membership

If a member wishes to withdraw from theatrical work for a period of a year or more, an inactive status is available. This enables the member to be excused from paying dues for that period of time. Under no circumstances, however, may members on inactive status work in Equity productions without special permission.

JOINING EQUITY

There are three basic ways to join:

1. *Signing an Equity contract.* If you audition in an Equity theater, and are offered a standard Equity contract, both you and the producer will sign. You will fill out a membership application form and send in an initiation fee, along with your first dues payment. Feel free to negotiate with the producer to see if he or she will pay the costly initiation fee. If not, don't push it. It's your responsibility. If full payment is not made, a weekly payroll deduction will be authorized, with full payment due within twenty-four months. To maintain an active Equity membership, you must pay dues semiannually, each May and November.

   Example: You are nonunion and audition for the touring company of *Chicago*, which is an Equity show, meaning everyone in the cast is a member of the union. If you're accepted into the cast, you'll have to join Equity too.

2. *Open-door policy.* If you are a member in good standing, for at least one year, of one of Equity's sister unions, you may join Equity without being in an Equity production. These include (1)AGMA; (2) AGVA; (3) AFTRA—the American Federation of Television and Radio Artists; (4) APATE—the Association of Puerto Rican Artists and Theatrical Employees; SAG—the Screen Actors Guild; IAG—the International Artists Guild; and HAU—the Hebrew Actors Union. You must pay the full initiation fee upon applying to join Equity in this way. But members of AGMA enjoy a reduction of up to half the cost of the remaining Equity fees, while members of the other sister unions benefit from reduced fees in lesser amounts as long as they remain members in good standing with their parent unions.

   Think it through before you dive in. Is it worth the money? Here again, you have to be sure you're ready to compete in the professional market. Just because you're doing television commercials doesn't mean producers and directors will be impressed by your stage talents. Get a second opinion.

3. *Membership candidate program.* An Equity membership candidate (EMC) is a nonprofessional interested in obtaining theater training with the intention of pursuing a career in the professional theater. It allows nonprofessional actors to gain experience in professional theaters while working toward membership in the Actors' Equity Association.

   Here's how to take part in this program: (a) Get a nonprofessional job at an Equity theater offering the program. (2) Complete the application form and submit it with the registration fee (currently $100). This fee not only gets you into the program but can be applied eventually toward paying the initiation fee when you join Actors' Equity. (3). After completing fifty weeks of working at an Equity theater, you will be eligible to join the Actors' Equity Association. The fifty weeks do not have to be consecutive.

Many Equity theaters offer this program to nonunion talent. If you are interested in it, call the theater whose show you'd like to join before auditioning and ask if it participates. But remember, as an EMC you are not actually a member of Actors' Equity Association and the protections and privileges of Actors' Equity do not apply to you. Another downside of the EMC program is its limited time period of fifty weeks. Once you've used it up, you may be forced to decide whether to join Equity. You don't want to make a hasty decision about this, so think out your moves ahead of time..

Following any of the three paths outlined above will get you your Equity card. But there are options other than immediately joining Equity that will allow you gain experience performing in theater. Let's examine some of those now.

FINDING NON-EQUITY WORK

The most obvious way to do this is to apply for work in non-Equity theaters. Just remember that in such theaters the employer's only obligation in regard to performers is to adhere to state and federal labor laws. Beyond that, anything goes. Pay may be low and the hours may be long. Protecting the artist isn't always the first priority. However, work like this can be a good way of developing your resume and making the kind of contacts you'll need to find work later on.

You can also look for nonunion work in an Equity theater. There is plenty of Equity theater work you can do and not be subject to a union contract. An Equity theater is required to hire a certain number of people under an Equity contract. Beyond that, it can use nonunion performers in various categories, especially if the venue is outside the major performing centers in the country. For example, the theater can hire local "jobbers," or residents of the community where the theater is located who are not actively pursuing theater careers. Just be aware that certain restrictions usually apply— for example, no jobber is to perform in more than two productions in any twelve-month period. And while Actors' Equity might let you dabble in a show or two, beyond that it will most likely question your future plans in regard to theater.

However, performing in a professional environment, building your resume, and having people see your work are important aspects of creating a successful career in the theater. And even without being a member of Equity you will benefit from the Equity rules. Nonunion performers may have to work some hours that union members won't don't, or attend more rehearsals. But for the most part, the Equity work rules will carry over and you'll benefit from the real-world experience.

As previously noted, some Equity theaters have an Equity Membership Candidate Program. You won't be obligated to participate, but there may be a limit on the number of shows you perform in at a given theater before having to join the program. In any case, your best bet is not to stay at one theater, but to perform at a number of them, networking and building up contacts that will be useful later in your career.

College Students and Interns

If you are a college student working toward a theater arts degree and your college or university is connected with a professional Equity theater, you will be able to perform in productions and not join the union. But this eligibility applies only as long as you remain a student.

The final option for fledgling performers is the Professional Intern Program, offered only at resident theaters. As an intern you are considered a member of Equity and receive most of the privileges and protections of union membership. But you receive 75 percent of the minimum salary of the other Equity contract performers and reduced benefits. After fifty weeks of work (twenty-five if you are an EMC) or two years, whichever comes first, you must be signed to a regular Equity contract as long as one or more of the following criteria are met:

1. The intern has completed at least twenty-five hours of work as an Equity Membership Candidate.
2. The intern has graduated from a college or university with at least a bachelor's degree in theater, or has completed an accredited professional theater training program.
3. The intern, in the judgment of the theater and Equity, is qualified to join on the basis of experience or training.

YOUNG PERFORMERS AND EQUITY

Kids under the age of 14 who are performers can pose a difficult decision regarding unions. Under Equity rules, if a child is under 14 and not under an Equity production contract, the producer may cast him or her in a child's role. In this case, Equity does not require the performer to join the union.

If, let us say, a young actress does get a production contract for the role of Mary Lennox in *The Secret Garden,* and the show closes, it is crucial for her parents to have a heart-to-heart talk with her. It has to be decided, with sensitivity and honesty, whether continued membership is a good idea during the years the young performer will be growing and exploring his or her future.

AMERICAN GUILD OF MUSICAL ARTISTS

Founded in 1936 to address the needs of musical artists in the United States, the American Guild of Musical Artists (AGMA) was established to eliminate the unfair practices and abuses facing the profession at the time, to promote mutual aims and interests of all musical artists, and to enhance the image of the musical arts and culture in the country. AGMA started out as an organization for solo musical artists, but quickly came to embrace not only soloists, but all opera, dance, oratorio, concert, and recital performers. In 1937, it became a branch of the Associated Actors and Artists of America (the Four A's). It is affiliated with the AFL-CIO, through which all performers' unions derive their jurisdictional charters. From the start, AGMA's growth has been steady, and it has been a leader in the struggle of musical artists to gain recognition as working professionals, achieve a living wage, and ensure a secure future.

AGMA currently represents more than 6,500 working members in six categories: solo artists (one of the world's great singers, Luciano Pavarotti, is an AGMA member), instrumentalists, stage directors, stage managers, chorus members, choreographers, and dancers. It deals with the nonprofit world of music performance, including all of the big opera and dance companies. Its members sing and dance for major organizations like the New York City Opera, New York's Metropolitan Opera, the Chicago Lyric Opera, the New York City Ballet, the Alvin Ailey American Dance Theater, the Merce Cunningham Dance Company, and Dance Theater of Harlem. Other members include singers with the Master Chorale in southern California, and soloists who sing in major concert halls around the country. AGMA also represents nonperforming personnel who work with these companies or in these halls like stage managers, stage directors, and choreographers.

AGMA has an open-door membership policy. You simply fill out a membership application, and pay an initiation fee and your first dues payment. Thereafter, dues are payable twice a year, February 1 and August 1. If you are a member in good standing of Actors' Equity or the Canadian Actors' Equity Association, you may join AGMA by paying half the initiation fee and your annual basic fees.

Benefits

Like all other performing unions, AGMA exists to serve its members, who benefit via legally binding collective bargaining contracts with employers and managers/agents. AGMA contracts establish minimum compensation (wages) for performers, the length of rehearsal hours and the number of rehearsals allowed for a production, the length and number of breaks allowed during rehearsals and performances, the maximum number of consecutive performances that can be required, the amount of overtime compensation, the amount of sick leave, travel conditions for performers on the road, and the security deposits needed to ensure that the terms of the agreements are adhered to. If an employer violates any provision of the basic contract, the performers have two weeks to file a claim. If the dispute cannot be settled directly by the performers and management, AGMA intervenes. It also looks out for the safety of performers involving all issues related to theater flooring and temperature as well as the health of the performing artists.

As Gerald Otte, president of AGMA, says, "You cannot sing for six solid hours. But there are some conductors who insist on this. We want our members to last and have a career, not burn out after three to five years."

AGMA also offers its members terrific benefits not directly related to performing, including a pension fund, health insurance, dental and optical plans, legal services, unemployment insurance, and worker's compensation. Its emergency relief fund assists members who because of age, infirmity, or other causes are unable to meet their primary financial obligations, including medical bills. AGMA also supports a program called Career Transition for Dancers, which helps dancers move on to other occupations once their performing days are over.

Should you join AGMA? Just remember, you're at the beginning of your career, so you have to go where the jobs are. You may initially find yourself working for a nonunion company. There are many out there, some of them truly outstanding. The time to join AGMA is when you're offered an AGMA contract.

MAKING A THOUGHTFUL CHOICE

That's it in a nutshell. While I can't tell you everything you'll have to know about union membership, feel free to call Equity or any of the other performing unions directly with specific questions you might have in advance of joining. Their phone numbers and addresses are listed in the Appendix.

In the meantime, keep in mind that as a performer, you have to plan for your future. You will probably find yourself turning right here, turning left there, or even backtracking. Just keep assessing the situation as you go. Take responsibility for yourself and your career. And remember that once you've joined a performers' union, you won't be able to test the waters in the nonunion world any longer.

Kathryn V. Lamkey, the central regional director of Actors' Equity Association, was extremely helpful in putting this chapter together. She sums it up with the following:

> It's a long process, but it's like any career. You may become a doctor at the end of your education, but there is still a continuing process. It is a business, and you have to attend to your own business as well. There is a time and place for the union. I think performers have to assess it, look at it, and not just let it happen to them. I hate the phrase "I had to join the union." I would rather they take a look at it and say, "I planned it, and this is where it happened." You may even turn down a union contract at some point—you really need to determine whether or not you are prepared for it. We would like to offer our protection to as many people as possible, because we think we can do that kind of thing. But you have to be at a point in your career when joining the union is good for you, when you know you can deal with it and be responsible for it.

10
Contracts and Other Legal Issues

In an ideal world, performers would not have to bother with contracts and would be free to spend all their time perfecting their art. Their agents would negotiate the best terms for them, and their lawyers would ensure that any contracts would be to the performers' advantage and free of loopholes. Unfortunately, such a world doesn't exist and probably never will. Beginning performers seldom have agents and usually cannot afford lawyers, so they are forced to handle their own contract issues. Even big-name stars, who do have agents and lawyers, often learn they must take an active role in contract matters or suffer the consequences. More than one overly trusting celebrity has discovered that most of their money has vanished, or that they're stuck with contract terms they don't like. In this imperfect world, performers had better understand basic principles of contract law, and take an active role in negotiating their contracts. We will discuss six principles relating to these issues in this chapter.

Performers often have the mistaken impression that contract disputes only arise when one of the parties is a "bad" or "dishonest" person who is trying to "take advantage of" the other party. Believing this, they do not see their own participation in negotiations as being very important because they know themselves to be "good" people and trust their instincts that the other party is "good" as well. This is flawed reasoning, and can lead to trouble. First, no one is a perfect judge of character, always able to tell the difference between "good" and "bad" people. Second, contrary to popular opinion, in most contract disputes both parties are actually "good" people who entered into the agreement in good faith but with entirely different understandings of one or more provisions of the contract. Most disputes over contracts could have been avoided had the affected parties paid more attention to what they were agreeing to during negotiations.

NEGOTIATING

Before entering into any negotiations, try to learn about the producer or agent you are dealing with. Word of mouth is a good indicator of his or her habits and track record regarding work, housing, schedules, and pay. Knowing that kind of information can give you a leg up in working out an agreement.

Negotiating a contractual relationship is comparable to the stages in a romantic relationship between two people. There's the first "date," where both sides put their best feet forward and are on their best behavior. The performer wants to be perceived as talented and physically attractive. He hopes that the producer won't notice any flaw in his abilities or that tiny wart on his chin. The producer (director, artistic director, or whoever is doing the hiring) for her part wants to be perceived as well-funded and highly professional. She hopes the performer won't notice the shabbiness of the office or the fact that things there aren't always perfectly organized. Later on comes the "marriage," when the performer and producer agree to work together. As in any marriage, the masks soon come off and each party sees the other very plainly, warts and all. In between are dates 2 through *n*, which can be compared to the negotiating process. The purpose of those later dates, as well as of negotiations, is to see how compatible the two parties really are and to iron out any differences between them. In the best scenario, the parties arrive at a clear understanding of their mutual needs and how to work around their differences. At the very least, they decide their differences are too large to bridge or get around and decide to part company before problems arise. Good negotiation skills, in other words, prevent later messy "divorces."

Being an Active Listener and Asking Questions

Unfortunately, to most people the word "negotiate" conjures up images of an adversarial test of wills. They view the process as what mathematicians call a "zero-sum equation," where one party can only gain something at the other side's expense. Because of that misperception, most people negotiate by desperately seeking to avoid any clash of wills. They want the relationship to work out. They want the other party to like them, and so won't risk removing their social "mask" for fear that the other party will find them petty or argumentative. They're afraid that the other party will become irritated and decide against entering into a contractual relationship. This results in people tending to hear only the positive things that reaffirm the relationship and to ignore any warning signs of problems to come, simply assuming that such problems can be worked out later. Unfortunately, such tactics work no better in negotiating contracts than they do in deciding whether to marry.

For example, a student of mine once auditioned for a cruise line. She was very excited when the company offered her a job. Reading through the terms of the agreement they mailed her, she noticed a vague reference to the fact that she would be required to do other "occasional light duties, as requested" about the ship. Now, she could have ignored that phrase and hoped for the best, which is what most people do. Instead, she asked around and found a friend of a friend who had worked for that cruise line. According to that friend, that "light duty" involved about two to four hours a day cleaning the ship, which was hardly "occasional" or "light" duty by her standards. She called the cruise line about this, received unsatisfactory answers, and ultimately decided against accepting the job.

Sometimes differences cannot be negotiated away, and the performer must decide to accept a job as offered or turn it down. This can be disappointing. But either option is preferable to accepting a job without being clear about what you're getting yourself into. Imagine accepting a cruise job thinking you'll be able to lounge in the sun during your nonperforming hours, only to learn that most of your free time must be spent pushing a mop.

My student practiced good negotiating skills. She read and listened closely and was not afraid to ask questions. She realized that the cruise line was not being morally "bad" in the sense of trying to trick people into cleaning the ship. (If the company were really that bad, the offer wouldn't have contained the language about "occasional light duties" in the first place. After all, it would be far easier to leave the language about the extra work out and simply surprise performers with those additional duties when the ship was at sea and there was no choice but to comply!) Instead of ignoring the possibility of conflict, the student approached the situation as an opportunity to negotiate, to explore the possibility of establishing a sound and pleasant working relationship with the cruise line. She knew her own expectations and needs, and clearly defined the cruise line's expectations about work duties. In the end, the negotiating did not lead to a job, but at least it didn't lead to what would have been, for her, a miserable time spent doing work she did not find appealing.

So be an active listener and ask questions. Remember, negotiating always involves determining the goals of both parties and clarifying the rights and responsibilities of each. It must also address the basic terms of salary and working conditions.

SIGNING CONTRACTS

The performer must understand what is required for a contract to be *binding*.

Shakespeare wrote that "a rose by any other name would smell as sweet." The same is true of contracts. Whatever it's called—a memo of understanding, a memo of agreement, or a letter of agreement—if a document contains terms a court of law would find legally binding and enforceable, it's a *contract*.

It is important, then, to understand the four legal requirements involved in entering into a contract: They are called the "offer," "acceptance," "consideration," and "capacity." Lawyers refer to them as the "elements" of a contract. As I explain to my students, they are similar to the ingredients of a recipe. If a recipe for chocolate cake lists seven ingredients, one of which is baking soda, and I faithfully follow the recipe with the exception of leaving out baking soda, I may have made brownies, but I have definitely not made a chocolate cake. Similarly, with contracts: The four elements are necessary for a contract to be legally binding, and if any one of those four is left out, the agreement is not an enforceable contract.

The Offer

The first requirement is a valid offer. As entertainment attorney Scott Prough observes, "For an offer to be valid, the *offeror* (the person making the offer) must have a serious intent to make that offer, and must communicate the offer to the *offeree* (the person receiving the offer) in reasonably clear and certain terms." Let's examine each of these concepts in a little more detail.

Intent and Lack of Intent Say I were producing *The Sound of Music*, and a performer named Susan auditioned for the role of one of the nuns. Suppose at the end of the audition I said, "Susan, you have such a lovely voice. I already had someone in mind to play the lead, Maria, but I'm curious as to whether you'd be interested if I offered you the role?" Ignoring the other issues noted by Scott Prough as being related to a legal understanding of the term "offer," could it be said that I "intended" to offer the role of Maria to Susan? If you answered "no," you're correct. If you answered "yes," reread my statement and concentrate on the use of the word "if." To say "if I offered you the role" establishes what English teachers refer to as the subjunctive tense. To most of us, that simply means the words are referring to something in a nebulous, possibly nonexistent future. To a lawyer, anything phrased in the subjunctive usually signals a lack of intent. Legally, intent means something has been offered to an offeree in such a way that any reasonable, disinterested person (that is, an average person who is not involved emotionally with the situation because he or she isn't dying to get the part) would conclude the offer is binding on the offeror. To phrase it another way, disinterested observers should be able to conclude that the offeror was expressing himself or herself in a way that showed a willingness to bind himself or herself to the terms of the offer in the immediate present as opposed to a nebulous future. If that willingness is clear, there is intent. If it is not, the offeror was simply indulging in preliminary negotiations or something else, not expressing intent.

Communication Whether the offeror has communicated the offer to the offeree is an easier issue to establish. The only questions in this regard are whether the offeror actually communicated the offer, and whether the offeree received the communication. Going back to the example of *The Sound of Music*, which I'm producing, suppose several days after the audition I decided to offer the role of Maria to Susan, and called her up saying, "Would you like to play Maria?" I've clearly communicated my offer, and Susan clearly received my communication. Or say I asked my assistant to convey the offer, and she asked her assistant, who asked her friend, who then asked Susan if she'd like to play the part. Would that count as "communicating the offer"? The answer is "yes." I intended that an offer be made and Susan received it, so it doesn't matter how it got to her.

Reasonably Clear and Certain Terms This element simply means that all the important terms of the offer must be stated in a reasonably clear and certain way. It does not mean that all of the terms must be so stated, only the important ones. For example, if I offered Susan the role of Maria, making it clear that she would be paid $500 per week for a twelve-week run, the fact that I neglected to mention the print size in which her name would appear on posters or programs or to say whether she would have a private dressing room would not matter. The important provisions of the agreement (the names of the parties bound to it, the role involved, the salary, the length of the show's run) were mentioned in reasonably clear and certain terms.

The Acceptance

The second legal requirement of entering into a contract requires that there be a valid acceptance. Acceptance has two problem areas, the first involving the nature of the acceptance, the second involving its timing.

Unequivocal Acceptance In order for an acceptance to be valid, it must be unequivocal and must totally match the terms of the offer. Let's return to the offer I made Susan: the role of Maria in *The Sound of Music*, at a salary of $500 per week for twelve weeks. If Susan responded that she needed $505 per week, her acceptance would not match my offer and would, therefore, not be an acceptance at all. Legally speaking, she would have made a counteroffer, a rejection of my offer coupled with a new offer of her own, and my original offer would be dead. She would now be the offeror and I would be the offeree. Say I rejected her counteroffer. Susan would not be able to return to my original offer and later accept it.

Now don't get confused here. Assuming I rejected Susan's counteroffer, there would be nothing to stop her from making *another* offer using my original terms. However, I would then be the person in the position of being able to accept or reject her offer instead of the other way around.

Learning about this rule tends initially to have a chilling effect on performers' interest in negotiating contracts. Understanding that making a counteroffer terminates the original offer, they fear that doing so could leave them out in the cold. Legally it could, if the other party chose to do so. Practically speaking, though, that is rarely the case. If a performer has demonstrated enough talent, energy, and stage presence for the producer to make an offer, no one is likely to lose a part simply for having raised a few issues during the negotiations. I, personally, am not aware of anyone who, having made a reasonable counteroffer and demonstrated a willingness to negotiate in good faith, has ever lost a part. I know plenty of people whose counteroffers were accepted and plenty more who ended up settling for the terms of the original offer, but none who lost out completely simply because they made a counteroffer.

Timely Acceptance It only makes sense that an offer should be accepted in a timely manner. For example, if I offered Susan the role of Maria, and she said she'd think about it but waited for six months to accept, that could be problematic for my production.

To avoid problems like that, all offers have a lifespan. Some lifespans are spelled out directly in the offers themselves. For example, when offering Susan the part I might have told her she had three days to accept or reject. In that case, I as the offeror determined that the lifespan of my offer was three days. Other offers do not openly spell out deadlines. Even so, their lifespans only extend for a reasonable time after they are made before they too die. Returning to my offer to Susan, a reasonable time for her to think it over might be a few days or a week, but clearly six months would be too long. By that time, no doubt, I would have offered the part to someone else, and Susan would be out of luck.

Finally, an offer must be accepted prior to any revocation by its offeror. Revocation occurs when the offeror withdraws or cancels his or her offer, which all offerors have the legal right to do. Of course the revocation must be clearly communicated to the offeree.

Consideration

The third element of a valid contract is known as consideration. This is the value provided by each party to the contract, and is required to help lawyers distinguish contractual obligations from gifts. For example, if I told Susan I would give her $500 per week for twelve weeks in return for nothing, I would be telling her I was giving her a gift. I would not be paying her for anything she was agreeing to do and my "offer" would amount to nothing more than a promise on my part alone. If I later changed my mind, she would learn that most promises of gifts are legally unenforceable. But my promise to pay Susan $500 per week for twelve weeks in return for her promise to play the role of Maria involves consideration. Any attempt by me to go back on my word would now fail. Susan would have the legal ability to enforce my promise.

Capacity

Finally, in order for a contract to be valid, both parties must have the legal capacity and authority to sign it. Legal capacity requires that a person be of legal age (18 years old in most cases) and have the requisite mental ability to enter into a contract. People who are mentally incapacitated or heavily intoxicated when they sign are deemed to lack the requisite capacity. Authority means that both signing parties are the principals in the contract or legally represent them, such as lawyers hired by the principals or the parents of minors.

WRITTEN VERSUS ORAL CONTRACTS

The performer needs to understand when written contracts are required and when they are valuable.

One of the biggest myths about contracts is that, to be enforceable, they must be in writing. That could not be further from the truth. Theoretically, oral contracts are every bit as valid as written ones. In fact, the only contracts legally required to be evidenced by a written agreement are those involving the sale or rental of land, homes, apartments, and other types of real estate; contracts which cannot be completed within one year (say I offered Susan the role of Maria for a twenty-four-month play run); contracts involving a promise to pay someone else's debts; contracts involving marriage; and contracts involving the sale of goods worth more than $500. (Don't get confused here. A contract involving services like acting and dancing is not a sale of goods.) Otherwise, oral contracts are considered as enforceable as written ones.

Scott Prough notes that "the reason most lawyers suggest that contracts be evidenced in writing has to do with the practical aspect of later proving the terms of the agreements. A verbal contract might be theoretically enforceable. Often, however, say because of a 'he said/she said' situation, a judge may be unable to determine the actual terms of an agreement unless it is in writing."

That being the case, I recommend that, whenever possible, performers get their agreements with producers and agents down in writing.

THE USE OF LAWYERS

You always want to know when, and whom, to call for help. If it's possible to consult a lawyer when drafting a written agreement, do so. Often, however, that isn't practical. But performers who find themselves in the position of having to draft an agreement without the aid of a lawyer should not be intimidated. Contrary to popular belief, a contract does not have to be written in archaic English using "thees" and "thous," full of convoluted sentences and multisyllable words. Nor does it have to be typed and ten pages long. To be valid an agreement just needs to state the names of the parties involved and its terms, and be signed.

Most of the time, in professional situations, even if lawyers are not directly involved the contracts will be standard ones drafted by lawyers originally. Because many performers assume that "standard contract" means "safe" and are intimidated by the legalese such documents are written in, they simply sign the agreements hoping for the best. At a minimum, however, performers should read each contract put before them and ask the agent or producer about anything needing clarification until they are fully satisfied they understand what the language means. Just because the contract is "standard" for the producer does not mean it is "standard" for a performer.

When dealing with a written agreement, if both parties agree to changes or clarifications, it is important that these changes be written down, preferably on the original agreement. There is nothing wrong with crossing out a word or phrase and writing in new words or phrases. Just remember to have both parties initial the changes. It's also important to remember that, in most instances, written agreements will trump anything agreed to orally.

Harkening back to that ideal world we'd all love to live in, it would be wonderful if lawyers were available for free consultations anytime we needed them. Obviously, though, that world does not exist. Lawyers cost money, and since performers may not have the cash needed to consult them in every instance, they must be able to gauge whether or not they really need a lawyer.

Two factors should be considered. First, the performer should weigh the potential income involved against the cost of consulting an attorney. A contract to sing at a wedding for $200 would probably not be worth the $100 to $200 it would cost to have a lawyer review its terms. On the other hand, a contract to star in a Broadway show, with a salary of $60,000 per year, probably should involve an attorney.

Second, if a performer does decide to consult an attorney, it's important to find one with the relevant knowledge and skills. Most attorneys specialize in particular areas of the law. A lawyer who is excellent at defending ax murderers is not likely to be well-versed in entertainment law.

If you have a legal issue concerning your career and aren't sure how to find the legal advice you need, a good source of assistance is the Volunteer Lawyers for the Arts (VLA). Its members offer legal advice and assistance to individual artists and art groups, including those in the performing arts. VLA is located in New York, and you can reach the organization by calling (212) 319-2910. Typically, your call will be returned within two working days, and you'll be referred to someone who can help you. Fees are minimal, depending on income, and the assistance can provide peace of mind.

CONTRACT PROVISIONS

Performers should fully understand what terms a contract should include and be aware at the outset that compromises are inevitable in contracts. Nobody gets everything he or she wants.

That said, there are some basics you must focus on. These include amount of salary, how often you'll be paid (every week, every two weeks, etc.), in what manner you'll be paid (in cash, by check, by direct deposit to your bank account, through your agent, etc.), provisions for compensation if the show closes ahead of schedule, the kind of billing you'll get, how the show will be advertised, and whether you can freelance elsewhere while the show is in production. If you're joining a tour, find out about a daily per diem, the sleeping and meal arrangements, and the type of transportation and who pays for it.

You must also check into rehearsal time, including how many hours per day and the number of weeks you'll be involved in rehearsals; the amount of overtime you can be required to put in and what you'll be paid for it; clothing (who supplies the costumes and who is responsible for cleaning them); security measures at the venue or venues where you'll be performing; dressing room arrangements; and whether or not you'll be required to do things other than perform (remember the earlier discussion of cleaning duties on the cruise ship).

I've already mentioned standard contracts. Over the years, performers' unions have evolved a variety of standard contracts and agreements aimed at protecting their members' interests. After the producer and performer sign a contract, a copy is filed with the appropriate union prior to starting rehearsals. Be aware that standard contracts can be modified by "riders" during negotiations. You, the party you're negotiating with, or both may want to add or change something, and you're legally entitled to do so as long as you both agree to the modification.

If you're a nonunion performer, you won't have the standard union contract to protect you. You'll either be offered a contract by your would-be employer, or you'll have to create one yourself. Such contracts do not carry the recognition or protection of the unions. So be very careful when entering into one of them or you might find yourself victimized somehow down the line.

PROBLEMS REGARDING A CONTRACT

Understand what your rights are and you will be better able to handle problems such as breach of contract and fraud.

Breach of contract occurs when someone does not do what was agreed to in the contract. Despite all your care, the producer or agent may fail to uphold her or his end of the bargain. Suppose you signed with the written or even verbal understanding that you'd have every other weekend off, but when you tried to take that time, you were told to work or be fired. That would be a breach of contract on the part of the producer. Another example might involve salary. If your first paycheck "shorted" you of the agreed-upon amount, that would violate the contract. You could get a lawyer and sue the producer. Or if it was too expensive to go that route, you could just walk away from the job. Breach of contract makes a contract null and void. It entitles you to declare the agreement dead, absolving you of your obligation to perform in the show. Of course, if *you're* the one not honoring the responsibilities you agreed to, the producer has the right to sue or remove you from the production.

Fraud occurs when someone misrepresents some aspect of the contract. Let's say you agree to tour the Midwest, performing in major cities like Chicago, Indianapolis, and St. Louis. The producer and promoter has guaranteed you great exposure, big crowds, even television coverage. Instead, you wind up in some backwater venues, performing in bus stops or trailer parks. That constitutes fraud, and entitles you to cancel the contract. You're not obligated to accept such obvious misrepresentation. In fact, if you choose, you can sue those perpetrating the fraud.

In this chapter, I've given you some basic guidelines regarding contracts—what they are, what they contain, how to negotiate them, what to watch out for in them. But remember, if you have any doubts about the legality of a contract, or your rights in regard to one, the safest thing to do is consult an attorney who specializes in entertainment law.

AGENTS, MANAGERS, AND CASTING DIRECTORS

In the performing world, there are union and nonunion jobs. There are also times when agents, managers, and casting directors are vital to a person's career, and times when they aren't necessary or even wouldn't be in the performer's best interest. At the beginning stages of most musical theater careers, when performers are looking for those initial jobs that will give them some professional experience, they're not needed. Instead, the performers need to go out and create their own opportunities; they need to test the waters by exploring nonunion venues. They can have the time of their life doing this, and in the process build an impressive professional resume.

For starters, there's summer work at a theme park. It's a perfect entry-level job, and there are many theme parks around the country to choose from. This work isn't restricted to summertime, either. Many of the parks are open year-round.

Beyond theme parks, there is work on cruise ships. More than twenty different cruise lines offer show work on their ships. It can be great fun, and a great way to see different parts of the world.

There's also work at resorts and gambling meccas. *Dirt Alert*, the Las Vegas trade paper, carries an abundance of audition notices for shows in Las Vegas, Branson, Missouri, and many other places. And each issue of *Back Stage* is filled with audition notices for summer stock jobs, nonunion bus and truck touring shows, and other exciting venues to explore.

The point at which most performers find themselves needing an agent or a manager, or needing to contact casting directors, is once they have those initial performing experiences under their belt and are moving into the world of musical theater proper. They find they need to join Actors' Equity, and they need someone to look out for their professional interests and find them jobs in a highly competitive work environment.

This chapter describes what performers need to know when they enter the world of agents, managers, and casting directors: what these people can do for performers, and what performers need to watch out for when dealing with them. And I'll discuss more than just musical theater. To survive financially, most musical theater performers do some TV commercials or roles in movies. Nathan Lane and Jason Alexander are prime examples of actors who did TV commercials on their way up the ladder. If you think of all the people who watch television, including agents, managers, casting directors, and their families and friends, it's a good way to get your face out there where it can be noticed. So this chapter also describes the roles of agents, managers, and casting directors in film and television as well as in theater.

AGENTS

The terms "agent" and "agency" are really synonymous. Some agents work for themselves, but most are members of multiagent companies, which can be large or small. The following discussion will cover agents in all those contexts, pointing out any differences in how they operate when necessary.

What are agents and what do they do? An agent is someone who looks after a performer's best interests. He or she makes sure the performer is dealing with legitimate directors, producers, and casting directors who are offering legitimate work; an agent sees to it that the performer fits the bill in auditioning for roles, gets paid once hired, and is treated fairly on the job. In other words, an agent is a salesperson who locates opportunities for the performer and sets up appointments with producers, casting directors, or whoever else is interested in seeing the performer for professional reasons.

Agents also negotiate money matters—not a skill most young performers or even many older ones have. This is one of the most important reasons for performers to have an agent. Young people especially are usually so excited about being paid to perform they're ready to jump at the first amount offered. But Lewis R. Chambers, of New York's Bethel Agency, has this to say about that first offer: "The actor will look at me and say, 'I want that.' I always pause and tell them they need to wait a minute, that they shouldn't jump at the first offer someone makes. Of course, the actor doesn't want to lose the job, and I'm not going to lose the job for him. But if I can get $1500 a week instead of $500, isn't it worth waiting and doing some negotiating? We have a cardinal rule around here. They will never pay you a quarter if they can buy you for a dime."

An agent can help performers avoid being bought off cheap. In the end he or she helps create a better relationship with the people the performers will be working for.

I want to point out, however, that agents are not employment agencies. Performers can expect agents to return their phone calls and treat them like professionals. Agents secure the auditions, but it's up to the performers to land the jobs.

If you're doing ensemble/chorus work, and being cast in small featured or cameo roles because of your singing, dancing, or acting strengths, it might be time to find an agent. But if you aren't yet being offered that kind of work, you should probably hold off until more roles like that come your way. Finding work in musical theater is all about marketing appeal. If you don't have anything special to sell, even the most exceptional salesperson (that is, an agent) won't be able to help. An agent might be able to stir up some initial interest, but, in this business, initial interest isn't enough. It's the talent on the stage that matters, and if you're too inexperienced or don't have what it takes to generate enthusiasm in those seeing you perform, spend more time polishing your talent and learn how to put a zing in what you do. The theatrical field is a close-knit business. No agent wants to be known for handling inexperienced performers, and you don't want to be perceived as an impostor.

How Agents Work

Agents find performers jobs. In return they receive a commission for each job they find, usually paid out of the performer's salary, which, of course, the agent has negotiated on behalf of the performer. They also do other things, depending on the status and needs of their clients. For example, they set up interviews with journalists and TV talk show appearances for well-known clients.

Some agencies are basically factories. They represent talent (industry lingo for performers) numbering in the hundreds, and divide those performers into what is commonly known in the business as the A, B, and C teams. Similarly to school grades, those labeled A are the top talents, those labeled B are the second tier, and those labeled C are considered mediocre. Unfortunately, if you wind up on a large agency's C team, you might never get sent out for an audition. As an example, take a casting director who calls an agency. Insisting she or he doesn't want a "cattle call" (an open audition for anyone interested in trying out) for the current project, the director tells the agency to send over only its top ten clients. The agency may have fifty qualified clients, but clearly it will send the ten with a track record of landing work. That means it will send the ones it has sent out before. If you're a beginner, you won't be among them. And if you're a beginner, no matter how good you are you might end up on the C team simply because you don't have the necessary track record to be considered A team material.

Breaking into the elite A team group of performers at the larger agencies can be very difficult. So as a beginner, it might be wise to sign right up with a smaller agency, where you might start out on the A or B team. If you're already with a large agency, monitor how much work it's finding for you, and if you're not satisfied, switch to a smaller one. Some agencies keep themselves intentionally small and like to see the careers of their clients grow with time. They don't sign you if you're hot and drop you if you're not. The agents work with their talent for years, and the continuity is reassuring for the performers.

A lot of agencies won't sign an actor immediately. Instead they freelance performers, also called handling performers "on consignment." Steve Unger, of the Gage Group Talent Agency in New York, has this to say about freelancing: "If I send people out, and they are not getting any callbacks because I'm thinking of them in the wrong way, being signed to my agency isn't going to do them any good." This "courting" period can benefit both the performer and the agency, allowing each side to see how they relate to each other. The agent determines if the performer is reliable about getting to auditions on time, prepared when he or she gets there, and, most importantly, if the performer is marketable. In turn, the performer decides whether she or he will be happy with the agency's representation over the long haul.

If you find yourself in this freelance situation, remember that the agent must call you prior to submitting your name for a job, in case another agent has already submitted it. The agency that gets you the job is the one that gets the commission.

Kinds of Agencies

Aside from large or small, there are three types of talent agencies. The first is union franchised and state licensed. You can find these in states such as California and New York where there is a large performing industry. The second is union franchised alone; these are located in states where the industry isn't considered large enough to require state regulation. The third type of agency is neither union franchised nor state licensed; these can operate anywhere, and are accountable to nothing outside themselves.

The important issue for performers is whether an agent is franchised through one of the performing unions—Equity and/or SAG/AFTRA—or not, so I'll concentrate on discussing those types here.

Equity Franchised Agents Actors' Equity Association, as we discussed in Chapter 9, is the union for theater performers, directors, and managers. If you are a member of Actors' Equity, you cannot be represented by a nonfranchised agent. Equity agents have clearly defined guidelines about what they must negotiate, can take no more than a 10 percent commission, and must follow certain rules spelled out by Equity in determining what monies connected with jobs they may receive commissions for. Say you're on the road making a per diem; your agent has the right to a commission based on the salary he or she has negotiated for you, but under Equity rules no right to any portion of the per diem.

Also under Equity rules, paychecks go directly to the performers. Other unions allow paychecks to go to the agents, who then pays the performers after deducting the commission. Most Broadway and regional theaters offer a service where they deduct the 10 percent commission from the paycheck and forward the rest to the performer.

SAG/AFTRA Franchised Agents As we also discussed in Chapter 9, the Screen Actors Guild is for performers in the movies, while the American Federation of Television and Radio Artists is for those who work in television and radio. Agents franchised by these unions are also limited to 10 percent commissions. SAG/AFTRA contracts offer three choices of payment: (1) All the salary goes directly to the performer, (2) all of it goes to the agent, or (3) two separate checks are written, the employer sending one check to the performer and a second to the agent. Most actors choose to have all of their salary go directly to their agent, who then pays them after deducting the commission. This is convenient because the agent also serves as a bookkeeper for tax purposes, giving them summaries at the end of each year as to how much they have earned as well as amounts paid out (like commissions) that are tax-deductible expenses. Other actors prefer getting their checks directly and handling their own financial recordkeeping.

SAG/AFTRA national contracts allow employers ten days to pay after the completion of work, while their regional or local contracts allow thirty days. This mostly has to do with work in commercials. The major film companies and producers of independent films usually negotiate their own arrangements with these unions.

Nonunion Agents Agents not franchised by the performing unions can still submit clients for union work so long as the submission is requested by someone affiliated with one of the unions—a producer, a casting director, or in the case of commercials someone from a union franchised ad agency. There are franchised production companies that prefer to work directly with franchised agencies. And under union rules those companies must contact local franchised agencies when they are looking for performers—that's part of the bonus for performers of being part of the SAG/AFTRA or Equity teams. However, in the SAG/AFTRA world, producers can also contact nonunion agencies and accept nonunion submissions. Nonunion performers cast in their first union jobs are sometimes able to "Taft–Hartley" those jobs (SAG/AFTRA terminology that refers to being permitted to work a first union job without joining the union). But often they must join the union involved or turn the job down.

Keep in mind that nonunion agents' fees aren't regulated in any way, and can range from the standard 10 percent to more than 25 percent. Higher fees are acceptable as long as they have been agreed to by both parties ahead of time and are clearly stated in the contract. If you decide to go this route, just make sure you know what portion of your paycheck is going to the agent before you sign the agent's contract and he or she starts finding you work. Spare yourself the shock of getting less money than you anticipated.

Also remember that nonunion agencies aren't regulated by the unions or the state and can hold on to your checks as long as they want to before paying you. Horror stories abound about talent not getting paid for their services, and the ensuing battles that had to be fought by performers to get money that was rightly theirs. One way to avoid that kind of problem is to work out an agreement on payments with your agent before you sign on, and have it added to the contract. For example, there might be a clause stipulating that employers will write two checks, one to you as the performer and a second to the agent paying her or his commission. You don't want to insult a potential agent by making unreasonable demands or saying, "These are the only terms I will accept." But you have nothing to lose by trying to protect yourself.

My own opinion is that you should consider nonunion agents only if you can't land a franchised agent for yourself, or if your town and nearby cities don't have any.

Agent Contracts

Performers and agents have professional relationships, and when you sign up with an agent you'll be signing a contract. You need to know what to expect.

Franchised Agent Contracts All the performing unions have standard contracts for you and your agent to sign. Whether you're on the East Coast, the West Coast, or in mid-America, they read the same for each union, and they're designed to protect you the performer. As in any contract, there are items that are not negotiable. These include the 10 percent limit on commissions and in Equity contracts certain types of payments such as per diems the agent will not be able to receive a commission on. Other items are negotiable. If there are things you and the agent want to change, you just note the changes before signing the document as a whole and initial them. The same goes for anything you want to add. These changes and additions can be made in the form of a rider. or an attachment, to the contract.

Nonunion Agent Contracts When signing with a nonunion agent, be especially careful. A nonunion contract can be anything: a memo of understanding, a letter of agreement, or a handwritten, do-it-yourself piece of paper signed by both parties. Read the contract closely, especially the fine print. Don't blindly sign because you're excited that an agent is willing to take you on as a client. Gail Nelson, who recently starred in *The Life and Times of Billie Holliday*, offered this warning: "Be very careful if an agent tries to get you to sign a contract in their office before you have a chance to really look at it. Don't ever accept someone's word on what's in the contract." If you're unsure or confused about the terms of the contract, it's best to have an attorney look it over. A few dollars spent at the outset can help avoid many headaches later on.

Smokey Joe's Cafe star Mathew Dickens offers the following advice:

> *Always make sure your contract has an "out" clause allowing either side to end it for good cause. What if the agency isn't doing anything for you, or hasn't sent you out on auditions for a long period of time? On the other hand, what if the agency sent you out and you didn't show up for the audition, or you haven't landed a job in a while? An "out" clause protects both you and the agency.*

Finding an Agent

If you're looking for a franchised agent, you can call a union office and request a list of them. These lists are broken down by states, are usually free of charge, and only list agents in good standing with the unions. You can find the SAG and AFTRA lists on their Internet homepages, www.sag.com and www.aftra.com, respectively.

If you're looking for a nonunion agent, all you have to do is open the Yellow Pages and look under "M" for modeling agencies or "T" for talent agencies. Just be very careful. Make sure to "preshop" by asking around for recommendations. Also, call the Better Business Bureau to see if any complaints have been filed against any of the agents you're thinking of contacting.

Agencies That Run Schools If an agency runs a school, be cautious. Remember, you don't have to take $1200 worth of classes to get an agent. You're in control. If the agency insists you take classes but you don't want them, say no and move on to the next agency.

Some of these agencies with schools are regulated, but it's not the same type of regulation that applies to a franchised agency. Instead the regulations usually have to do with the school. The ad in the Yellow Pages will say something like "Approved and regulated by the (state) division of occupational schools and the department of higher learning." If the agency does happen to be franchised, it will list its union affiliations in the ad.

To casting directors and agents, this type of licensing is a joke as some of the "schools" are nothing more than glorified charm schools. There are no federal or state regulatory bodies to check the certification of teachers. Many times the schools just hire people off the street who are willing to say, "Yes, I acted and modeled," not even bothering to check their credentials.

These agencies push not only the classes they offer, but their in-house services too. These can include in-house photographers, makeup consultants, and directories you can be listed in with the promise that casting directors use them to find talent. Performers have walked into these kinds of agencies with perfectly good headshots, only to be told that they would have to use a picture shot by the in-house photographer in order for the agency to represent them. But the real reason for the new headshot was the kickback the agency received from the photographer—and the same went for the makeup consultant and any other "services" the agency recommended or insisted the performers use. I'm not saying that all photographers or consultants who work for agency-run schools are fraudulent. But if the costs for the photographer, say, run around $400 to $500, you're probably getting ripped off.

Agencies that offer training and other services have obvious attractions for beginners. It's virtually impossible for someone with no working knowledge of the entertainment industry, with no pictures, no resume, and no demo tape, to just walk into an agency and immediately be sent out to auditions. I'm not saying no one should go this route. I'm just saying it's the performer's choice of where, how, and with whom that training will happen. If you decide this is right for you, it's best (as always) to shop around and ask for information about the agency you're interested in. Check with the Better Business Bureau for any complaints. Make sure the school has some graduates that have actually found work as entertainers. Protect yourself so you're not throwing your money away.

Landing an Agent

I perceive seven steps in the process of finding and signing with an agent. Here they are.

Step 1: Homework Before making your initial call to an agent, first do a little homework. Get some referrals from people in the business who know the agents that are out there. You want to know which ones are reputable and which aren't. You want to know which agents handle which types of performers. You want to know in which media they specialize.

Agents often specialize. Among the categories in which they specialize: theater, television, film, commercial, broadcast, print, production. As a performer, you have to understand those terms. Don't be embarrassed because you don't know something. Find a reliable source to ask, and learn the answer. It's not uncommon in this business for a performer to have four or five different agents handle different categories of work for them— a commercial agent, a theatrical agent, a film and television agent, and so on. Very few agencies are able to handle all of the different performing specialties under one roof. It's also a case of specialties within specialties. If you're looking for theatrical representation, you'll have to find an agent who not only specializes in theater, but in the specific kinds of jobs you're interested in. Remember, in this business you don't walk into an apple store to buy bananas.

Step 2: Initial Call You've done your homework. Now it's time for you to make the initial call. Actually, it's very simple. Just pick up the phone, dial the number, and ask the person at the other end two basic questions: (1) "What categories of actors do you represent?" (2) "Are you accepting submissions for new talent at this time, and, if so, who handles the submissions?" The answer to the second question will tell you who to address your cover letter to when you send the agency your picture and resume.

Step 3: Send Materials Once the initial phone call is completed and you know the name of the person at the agency to contact, prepare the material you want to send them and mail it:

1. Glue your resume to the back of your picture, making sure to write your name on the back of the picture first in case they become separated. (Reread the tips in Chapter 8 on writing resumes, if necessary.)
2. Write a cover letter, addressing it to the contact person the agency told you to send it to so it sounds more personal. (Again, see the tips on writing cover letters in Chapter 8, if needed.)
3. Buy a mailer big enough to hold everything. The mailer should also be padded or have cardboard inserts to protect the enclosed material from being damaged in the mail.
4. Paper clip the cover letter to the picture before inserting it in the mailer. Type a mailing label and attach it to the mailer—no handwritten addresses! Also make sure you've spelled the person's name correctly and are sending it to the right address and zip code.
5. Once the package is ready, mail it. Just remember the advice K. Callan gives in her book *How to Sell Yourself as an Actor*: "Mail your letter so it arrives on Wednesday or Thursday, away from the first of the week rush. On Monday, not only is the agent catching up from the weekend, so are your rivals, and the agent's desk is full. If your letter arrives later in the week it will have less competition."

Step 4: Follow Up About seven days after you mail the package, follow up with a phone call to the person at the agency you addressed the envelope to. Make the call brief, asking if the person received your picture and resume. If the agency is interested, arrange for an interview. If the agency isn't interested, the person will say so right then. Don't take a lack of interest personally. Just move on to the next agency. Always be courteous on the phone, letting the person at the other end do most of the talking. Don't interrupt or try to talk over his or her voice.

Step 5: First Impression Once you've landed an interview, take some time to plan what you're going to wear. Remember, the first impression the agent has of you when both of you meet counts. If you look and act like a slob, you'll be perceived as a slob. Make sure you dress professionally.

Step 6: Interview the Agent Go to the interview, being careful to arrive on time. During the interview, always remember that you operate from a position of power, that agents don't make any money unless they have clients and can secure auditions for them. The agent may be deciding if you're right for the agency, but you're also deciding if the agency is right for you. Therefore, while the agent is examining your background, you should be determining what the agency has to offer you.

Ask yourself if the person you're talking to feels right, if you'll be comfortable working with him or her. Ask questions such as "How many people have you booked in the last three months?" "What kinds of projects did you book them into?" "Who were some of the performers you placed in those projects?" If the jobs were in musical theater, find out how many clients he or she found work for in major productions like *Cats* or *Les Misérables.*

In this business you have to ask questions and push to get the answers. Some agents just aren't involved in that many projects. Make sure you're with an agent who succeeds in booking people, who has a good client list, who has the power to get you jobs. It's no good to sign with someone who makes claims they can't deliver on. It's also no good to sign with someone whose vision of where you should be going in your career doesn't agree with yours. As K. Callan says in *How to Sell Yourself as an Actor:*"For a successful partnership, you and your agent must have the same goals and visions. If you think you can be a star and your agent doesn't, or if he sees you as a star and you want a different kind of career, you're both going to be frustrated and the relationship won't work."

Keep in mind that sometimes agents agree to go to showcases and college shows to see new talent instead of interviewing the prospective clients in their offices. But it better be something worth their time to see. Agent Steve Unger says, "Some talents think you have to get into something big to be seen by an agent. Well, that's just a myth. You have to get into something respectable and worthwhile. For an agent to come and watch somebody do bad work in a bad show isn't going to get anyone an agent. Our time is valuable. I'd rather you come into my office and do a monologue or a scene, or bring in your reel, if available. It's better for me than sitting through a bad three-hour show."

Step 7: Think It Over Even if your research has gone well and you know this is a good and reputable agency, even if you have friends represented by the agency, even if your interview goes well, even if you know you want to sign with the agency, it's still a good idea to look the contract over and think about it for a few days. Never sign a contract blindly, even if the agency is reputable. You have to know what you're getting into, and that everything in the contract you're about to sign is in your best interest.

After You've Signed

You've signed a contract and have an agent. Now the job of you two working together has just begun. Both of you are working toward a common goal, so tell your agent up front what you will and won't do. If you have sensitive issues that could directly affect the kinds of auditions you attend, tell your agent immediately so there's no mis-understanding later on. Don't be afraid to be honest, and don't lead your agent on.

A lot of performers think they should check in with their agent every week. It's OK to check in with your agent periodically, but find out what their policy about this is. When you do check in, be positive and brief. Let her or him know what you yourself are doing to move your career along. Don't sit back and expect the agent to do all the work for you. You can't say to yourself, "I have an agent, so let it happen." If you expect that simply having an agent is going to secure your future, and that you'll soon be a "star," you're just kidding yourself and setting yourself up for a lot of disappointment and resentment.

An effective way to stay in contact with your agent is to buy some mailer cards and occasionally drop him or her a line. You should buy either 4 by 6 or 5 by 7 head-shot cards that you can also use as postcards. Professional actors use them a lot. On the back, jot down something like "That Pepsi commercial you sent me on went very well!" or "Just back from the industrial with Dayton Tires." You might send a card when you're going to appear in a play. That's a great way to say, "Hey, I hope you can catch the show. I'd love to comp your seats for you." By staying in touch this way, you don't have to make many phone calls and risk interrupting the agent at times she or he may be very busy.

Don't forget, even with an agent *you* still have to promote your own talent package. No one can do that better than you. In some job markets there simply isn't a lot of work. Auditions are limited and your agent might not call you very often. But remember that when you do locate a job opportunity, it's wise to call your agent and ask if he or she thinks you should try out for it. Maintain an open line of communication. You don't want the agent finding out down the road that you're finding work behind her or his back. Besides, unless you're freelancing, whether you find a job on your own or through your agent, the agent is entitled to a percentage of the pay. That's the way virtually all agent contracts read (check your own contract on this point). It's only good business sense to honor the clauses of the contract, especially the financial ones, so you don't have any trouble down the line between you and your agent.

Why Agents and Performers Part Company

Dissatisfaction in the agent–performer relationship can come from either side. Say your agent sends you out on three or four auditions, and gets word that your performances weren't up to par. She talks to you about this, pointing out ways you might improve based on the comments she's heard from the casting directors. You should *want* the agent to be honest with you. You want jobs, and the agent doesn't want to jeopardize her reputation with producers, directors, and casting people by sending them low-caliber performers. She also wants you to bring in some money for the agency. If you don't improve, if you're not doing anything for the agency, the agent will ultimately drop you.

On the other hand, maybe *you* feel your agent hasn't been sending you to enough auditions, or hasn't been sending you to auditions for the roles or kind of work you feel you're best qualified for. Maybe you feel you were too young to play a certain part, or the fact that you have big ears and a bulbous nose does not mean you should only be trying out for the "funny guy next door" kind of characters. You should always be honest about this, as the two of you are in this job hunt together and need to maintain good communications. The truth is that agents don't always have a clear fix on what the performers they represent are capable of doing and should be told if they're off the mark. But if the agent doesn't respond in a way that meets your needs, it may be time to find another agent.

Always exercise patience in your dealings with your agent. A lot of performers feel very impatient, and even hostile, toward their agents if they don't think the agents are doing enough to further their careers. But make sure the problem is not just a matter of poor communications before you decide to move on. And if you do leave, make sure it's on friendly terms. Don't burn your bridges. You never know when an agent will decide to move to a studio or production company working as a personnel staffer, assistant, or associate producer. If you show up at one of the auditions where your former agent is now doing the casting, it won't help your chances of being hired if you previously told the person: "Get lost! I can do better on my own." Besides, this is a tightly knit business. You don't want an offended agent telling everyone you have an unprofessional, nasty attitude.

Nonunion Agent Scams to Beware

"The biggest scam is one that has been around for ages," says Caryn Kocel, a casting director and television actress who appears in *U.S.A. High.* It usually goes something like this: An ad in your local newspaper says something to the effect of: "Need actors, dancers, singers, and models from ages 8 to 80 for work in theater, television, and movies. NO EXPERIENCE NECESSARY." This leads you to believe the agency needs people for auditions. As it turns out, there are fees you have to pay to sign with that agency. Because the ad said that no experience was necessary, you hear the following pitch: "First, you'll need a picture. We have our own photographer on the premises, and for only $400 he'll take your headshot. For just $100 more, we'll put your resume together. And our training classes cost only another $500. Take them and you'll be on your way to stardom. If you fall for this line, by the time you're done you'll have spent $1000 with little of value to show for it."

The people who run these scams manipulate the truth for their benefit. As a performer you do need a headshot and a resume; it's also good to have an agent. But don't be suckered by these show business buzz words. These "agencies" will do nothing to further your career.

Another kind of scam involves talent directories some agents recommend: You pay to have your picture and a short bio included, so that, supposedly, you'll be noticed by the "right people" in the industry who use the directory. Sometimes these pitches aren't scams—people casting commercials actually use such directories, and they can be helpful to performers who are interested in doing commercials. But they are rarely used by casting people in film, television, and theater. So before parting with your money, check out the directory being recommended thoroughly and make sure it will be helpful to you and your career.

Remember, it's hard to find a good agent. They may not even exist in smaller cities that have little to offer in the way of entertainment work, and in major cities like Los Angeles or New York agents are so inundated with people wanting representation they put up barriers to protect themselves. But if you work to develop your talent so that it's marketable, if you network to connect with people who can help you move past the barriers you find in your way, if you have drive and determination in locating the right agent for you, you will eventually gain representation.

MANAGERS

Show business managers come in two types: the personal manager who handles aspects of a performer's personal life and career, and the business manager who handles the financial aspects of a performer's life, including money, banking, and taxes. Managers aren't a necessity in a performer's life. Hiring them is a decision each performer has to make for himself or herself based on personal and professional needs.

The basic question to be answered before hiring a manager is: "Do I have anything that needs managing by anyone besides me?" That is, just how complicated are your career and finances? The second question is: "Am I at an income level that can support paying managers as well as all my other expenses?" The commission for personal managers is usually in the range of 15 percent of your income, the fee for business managers is usually around 5 percent, and the commission for agents another 10 percent. By the time you add in taxes—federal, state, social security, and so forth—it adds up to about half your income.

The work business managers do and their qualifications to do it are fairly clearcut. Here we'll focus on the role of personal managers. Just what do they do? How does it differ from what agents do?

Personal Managers

Kathleen Mann, a personal manager in the Los Angeles movie and commercial industry, notes, "A lot of kids are getting personal managers instead of agents because they work harder for them." But there's a rub to this. Personal managers can find jobs for their clients, but in locales where agents are licensed by the state, they still have to call an agent to negotiate the deals and sign the contracts, and the agent still gets a 10 percent commission for doing this even though he or she isn't representing the performer in any other way. Only a few states license agents, but they include important ones for performers like New York and California—California being the home state of Kathleen Mann. If you live in a state that doesn't license agents, say Texas or Oklahoma, a personal manager can negotiate and sign a contract on your behalf. Just remember the following important rule: Where agents *are* licensed by the state, a manager is not allowed to sign, or even negotiate, a contract on your behalf.

Nevertheless, Kathleen Mann's comment points up a real difference between personal managers and agents. Managers are dreamers, visionaries, people who plot the future of their clients. They see the special qualities a performer has and explore that individual's potential with an eye toward helping her or him climb the career ladder. They look ahead to venues like Carnegie Hall, Radio City Music Hall, and Broadway and plan ways to get their clients hired there as performers. In effect, they devise career plans for performers from the "infancy" to the "maturity" of their careers.

One of the best managers in the business is Jim Halsey, who has represented stars such as George Jones and Tammy Wynette. In his opinion,

> *Timing is so important, and to be a manager you have to be as imaginative and creative as the artist that you represent. A manager has to focus on each individual's career and, with that in mind, he or she should never have more than ten fledgling clients. It doesn't serve either party well if the number is greater. By spreading himself or herself too thin, a manager doesn't have the time or energy needed to concentrate on what each new performer needs to succeed, and it's the performers' careers that suffer.*

What a Personal Manager Does If you hire a personal manager, it's her or his job to advance your career. To do this, personal managers rely on their connections. They pick up the phone and call contacts in show business, looking to make record, television, or movie deals for you, to slot you into Broadway shows, to find you work doing commercials, or to arrange for you to appear as a guest on TV and radio talk shows.

Once you reach a high enough professional level as a performing artist, you'll be busy doing things you never imagined, and this is when you'll find the help of a personal manager invaluable.

It's also the personal manager's job to work on your image—to work with you on how you dress, how you style your hair, what makeup you wear, whatever it takes to make you marketable. A manager has to be directly involved in your career, making sure it's moving in the right direction by arranging things like press conferences and interviews. She or he even takes care of seemingly small details such as reminding you of appointments or seeing that you make it to rehearsals on time. In regard to your career, nothing should escape a manager's scrutiny.

In short, a personal manager looks after your best interests. If you hire one, he or she will be a very significant person in your career.

Personal Management Agencies

There are individual personal managers, and there are those affiliated with management agencies. The main advantage of managing agencies is their clout. Managers who work for agencies can call up just about anybody in show business from directors to producers to studio executives and know their recommendations will be taken seriously. Managers who work for themselves are fine if you want to go that route—just make sure the person you're thinking of hiring has the same kind of clout as a managing agency.

Managers and Agents: The Differences

We've already discussed one difference between personal managers and agents: In states where agents are licensed, managers cannot negotiate or sign contracts on your behalf. They must go through an agent for that. But there are other differences as well. For example, an agent's commission is a percentage of the salary for jobs he or she negotiates for you. A personal manager's commission, however, is 15 to 20 percent of your earnings whether his or her efforts land you paying work or not. This means agents and personal managers have very different perspectives about the people they represent. Agents are likely to go where the money is for their clients. Personal managers have other considerations. Good personal managers think about the long haul. They provide their clients with reliable professional guidance and support, and performers in turn give those managers the right to speak for them professionally. Since managers aren't always paid out of fees they receive for jobs signed, they may turn down work they don't think is in a client's best interests. Or they may get a performer involved in benefit concerts or performances that don't bring in any immediate money but provide exposure to large audiences numbering from hundreds or thousands in concert halls to millions on TV.

Despite their different perspectives, personal managers and agents usually work closely together. Good managers refer performers to agents when they need them, and agents rely on managers for help with casting directors or other talent buyers when necessary. Both have their place in a performer's career. It's just up to you to decide whether and when you need both. For beginners, an agent alone is probably enough.

Finding a Personal Manager

Anyone can call himself or herself a personal manager. There's no board certification or licensing for this job. Which means you have to do some research to find a good one. The first step is talking to agents and other performers. Find out who represents your performer friends and acquaintances. Good managers usually don't advertise. They don't need to—they have more than enough clients, and word of mouth leads people to them.

If you have questions regarding a specific manager, you can phone or write an organization called the National Conference of Personal Managers, which has offices on both the East and West Coasts (see contact information in the Appendix). Not all personal managers belong to this organization. According to its president, Gerard W. Purcell: "Eighty percent of personal managers who apply to our organization are turned down. Most of them are just interested in being affiliated with schools, and getting a lot of money out of the artists by telling them that they need this and that. That tells you how many bad managers there are out there." Nevertheless, not belonging to the organization does not imply something unprofessional or unethical about a particular manager in whom you may be interested. The person may simply not have applied for membership.

After you have a few names of potential managers, you'll have to go out and interview them, just as you would agents. And there are a few things to watch out for, especially if you're a beginner in the business. The primary red flag is if someone asks you for money up-front. Jim Halsey notes, "Everybody works on a percentage. Many times a manager will bankroll an artist at the onset of his or her career because, typically, the newcomer has no money. The performer then reimburses the manager as soon as he or she starts working. But suppose someone comes up to you and says, 'Listen, sweetheart, I think you're really terrific. Now I need $10,000 to put up as earnest money to get you a deal'? Move on. It's a scam. If a record company wants to record you, they'll pay *you*. You don't pay *them*."

This is not to say there haven't been legitimate deals where beginners have put up $10,000 earnest money with a good manager who then proceeded to turn them into stars. But these success stories are few and far between. So as I stated before, never pay anyone up-front money of any kind.

Once you have a personal manager, another thing to watch out for is whether she or he lives up to her or his end of the bargain. If you feel your manager's not on the right track and is telling you to do things you don't think are helping your career, let her or him know. If you paid your manager money to get your picture out there but no casting people have called you to audition in the last three months, hit the brakes. Let the manager know that you're dissatisfied with the job he or she is doing and intend to move on if things don't change.

CASTING DIRECTORS

The role of casting directors is often misunderstood. In fact, most young performers have no idea of the part these people will play in their professional lives. Read on to learn just how important casting directors really are.

Casting directors know *talent*; think of them as talent brokers. They're head-hunters for producers and directors who need performers, and they know what performers are available and what they can do. If they don't have someone readily available to fit a particular role, they know how to search until they do find the right person by contacting talent agents, managers, dance and vocal schools, universities, and anyone or anywhere else they can think of. For roles like the Annie character in the musical *Annie* or Maddie in *Paper Moon*, where a regional dialect is critical, they may conduct national searches to find just the right person.

Casting directors act as liaisons between the agents who have performers needing jobs and the theatrical production companies or film companies that need performers for the plays, musicals, or movies they are producing. They advise both parties and facilitate the initial audition process.

Many people think it's the director who does this for the acting and singing roles and the choreographer who does it for the dancing roles. But especially for big productions it's the casting director who weeds out the bad talent or those not suited for particular roles, then passes along the cream of the performers to the director or choreographer to make the final casting decisions. This frees up the production staff to concentrate on the creative aspects of a production until the final casting process.

Once the initial auditions are completed, the casting director's work is usually done. He or she may stay on for negotiations, but that's rare. Most of the time, casting directors don't have the final say about who actually winds up in the cast.

Most casting directors for theater are located in New York, and they are used mainly for Broadway shows and for the touring companies that stem from those shows. Dinner theaters, regional theaters, and summer stock productions sometimes use casting directors if they need Equity members for the shows they're doing. The directors of these theaters or productions consult with the casting directors via phone, or in person by flying to their offices in New York. They cast everyone else without the help of casting directors. Cruise ships and theme parks seldom use casting directors, leaving it all up to the production companies that put on their shows.

How Casting Directors Work

When a casting director is hired by a production company or theater to find the performing talent it needs, the first thing he or she does is to put together a list of information about the production, including the names of the production staff—director, music director, and choreographer, if any—and a "breakdown" of all the available parts. This information is then sent to a "breakdown service" provider, which e-mails or faxes it to the agents who subscribe to the service. A breakdown might include descriptions such as "clean cut all-American type actors" or "two American Indians."

The breakdown service usually has the information to the agents by 5 o'clock the morning after receiving it from the casting director. The agents then go through their files the first thing that day, and by midmorning will have submitted to the casting director the pictures and resumes of their clients (called the "talent") they think appropriate for the parts. By midday the casting director might have received as many as six hundred pictures and resumes for one particular role.

With so many pictures and resumes to deal with, the casting director will most likely leave the initial weeding-out process to an assistant, who will first eliminate the obviously unacceptable entries—those who don't look the part or don't have the necessary experience to play the role for which their names have been submitted. Next, the assistant will toss out those performers the production company specifically doesn't want. As an example, say the company has clearly said it doesn't want any television soap actors for this project. The assistant will eliminate all the performers whose resumes indicate they act on soaps. This leaves the performers whose pictures and resumes indicate they might fit the particular roles for which they're being considered.

Remember, all this is done without seeing the talent actually perform. But once the assistant has assembled a manageable number of performers who might be suitable for each role, the casting director calls the various agents involved and sets up auditions. The agents then call the talent (their clients) about the auditions, notifying them of the time and location, and providing any necessary information about the parts for which they're auditioning.

Casting directors don't make the final casting decisions, but performers should understand that auditioning for a casting director is no different from auditioning directly for the director, producer, or music director or choreographer of a show. Nor is it any less important. Casting directors can really make or break your career. You have to impress them just as much as anyone else or you won't get to the next callback. If you don't pass this first hurdle, you'll never be seen by anyone directly connected to the show for which you're auditioning.

Also keep in mind that the reputations of casting directors are constantly at stake. Production people rely on their judgment about performers, and they are out to protect those reputations. If a casting director gets a bad feeling about you, for whatever reason, you're in trouble. Say you were rude in the lobby or showed up at the audition with an attitude. Say you got kicked out of another show for something you did or didn't do. The casting director is going to protect his or her client from hiring a performer who might cause problems, who has a bad reputation, or who simply can't do the job. So make sure you're not the performer who loses out on that account.

At the audition, the casting director observes all the performers trying out, taking notes on each. These notes are not just used in reference to the current production, but go into her or his file for future use. Let's say you audition for *Phantom of the*

Opera, but the casting director doesn't think you're right for that show. However, she does think you're perfect for *Cats*. She will note that down. Later it will be added to the computer files she keeps on all the performers she has seen over the years. Say a year later she is hired to help cast a production of *Cats*. Even if your name isn't submitted by your agent for an audition, it will pop up from her files as a performer she thinks might be right for a part in the show. On the other hand, if your singing is poor and your dancing atrocious, that too will be noted down and find its way into her files. In that case, she'll probably never agree to audition you again.

So you see, both offstage and on, first impressions really matter. Human nature dictates that once someone forms an opinion about you as a person or performer, that opinion is not likely to change. Make sure that casting directors form good opinions about you because once they form a bad opinion it's difficult to undo the damage.

Contacting Casting Directors Directly

In general, for the principal roles in Broadway shows casting directors only consider performers agents have submitted. If you're young and new to the business, you may not yet have an agent. So if you're interested in performing on Broadway, read the trades and find a role or production for which auditions are being held that you would like to try out for. Buy a copy of *Ross Report*, look up the casting director handling the particular show you're interested in, and follow the guidelines for submitting your picture, resume, and anything else called for. In the cover letter state what role you'd like to audition for.

Just remember that casting directors are very busy people. Be professional. Send only what's required. If you send too much material, the casting director and his or her staff are likely to ignore it, and you. If you stick to the guidelines and only send what they want, they'll perceive you as an obviously sharp pro and probably look at your material more closely. For theater jobs, don't send a promo tape. Also, never send clippings. If you're a singer and have done jingles, a musical casting director may appreciate an audiotape to hear what your voice sounds like. Also, make sure your talents match the part you want to try out for. You don't want to try out for a chorus dancer or a dancing role if nothing in your training has prepared you for that sort of job. It will just prejudice the casting director against auditioning you for anything else.

If you're not contacted about an audition, you can call the casting director's office. But don't be obnoxious or a pest, or your efforts will backfire. The casting director may not agree to see you personally, but he or she may tell you to show up at the next open call.

There are a couple of ways performers sometimes contact casting directors that casting directors don't like at all because it puts them in an awkward position. The first is calls from talent unhappy with their agents. This can happen for a variety of reasons, but usually has to do with performers who think their agents aren't submitting their names for auditions frequently enough. The talent will call the casting office to see if they have missed any calls for the types of roles they think appropriate for themselves. The casting director then has to decide whether to point the finger at a valued talent agent or risk alienating a strong talent who might be the right performer for the next job.

Never place a casting director in that position by complaining about your agent. If your agent didn't submit your name for a role or production you're interested in, send the casting director your picture and resume with a note reading along the lines of "Hello I'm John Doe, currently listed with XYZ Talent Agency. I look forward to auditioning with you soon." This way the casting director gets to see your smiling face and your work history. He or she will probably add your name to the file listing your "type," where it will be available for future auditions.

Some performers dissatisfied with their agents also make the mistake of neglecting to tell those agents they've moved on to someone else. This causes trouble when both agents submit the name of a performer for a role or project and the casting director finds herself or himself in the unenviable position of having to inform one of them that the performer has already been recommended by someone else. This happens a lot in situations where agents are handling clients on a freelance or consignment basis. The tension this causes for everyone usually results in the talent getting the boot by both agents and casting director.

In conclusion, let me say: Casting directors are powerful people who lead very busy lives, put their professional reputations on the line every day in terms of the recommendations they make to their clients, and don't like to be put in uncomfortable positions. But they also know how hard it is to break into the business or to get an agent, and they're not inaccessible to new talent. Geoffrey Johnson, New York Casting Director for *Les Misérables*, *Phantom of the Opera*, *Miss Saigon*, and *Cats*, says, "I think a lot of young actors worry about being in the unions. But we are always looking for talent. We don't care whether people are union or not, because we know there are a lot of nonunion people who are very talented, and there are a lot of union people who aren't so talented." The bottom line: Casting directors are looking for talent wherever they can find it. If you do your homework, handle yourself professionally, and are persistent, you'll find casting directors willing to consider you for theater work.

12

Proving Your Talent in Paying Jobs

O ver and over, as if following some herd instinct, countless numbers of young performers flock to New York City, hoping to be "discovered" and land jobs on Broadway without testing the waters and exploring other options that generally serve as the stepping stones to working on Broadway. But hustling off to New York before you're ready, without a solid resume to demonstrate the level of your skills, without an agent to advise you and point the way into concrete job possibilities, and without a network of contacts in the theater world to ease your way through a highly competitive profession, is not a wise move. Not only will you likely fail in landing work on Broadway, but you will probably fail to find paying work of any kind in your chosen field.

Broadway is a business first and a form of entertainment second. Getting a job on Broadway takes *proven* talent. Proving your talent to the Broadway people who count—producers and directors—means understanding how Broadway works from their angle. And making a living as a performer—not as a waiter or salesclerk or clerical temp—means understanding where to find the jobs that will pay you as a performer while you're building the resume and contacts that will eventually land you your roles on Broadway.

In this chapter, we'll take a look at several theater-related venues in which young performers can prove their talent, build their resumes and contacts, and, at the same time, be paid to perform. These include theme parks, industrials, cruise ships, and Las Vegas. In Chapter 13, we'll turn to non-Broadway theater venues that usually serve as direct precursors to working on Broadway—dinner theater, summer stock, regional theater, and touring companies. We'll explore the kinds of jobs those venues offer, how to land them, what kinds of work they involve, and how to build on them to further your career.

As a lead-in to both chapters, I'll discuss a couple of issues every performer interested in Broadway needs to understand: the business aspects of Broadway, and the development of good habits and attitudes that will mark you as a professional in the eyes of the people you need to impress to land a job.

UNDERSTANDING THE BUSINESS OF BROADWAY

There was a time when anything was possible on Broadway, when both producers and audiences were willing to take risks. Many shows were newly minted projects that were considered successful if they broke even at the box office. Things have changed. Today, Broadway doesn't take many risks, simply because it's so expensive to mount a show. A bare-bones show, at minimum, will cost upwards of a million dollars. Even proven winners like *Beauty and the Beast*, one of today's most successful productions, cost many millions of dollars to open, and even more to keep going. Then there are the costs for the theatergoers. Here's an average breakdown of what a suburban couple today spends on a night at a Broadway theater:

Two orchestra-seat tickets: $150

Parking: at least $20 to $30

Something to eat afterward: $30 to $80

By the time the evening is over, this couple may have "dropped" $250 to $300. People have gotten to the point that, unless they're sure they'll have a good time, they won't spend that kind of money for an evening's entertainment. And the backers of Broadway shows, even if they're huge corporate conglomerates, aren't willing to throw money at something they don't think will pay them back their investment as well as some profit.

This situation is one of the reasons why so many revivals are appearing on Broadway these days. A revival is as close to a "sure thing" as you'll find in the performance world. People who saw the show thirty years ago may have loved the music and want to recapture the pleasure and enthusiasm they felt so long ago. They say, "I loved it. Let's go again." They recommend it to others.

It is also the reason producers tend to hire performers well known from other Broadway plays, TV, or the movies for the starring roles. Some shows like *The Lion King*, *Miss Saigon*, *Les Misérables*, or *Cats* have for various reasons proven to be successes without big-name stars. But these are the exceptions. New shows, especially those with shaky reviews, usually need bankable personalities to draw people to the theater.

The hard-nosed business aspects of finding work on Broadway are very simple: Producers and directors are not going to use new, untested talent if they can use proven performers—people they know have the experience and credentials to do the job. And this goes for performers across the board: stars, supporting actors, or members of the chorus. The trusted few get first crack at everything, leaving the scraps for everyone else. Unpleasant, but there it is. From the performer's side, it means that the number of jobs on Broadway available for new talent is not very large. There are a great many performers in New York competing for each Broadway job, and the ones most likely to be hired are those who have been hired before—and before.

What are the alternatives? Well, in the Big Apple, there are many other kinds of paying jobs available—waiting on tables, clerking in a store, temping as a secretary—the jobs I have mentioned earlier. But in other spots around the country, there are many paying jobs available for performers as singers, dancers, and actors. True, they're not in New York. But isn't working at your craft in St. Louis far better than waiting tables in Greenwich Village? And take the advice of Jack Tygett, veteran Broadway and film dancer: "Don't set your heart on being a star. Be a doer, not a quitter. Go for your dream with all your might—you'll love your life and like yourself better."

That said, let's turn to a discussion of developing the habits and attitudes necessary to mark you as a professional. Not surprisingly, as with so many other theater-related talents and abilities, that development should start early on. And one of the best places to start developing the proper habits and attitudes is in high school.

LEARNING PROFESSIONAL ATTITUDES IN HIGH SCHOOL

I know most of you are thinking, "Why is he bringing up high school? He described public high school drama programs (in Chapter 6) as not being very good on the whole. And besides, why should we spend time discussing high school shows when there are more important jobs to consider, jobs that actually pay money?"

Yes, high school drama programs and shows have their drawbacks. But to be honest, most young aspiring performers attend public high schools, and many of their early performing experiences take place in high school productions. So high school is the breeding ground for much of the behavior and most of the habits and attitudes we carry later on into our professional lives. That baggage can be good or bad, and it certainly has an effect on the success or failure we find as professional performers. So let's take a glance at how to develop *good* habits and attitudes by examining some typical issues that arise in high school productions. As you'll see, they're not very different from the issues that arise in any theater situation, from high school to Broadway.

Making Sure You're Prepared

A few years ago I was casting for a high school production of *Annie* and had some sixty-five kids, between the ninth and twelfth grades, show up to snatch a role for themselves. Before the audition started, I spoke to the group and asked how many of them were thinking of doing this eventually for a living. Almost all the girls raised their hands. When they filled out their sign-in forms, most of them wrote that they were there to audition for major roles in the show.

As I watched the kids audition, I found myself wondering why many of them were even trying out. They clearly hadn't taken any voice, dance, or acting lessons. Why did they think they could land the lead or even a major role in this musical when they were so badly prepared? Was the concept of "being prepared" so difficult for the kids and their parents to grasp?

Even at the high school level, if you attend an audition unprepared, you'll be blown out of the water by someone who is prepared. It's that simple. For example, the girl who landed the role of Grace in that production of *Annie* was so good she easily dismantled the hopes and chances of any other girl trying out for that role. There was no competition once you heard her sing, watched her dance, and took note of her acting abilities. Why was she such a standout? Because she was prepared. Because she took her ambitions seriously and attended weekly lessons in the areas she need-ed to know in order to be a good performer. Because the audition demonstrated that she knew what she wanted to do with her life and was doing everything in her power to make her dreams come true.

Learning to Be Flexible About Roles

There is no role too small for you. Repeat that sentence to yourself, over and over!

Too many times high school kids who audition think it's an outrage for them to be offered a role in the chorus, or the role of a minor character with only a line or two of dialogue. They figure they have to be the lead, the star. But you have to be realistic in thinking about your career. This also goes when you're starting out in the business as a professional. Say you're auditioning for a play being put on by a dinner theater. Remember that you'll be competing against regional performers who have already proven themselves to the director. What kinds of roles can you expect to get? Most likely you'll usually be offered a part in the chorus. This is how most professional careers start, so don't take offense if yours does also. If you're offered a spot in the chorus, take it and be proud. It's a wonderful part. And it can lead to better things.

Learning to Network

Many of the kids trying out for the shows I direct also take dance lessons from me, in hopes that it will give them an edge. Well, it does. And it's no different in the pro-fessional world. Contacts help. Remember that in show business part of your job is getting to know casting people, getting to know choreographers, getting to know musical directors so that when you go up to audition for them they already have a sense of who you are and the range of your talents. That contact can come in many ways—taking lessons from them, auditioning for them on previous occasions, or knowing them in some other manner. But with the large numbers of people you'll be up against when going after the role you feel is meant just for you, you can be easily overlooked if the people watching you audition have no idea who you are.

In regard to my own students, I find out, on a weekly basis, what they can and cannot do. To determine how their voices are coming along, I have them periodi-cally sing their audition pieces for me. To observe their acting abilities, I may have them perform monologues or read from a script. I know their abilities, and they know me. When it comes to casting the shows I direct, this kind of professional familiarity benefits everyone involved. However, keep in mind that no matter how well someone knows me, he or she has to be right for the part in order for me to cast the person in the role. The student must be able to sing, act, and dance the role properly or he or she doesn't get the part.

This is true of most directors. Even though they may have someone in mind for a part, they wait to see all those auditioning before coming to a final decision. Of course the star system can short-circuit this process. On Broadway, as I said earlier, financial pressures often lead to the casting of big names in the leading roles, and if you're not a big name you don't have a big chance of landing those roles. Even in high school productions drama teachers often cast the same people as leads year after year. But networking is still a must. You must bring yourself to the attention of the people who can hire you for the roles you want, and you should learn the habit and skill of networking as early as possible.

Learning to Be Committed

So many times at high school auditions, kids will note on the forms that they have other commitments that will conflict with their being in the show. Their idea of preparing for a performance is attending rehearsals whenever they please.

Although some high schools may go along with this type of thinking, it does the performers themselves no good whatsoever, especially those hoping to pursue professional careers. Preparing for a musical is time-driven. High school productions usually have more generous rehearsal schedules than professional shows—up to eight weeks versus one or two weeks. But not even a high school musical can afford to have its performers roaming in and out of rehearsals if a professional looking production is the goal. So if you want a career in theater, learn to commit. If being a cheerleader, a football player, or a member of the debating team is more important, stay away. And by all means don't learn the bad habit of asking for special favors. It will get you nowhere in the world of professional theater.

Learning to Build a Professional Reputation

Reputation begins at an early age, but definitely breaks through in high school. And bad reputations continue to follow you. One girl who had been cast for important roles in my two previous shows, *Evita* and *The Wiz*, and then dropped out within the first two weeks of rehearsals for both, showed up to audition for *Annie*. (Takes nerve, don't you think?) She had already shown herself to be unreliable, so I wouldn't consider her for a leading role. Had she acted that way in the professional world, she would never be considered again by that director for *any* role, nor would she be considered for any role by any professional acquaintances to whom the director told the story. Remember that this business is small. Everybody knows each other, and every unprofessional move you make will damage your chance of success—in the future you might have had.

Other kinds of behavior are just as harmful. One girl who was trying out for the part of Lily in *Annie* told a friend the evening before the audition that I would never cast a certain student for the part of Annie because I thought she was ugly. This was an outright lie. The girl then went on to declare that if she didn't get the lead herself, she wouldn't do the show. As it turned out, I thought the "certain student" excellent for the lead and gave her the part (she was outstanding in the role), while the girl who was busy spreading malicious rumors got nothing. The story got back to me, and she never stood a chance. There's a lesson here: When you speak badly of someone else, it will most likely get back to the person. If you're making up falsehoods about the director, once she or he gets wind of it your chances of being cast are pretty slim. This is not just a question of vanity. Most directors don't like people who snipe at others, or tell lies because more than likely it means those individuals will cause headaches later on. If you're caught in this type of behavior by those who have the power to cast you in a show, don't expect a good outcome.

Another example of problem behavior: A girl wrote on her sign-in sheet, "If I'm not cast in either of the above parts, I don't want to be in the cast." Then, in big letters, she added, "DON'T CAST ME IN THE CHORUS." While it's all right to turn down a part in the chorus, that kind of childish emphasis tells the director this person has an attitude problem and should not be cast in any part. In the professional world, word like that is likely to spread—and this time it won't be a malicious rumor, but a story that will hurt your reputation in more ways than you'll ever know.

Learning Not to Try Pressure Tactics

At the high school level, this would probably involve having your parents complain to the school administration that you aren't getting the parts you deserve, or perhaps coming to the school in person and demanding from the drama teacher or director that you be given a particular part. This will probably not lead to your getting the part you want. And the tactics could permanently damage your relationship to the teacher, or the professional director engaged for the show. You may need the teacher to write a recommendation for your application to attend a conservatory or college theater department. You may meet up with the director later on in your career. You may not always trust that the people in charge know what they're doing, but you must learn to live with their decisions. If you don't get the part you want, so be it. It's not the end of the world, and it's best just to move on. And this attitude is especially important once you're in the professional world, where a reputation for complaining and trying to go behind the backs of directors to get the parts you want—say through producers or backers of shows—will get you nowhere at all.

Four Rules

Learning good theater habits while in high school will help you immeasurably later on. And learning those habits can be boiled down to the following four rules:

1. Prepare yourself professionally. Take lessons in voice, dance, and acting if you want to be cast in a show, especially as a principal performer.
2. Go to auditions prepared by knowing your material, and if cast be ready to commit to the production one hundred percent.
3. Act professionally both before and after auditions, rehearsals, and performances. Don't bad-mouth other students, teachers, or directors. If you don't

get the part you wanted, accept the fact and move on. Let the people you work with know that you are someone who is worth working with, not someone who causes trouble.

4. If you don't get the part you want, never ask others to intervene on your behalf. This will cause you problems even in high school, and in the professional theater world will probably eliminate your being considered for any future roles.

In Chapter 13, I will look at another proving-ground for young performers—one that, like high school, is right in your local area: Community theater, where one is not paid but where valuable lessons similar to the ones I have mentioned here can be learned.

Having said all that, let's now turn to the different *paying* venues available to young performers. The following discussion is aimed at providing you with the knowledge and tools necessary to go out and find jobs that will allow you to earn your living as a performer while building the foundation for a long and successful career in musical theater.

THEME PARKS

Don't you love spending a day at a theme park, where there's so much to see and do? From riding a death-defying roller coaster, to playing one of the games on the midway in an effort to win a stuffed animal, to just walking around and observing the people, it's great to take it all in.

After awhile, however, most people get tired of all the commotion and noise. And where do they go for a break? You guessed it—the shows.

Whether located in a theater, on a platform in a restaurant, or in a covered park, shows draw large audiences throughout the day, offering a place for weary visitors to recharge their batteries. Most people don't really care what the show is, either. As long as it's clean, wholesome, family fun, they're happy to spend thirty to sixty minutes being entertained by those on the stage.

Performing in a theme park is a great way to start your career, especially if you're in high school. Some parks require performers to be at least 18 years of age, but many hire people as young as 16 or 17. That's not to say it's easy work. You may have five performances (called "sets") a day, with the first performance beginning at noon and the last at 7:15 P.M., meaning you finish your work day well after 8 P.M. Your actual time onstage may only total three or four hours, giving you plenty of free time between sets. But this schedule will force you to hang around the park for eight or nine hours, and as the summer wears on those hours of performing and waiting around will probably catch up with you.

But, hey, that's show biz. You're proving yourself, earning money performing, and building your resume and list of contacts—all of which are valuable at the start of your career.

Theme parks, such as Cedar Point Park, in Sandusky, Ohio, can be great starting points in developing singing or dancing careers. While some theme parks hire performers as young as age 16, others have a minimum age limit of 18.

Types of Theme Parks

There are literally hundreds of theme parks across the country that feature live entertainment. It's your job to research the opportunities available to you. Among the factors to consider when deciding on the theme park you want to apply to: union versus nonunion, location, seasons during which the park is open, whether it's entertainment-oriented or ride and retail-oriented.

Some of the largest parks in the country—Six Flags, Hershey Park, Busch Gardens, Cedar Point, Elitch Gardens, Paramount Parks, Premier Parks, and Silver Dollar City—are nonunion, which means the work rules and pay scales are not regulated by union contracts. Performers must abide by the park rules, and, of course, accept their pay scales. Then there are Disneyland (in California) and Disney World (in Florida). Disneyland is a union park whose performers are covered by the American Guild of Variety Artists. Pay scales, length of breaks, number of rehearsal hours, safety and sanitation conditions, vacation days, and holidays are all spelled out in AGVA contracts. Disney World is also a union park whose performers are protected by Actors' Equity contracts with provisions similar to those of AGVA contracts. But Florida is a so-called right-to-work state, which means performers don't have to join Equity in order to work at Disney World, even though the park honors Equity provisions for every performer who works there.

Location is important in terms of when the parks are open—year-round, or just during warm weather. You may want to take a break in your education after high school and work full time for a while, or you may just want summer work while attending high school, college, or a conservatory the rest of the year.

Then there are the parks that are basically entertainment-oriented versus those that emphasize rides and retail over entertainment. This difference is important to consider when securing employment. A park that puts entertainment first produces higher-quality shows and offers performers better pay. They often have better production staffs who run interesting programs that are updated from time to time with fresh material.

If you live near a theme park, call its main number and ask for brochures or booklets giving information on its hiring policies, along with an application. Talk to people who have worked there. For parks out of your area, call long-distance information for their numbers and contact them in the same way. Go to the library and look in the *Summer Theatre Directory* and the *Back Stage Handbook for the Performing Artist* (see the Appendix for information on buying your own copies of these important books). You can probably find information about the larger parks on the Internet. Most likely there are even chat rooms where you can learn more.

What Theme Parks Look For

Performing jobs at theme parks are considered entry level. As I mentioned earlier, the minimum age is usually 16, although you should check directly with the Disney Corporation parks since their employment rules are governed by their union affiliations. There are no upper age limits on those they will hire. But since people who are older aren't usually willing to settle for theme park wages, most performers are between the ages of 17 and 25, with the highest concentration being between 17 and 21.

In terms of skills, theme parks generally need singer/dancers; stunt performers; a variety of street performers, including mimes, jugglers, puppeteers; actors with strong improvisational skills; and magicians. They look for self-motivated people who have excellent people skills.

Theme Park Auditions

Finding out about theme park auditions is relatively easy. You can start with the trade papers, such as *Back Stage* and *Dirt Alert*. They list these types of auditions in some detail, especially beginning in January. Or you can contact theme parks directly by finding out their addresses or the addresses of the production companies that put on their shows in the *Summer Theatre Directory* or the *Back Stage Handbook for the Performing Artist*. All you have to do is send off a neat, typewritten letter to each theme park or production company asking it to put you on its audition mailing list. Long before any of them start their local or national tour auditions for the coming season, you will receive all the pertinent information in the mail. That information will include the location of each audition, the time it will be held, and a phone number to call for details about the type of show the audition will be for and what kinds of clothing or costumes to bring with you. These details are usually provided on a taped message. If there is no message providing these details, just go to the audition prepared as you would be for any audition, with your dance bag, your resume and picture, and songs you've prepared to perform.

Where Auditions Are Held Many theme parks prefer live auditions. Most parks these days conduct national casting tours, where the casting people travel from one city to another on the lookout for talent. Others send their casting people to regional theater conferences. A few allow only live auditions, and conduct them in-house where they're located. In that case, if you're really serious about working at one of those parks, be prepared to spend the money for a plane ticket to attend the audition.

If you live a long distance from the park for which you want to audition, some of them will allow you to send a videotape that showcases your abilities (reread the section in Chapter 8 on making a promotional tape). First send them your resume and picture, along with a cover letter explaining the season and types of work you're interested in as well as the reason you can't audition in person. Send the tape promptly if they request it. They will review the tape to determine if your talents, showmanship, height, and weight fit the needs of any of the shows for which they are casting. If they can't use you for the time being but like your work, they'll usually keep the tape, resume, and picture on file so they can contact you later if something suitable does come along.

Be aware that if you're cast by a theme park chain, they will place you in the location where they think you will fit best. So be prepared to relocate.

Levels of Audition Experience Because theme park jobs are mostly entry level, the casting people realize there are many beginners who show up at their auditions simply to learn how to audition. Nevertheless, you should really have a certain training under your belt before showing up at a theme park audition. The casting people like performers who know something about the basics of how to audition. They find it especially annoying when performers aren't prepared to demonstrate onstage what their resumes say they've been trained to do.

Finding the Right Audition Songs Let's say that one of the shows you're auditioning for will be a 1950s retrospective, and the second a country & western show. You don't want to show up and sing something from *Phantom of the Opera* or *Cats*. Instead, you want to tailor your songs to the types of shows being done. Remember that having the proper audition pieces is a very important step in helping you to secure the job you want. So plan ahead. Make sure your audition songs are in keeping with the show you're auditioning for.

Also, it is very important to be imaginative with your material, and to know how to deliver and interpret the lyrics. Even if you have the right kind of songs, you don't want to stand there blank-faced, just singing a bunch of notes.

Elements of the Audition Process Auditioning involves at least five elements, which are summarized below.

1. *Signing in.* When you enter the audition hall, you'll be asked to sign in and fill out a form. Sometimes the monitor (the person you signed in with) takes each hopeful into the audition room person by person, where he or she performs for the casting people, include members of the production staff like the music director, the choreographer, and the theme park's entertainment director. At other times the monitor ushers in the hopefuls in groups of five, ten, or fifteen, where they will all be seated and watch each other audition along with the casting people.

2. *Typing Out.* This term means sorting out those auditioning into the types of characters they resemble most. Usually, theme parks don't type out. They tend to do so only if they're casting for a show with definite characters or character types. But in general their only basic requirement is that you actually be able to sing if you're being cast in a singing role, be able to dance if you're being cast in a dancing role, and so forth. They don't require that you look a specific way to play the part you're trying out for.

3. *Singing Auditions.* Those performers who are auditioning as singers will be called onstage one by one and asked to sing their song. The casting people will be checking to see that you prepared a song compatible with the show they're putting on, that you know how to dress appropriately, that you sing clearly, and that you fill the theater or audition room with sound. Unfortunately, many voice teachers these days are letting their students attend auditions and sing with small, breathy voices. I don't know why, since the sound isn't marketable. If you can't sing out so everyone can hear you clearly, you will not be hired.

You have to be able to deliver your song instantly, from the introduction to your stopping point. And don't sing the entire song. Sixteen bars is enough. The casting people for theme parks would rather hear you sing sixteen great bars than twenty-five rambling ones. After finishing, you might be asked to sing the song again, this time in a different way. This usually means the casting people are checking to see if you can take directions or are difficult to work with.

Theme parks don't pay cruise line wages, so they realize that most likely they'll be getting singers who don't dance. However, they do prefer singers who can at least move, that is, who can follow some kind of simple choreography. And they're always hoping to find triple threats, even though that's rare.

4. *Dancing Auditions.* After the singing auditions are over, you'll be given time to change into your dance clothes. The choreographer will then spread everyone out on the stage and teach a dance combination. After teaching the combination, she or he will break the large groups down into smaller groups of four or five. One group at a time, they will be asked to perform the combination. After everyone has gone twice, the choreographer may ask each person auditioning to step forward and execute a double jazz pirouette.

Some parks also conduct tiered dance auditions. These are for roles where the performers must be able to move, although not necessarily to dance. The casting people divide the auditioners into different groups according to their abilities: singers who can move, singers who can dance, and the straight dancers, who won't need to sing at all.

5. *Callbacks.* Usually, after the dance audition, the casting people take a few minutes to go through the pictures, resumes, and the forms that were filled out at the start to see who might be right for the shows the theme park will be producing and to check for conflicts that might get in the way of those they're thinking of hiring. After a few minutes, the person in charge will announce the names of those performers wanted for callbacks. He or she then thanks everyone for coming, and apologizes for not being able to use everyone.

At callbacks, the job is to match the right talent to the right show. Everyone will be asked to sing and dance again. The process usually takes a few hours. Those hired are asked to stay, while the rest are thanked and dismissed. On some national casting tours, the performers who make it to the final callback are videotaped. The tape is then taken back to the park, where it is viewed by the production staff members who weren't on the audition tour, and the final decisions are made.

Some theme parks carry out the initial auditions and the callbacks all in one day. This is usually the case when they're doing a national tour, traveling from city to city. Others hold the callbacks on another day, usually when they're conducting the auditions in-house, at the park itself.

Keep in mind that there are variations to the audition process. The point is to be prepared for anything.

Theme Park Work as a Learning Experience

Theme parks look for performers they see as directable. That is, they know that young performers are not particularly experienced yet, but they want cast members who are open minded and willing to try different things. They don't want people who just go through the motions of performing, or who are hypercompetitive and unwilling to work as part of a team. They *do* want performers who have good people skills, who interact well not just with other cast members but with audiences.

These could be called performing "instincts," and are what you as the performer will bring to working at a theme park. They are detectable by good casting people as early as the first audition, and if the casting staff perceives you as *not* having them—as likely to cause problems or be a troublemaker—you can be sure you won't be called back or hired.

But there are also valuable skills you will learn through the experience of working at a theme park. These include learning how to meet your call time for each performance, how to hone your people skills as you work each day with other cast members and interact with the public, and how to keep a show fresh, day after day, week after week. This is especially important if your eventual goal is work on Broadway, where you will repeat your role performance after performance for weeks, months, or even years at a time yet must always manage to keep it fresh for each new audience.

Salaries

On the low end, you may earn about around $250 a week. At the high end, the range may be $350 to $450. If your salary is at the low end, don't be jarred by the deductions taken out, which can reduce that $250 to $175 in take-home pay. If you fulfill your contract by staying the full season, some theme parks give a bonus. Also, you will make more if you work at one of the Disney corporation parks which, because of their union affiliations, have higher pay scales than the nonunion parks.

INDUSTRIALS

One of the best kept secrets in the business is the industrial, also known as business theater. For performers it is also potentially one of the most lucrative jobs. Industrials keep a lot of singers and dancers employed. They're also good for networking and a great way to build your resume.

An industrial is a custom-produced show written specifically for a corporation, perhaps to launch a new product, or to implement a new business policy. It can be a modest production that involves no more than a local entertainer who tells some jokes at an in-house buffet luncheon before a company spokesman steps in front of the microphone to make an important announcement to employees. It can be something elaborate that costs millions of dollars to put on, involving well-known celebrities, singers, dancers, and specialty acts and aimed at maximizing the impact of a new product or corporate decision on a grand scale. Or it can be something in between.

For the more extravagant industrials, corporations usually hire industrial production companies, which have their own in-house writers, directors, choreographers, music directors, costumers, and other theater specialists. Within a budget specified by the corporation, the production company writes and produces a show that gets out the message the corporation wants to promote.

Types of Industrials

Industrials are held in ballrooms, theaters, convention centers, or whatever other location best suits the purpose, and are attended by invitation-only audiences. They can be broken down into several types:

The first type is a show offered as part of a reward for people within a corporation who have done outstanding work—say the top salespeople within a company who reached or surpassed their quotas during the last year. The corporation has arranged a special day for these individuals, and perhaps their spouses, which involves a business meeting in the morning, golf or sailing in the afternoon, and a show in the evening following a dinner at which everyone is congratulated for a job well done.

A second type involves the introduction of a new product. The show targets both the people involved in producing the item and potential customers, which means the audience is composed of both.

A third type is a video production, actually an industrial movie, which explains something about the corporation itself, either to employees or customers.

The fourth type of industrial uses a theatrical format to deliver a message. Say employee turnover at a corporation is high, and upper management wants to train lower-level managers on good supervisory techniques. (This can be also be done through a video.)

Required Talents and Other Qualifications

Industrials require a special breed of performers. First and foremost the actors (or singers or dancers) need to be quick studies, able to pick things up in a hurry as they might have just a week to prepare for the show. Sharon Allyson of Rave Review, an industrial production company in Denver, says, "I look for people who are flexible and willing to work, people who aren't rigid. It's a real team effort and you have to be a team player, not a prima donna. Everyone has their job to do and you can't cater to any single performer. So I look for people that are easy to work with."

Since every industrial is different, a company may have four or five full-time performers on staff, auditioning for others as needed for each specific event. Production companies prefer performers who are cross-talented—that is, singers with some dance skills, or dancers who can also emcee a show, actors who can also sing and dance. The more you can do, the more valuable production companies will find you. (Again, notice the importance of being a triple-threat performer.)

There are really no age limits on performers in industrials since people of all ages are needed. Corporations have people in every age group working for them, and the production companies cast to reflect this. In effect, the performers are portraying real people, albeit in an elevated manner. The audience wants to see people like themselves, not just 25-year-olds with perfect bodies, up on the stage. This means people of different ages, body types, and talents are welcomed in this sort of work. If you have the abilities needed and the stamina to perform, the opportunities are limitless.

Finding Out About Jobs in Industrials

Finding out about industrials is more word-of-mouth than anything. Agents who deal with live theater usually know about these kinds of jobs. If you don't have an agent, you'll have to research them yourself. The trade papers list those in the big cities. If you don't live in a major metropolitan area, ask about opportunities from colleagues and casting people as you make the auditioning rounds.

Earnings

Industrial jobs can be either union or nonunion. It depends on the contract in a particular city. Union contracts for live stage industrials are governed by Actors' Equity rules, while those for industrial videos are governed by either Screen Actors Guild or American Federation of Television and Radio Artists rules.

Pay scales vary by locale. In a city the size of Denver, they range from $500 to $2000 for a week of rehearsals and performances. In larger cities, the pay trends to be higher. How you get paid depends on what kind of experience you have and how long you've worked with the production company.

CRUISE LINES

If there's one job in show business that sounds exciting for beginners, it has to be the cruise line adventure. Just think: You're out at sea, earning money as a performer, meeting interesting people, enjoying great food, enjoying room and board as part of the job package, and getting to see new parts of the world.

Sounds fantastic, doesn't it? While there's a lot of truth to this picture, that's not all there is to it. Let's do a little exploring to see if it's a job for you.

Pros and Cons of Cruise Work

There are certainly pros here, but I'll start with the cons.

While it may seem like a dream job, working on a cruise line isn't for everyone. Why? Let's start with the simple fact that you're confined to a ship. It's like living in a hotel, only you can't leave should you want to. Your free time shares the same space as your work time. While it may be exciting at first, seeing the same people and doing the same things over and over again, without any alternatives, can adversely affect some people.

Another problem is that you have to be willing to leave your own home for up to nine months at a time. Not only will you be out of touch with family and friends, but if you're living on your own you'll have to sublet your apartment or continue to pay rent and any other bills that might accrue.

Then there's the constant motion of the ship. No matter what measures they take, some people can't escape getting seasick. If you suffer from motion sickness, and if being miserable for long stretches of time doesn't appeal to you, cruise ship work is not for you.

You also have to abide by certain rules on a cruise ship. You are part of the crew, and must know all about the safety procedures and guidelines applicable to crew members. Crew members are also subject to dress codes and curfews. As a high-profile individual onboard the ship—an entertainer—the passengers will turn to you for help during any crisis. At the same time, since you're *not* a passenger yourself, you won't be allowed in the guest areas during certain hours of the day and night. You won't be allowed to cook in your room—not even on a hotplate. You may be allowed to eat in the dining room with the passengers on some occasions, but at other times you'll have to eat with the crew. Food for the crew and entertainers can range from very good to downright horrible. Every ship has its own rules about how entertainers eat their meals, so be sure to ask before you sign up with any cruise line.

As an entertainer, you will be watched more closely than the other employees by the ship's officers. It's human nature that those in charge will think you have it easy and as an entertainer you don't really work hard. They may believe that you take advantage of the rules and just do what you want. On the other hand, entertainers on some cruise ships are assigned nonentertainment duties that take up much of the time they're not on-stage. Also ask about that kind of arrangement before you sign up. It may not be for you.

It will also be hard to continue lessons while on a ship. You might find yourself in a port with a studio nearby, or you might be able to take classes on the ship, but both are pretty iffy.

Finally, when off the stage, you might find yourself tempted to feel and act as if you're on vacation just like the passengers. Yet your time on a cruise ship is work time, with all the rules and responsibilities any job entails.

Of course there is an *upside* to working a cruise line as well. You don't have to pay for room and board. When the ship is docked, you can take a walk, check out the town, spend time on the beach, and eat at a restaurant of your choosing. On some ships all you'll be expected to do is perform in shows at night, leaving you free to do what you like during the day, exploring the ship or various ports and having fun. There will be times when you *can* feel like you're on a vacation. And of course the best part of it is that you'll be working at and getting paid for doing something you love, developing your talents, and building your resume.

Finding Cruise Line Jobs

Cruise ships always advertise in the trades. Your subscriptions to *Back Stage*, *Back Stage West*, and *Dirt Alert* will keep you current. There are so many cruise ships these days, with new ones being built all the time, that you'll see auditions listed every three months or so. It's a booming industry.

Since the cruise lines themselves don't have the expertise to put together shows, the majority of them are put together and cast through production companies. The production companies also place the ads in the trades, so it's fairly easy to find out their names and addresses. If you can't attend the audition that caught your eye but you'd like to work in one of the shows that company puts on, send along your picture, resume, and promotional tape, with a cover letter explaining the kind of job you want. Just be aware that these production companies get hundreds of tapes a week. It's a big help if you know someone in the industry who can help push your tape to the attention of the casting people. If you don't have an industry connection, be sure to phone the company a couple of weeks after mailing the package to make sure the people there have looked at your tape. Then ask for an audition. Remember that in this, as in every other aspect of your career, you have to take an active part in making things happen.

There are a few cruise ships that produce their own shows in-house. You can get this information by calling the cruise lines directly and listening to their recorded messages, which will include the names of those in charge of their entertainment departments, the addresses at which to contact them, and the types of material to send for them to determine if they want to audition you. Cruise lines that don't produce their own shows may well give you the number of the production company you need to contact.

Requirements of Performers

There's no doubt that, with the wide variety of shows on cruise lines, you can find some kind of job that will suit your talents. You may find some shows where you'll only need to sing but not dance, or where you'll only need to dance and not sing. But that doesn't happen often. Just as in theater jobs on land, specialization can be a drawback in finding work on cruise ships.

You can't be physically out of shape or carry too many extra pounds and work successfully as an entertainer on a ship. However, many entertainers gain weight on cruises because of the immense volume of food that's available, or because they start drinking. Many ships hold weigh-ins on a regular basis, and if you start putting on too many pounds you may find yourself out of a job.

Height requirements vary. Some cruise lines like their performers—especially their dancers—to be tall and statuesque, while others don't care. That means there's always work for shorter dancers, too. For the most part, they like attractive female performers and handsome male performers.

Living Arrangements Onboard

"Will I get my own cabin?" you might be asking. And the answer to that question is an emphatic "No!" At least not if you're a cast member. If you're a lead singer or a headliner, you will. If you're a dance captain or company manager, you might. But as a singer/dancer or dancer/singer, you'll be sharing your cabin with a roommate. Did I say "cabin"? Don't forget, this is a ship, so your living quarters may amount to little more than a walk-in closet with a shower and two beds.

Of course living conditions on cruise ships vary, and some cruise lines treat their performers better than others. One that performers consistently rave about is Crystal

Cruise Line. It treats its employees well, gives them decent-sized cabins they don't have to share with roommates, and pays good salaries. Unfortunately, these kinds of cruise lines seem to be the exception to the rule.

Salaries

Pay varies from ship to ship, from production company to production company. It also depends on the type of show, and what you're doing in it. Sometimes everyone is paid the same amount, usually starting at $600 a week. If you renew your contract, your salary goes up. On other ships, singers are paid differently from dancers. For example, a lead singer might earn more than a dancer, with a singer/dancer earning something in between. The highest paid performers are the headliners, lead singers, and the variety acts that perform thirty- to forty-five-minute shows.

Nonentertainment Duties

On some ships, you'll be assigned other responsibilities in addition to performing in the stage show. You might have to conduct bingo games, teach an aerobics class, play background piano in the lounge, or host the karaoke bar. On some ships performers are required to carry out some of the housekeeping duties. You might have to do these things every day, or just once a week. In some cases these duties will be part of your contract and nonnegotiable once you've signed it. In other cases the contract will state that you don't have to perform any extra duties unless you want to, and that you'll be paid extra if you do perform them. Check into this before you sign your contract, because once the ship is at sea you'll have no choice but to comply with these demands.

The Bottom Line

Cruise ship work isn't for everyone. Some cruise lines offer low pay, put on poor shows, and require performers to carry out plenty of nonentertainment duties. Others are terrific to work for. Remember, there's a hierarchy on a ship and you'll be low on the totem pole. There will be rules, and a lot of performers don't like to follow rules. They don't like being told when to be in bed, that lunch is strictly between 12 noon and 1 P.M. and dinner strictly from 6 P.M. to 7 P.M., or that they can drink beer but not wine.

Performers on cruise ships *are* on a strict schedules, and must toe the line in some respects. But on the whole it can be a good job if you know and like what you're getting into. If you're a young performer, you can use cruise ship work to save up some money and serve as a stepping stone in your career.

LAS VEGAS

I mention working in Las Vegas many times in this book. I worked there, and loved it. I loved the shows, the people, and the twenty-four-hour nonstop excitement you can't find anywhere else. Just keep in mind that Las Vegas is easy to visit, but getting a job there is another matter. If you're interested in working as a performer in Vegas, this section is aimed at helping you prepare in advance, so you'll be set to find work when you arrive.

Auditioning in Las Vegas

If you're thinking about working in Vegas but don't live there, you should visit for a weekend, to get a feel for the size, the climate, the city's layout in general. If you decide it's the right place for you, it shouldn't be hard to find an apartment, locate dance, voice, and acting classes, and start looking for auditions. Las Vegas has outstanding voice and dance teachers, as well as fine acting teachers. It is excellent for networking with people in show business who can help your career in many ways, and compared to New York, for example, it's a very reasonably priced place to live.

You should plan on an initial auditioning process of six months to a year. Apartment rentals are quite reasonable in Vegas. You might pay between $800 to $1200 a month for a studio apartment in New York, while a one-bedroom apartment will run between $400 to $500 a month in Las Vegas. Other costs are also low. Eating out can be so cheap that a lot of performers don't even bother to cook at home. All this is important, as you won't find yourself depleting your savings drastically as you look for work.

Types of Work to Audition For You can audition for a smorgasbord of jobs in Vegas, from floor shows to cruise lines to touring companies, to productions that play all over the world. The town probably has more singer–dancers employed on a full-time basis than any other city in the country, including New York.

There's also the matter of job longevity. In New York you might be able to perform in a long-running show like *Cats* for ten years or so. But that's an exception to the rule that most theater jobs in New York are only short term because most shows run for only short lengths of time. On the other hand, in Vegas you can work fifty-two weeks a year, if you want to, because many shows run for years at a time. That basically means full-time employment with extensive benefits, including health insurance and paid vacations, among other things.

Finding Out About Auditions A subscription to *Dirt Alert* (see Appendix) is probably the best way to keep up on Vegas auditions. Notices about auditions and job openings are also sometimes posted at dance, voice, and acting studios. But there is another route. If you know of some specific shows that you want to audition for, you can go to the stage door and ask to speak with the stage manager or dance captain, either before the first show of the evening, or in between shows. If a show is looking for new cast members, those in charge might audition you on the spot, or ask you come back the next day. If the show doesn't have any openings at the moment, the person you talk to will probably tell you about the next open call, and ask you to check *Dirt Alert* for details.

Allowing performers to audition at a moment's notice may seem like a very casual system, and it can be a very convenient way to find a job. But remember that you still need to do your homework before showing up at the stage door. As always, be prepared. If you don't present yourself as a professional from the beginning, you won't get an audition, much less a job.

Dancers in Las Vegas Shows

The first question most dancers interested in working in Las Vegas ask themselves is: Do I have to be tall to be hired? In the old days, every hotel had both a main stage show and a lounge show. The short and medium-height dancers worked the lounge, while the taller ones appeared on the main stage. Then the hotels began to eliminate the lounge shows, which meant they wanted all the dancers to be tall— in the range of 5 feet 11 inches or 6 feet for male dancers, and at least 5 feet 8 inches for female dancers. If you didn't measure up, you just didn't work. That has changed again. There are still shows, such as Donn Arden's *Jubilee*, where dancers must be tall to be hired, but in general these days Vegas is much more open to different heights. The *Siegfried and Roy* show, for example, uses dancers of all different heights, as does the *Enter the Night* production at the Stardust Hotel.

Working in Las Vegas is a great way to build your resume and make contacts. Shows such as "Enter the Night," at the Stardust Hotel, make you aware of the physical and height requirements necessary to land certain kinds of jobs.

Dance Work for Women The first type of female dancer most people associate with Las Vegas is what is often called the "showgirl." These dancers wear skimpy costumes, and in the past often performed topless or even nude. Showgirls are still around in abundance in Vegas. However, topless women dancers may be on their way out. This is because the direction is increasingly toward family-oriented entertainment in Vegas, especially during the early evening shows. Only a handful of shows still cast for topless or nude parts, among them *Jubilee* and *Enter the Night*. In virtually every other show, female dancers are "covered."

Vegas shows usually cast tall female dancers—say 5 feet 8 inches and over in height—as showgirls, and these are the women most likely asked to go topless if the show has topless dancers. Showgirls don't usually find themselves doing heavy duty dancing, even if they're well-trained dancers. Instead they parade around in elegant and glamorous outfits. Keep this in mind before accepting a job in the "showgirl" category since if you're a dancer it can obviously be frustrating to do work that doesn't allow you to use your dance talents.

Also keep in mind that if you're asked to go topless, you don't have to agree. At the very least, you can look elsewhere for work. And if you *do* accept the job, you won't be doing any erotic movements as in a burlesque house—no bumps and grinds. There's nothing sleazy about it. It's done tastefully, and the performers actually take pride in their work. Topless work also includes the monetary incentive of extra pay.

If you audition for a topless job, you'll be asked to remove your top privately for the show's director alone, not publicly in front of the other performers at the audition.

"Covered" female dancers do not go topless, but must still be physically fit and trim because their costumes can also be very revealing—the lower halves often being no more than G-strings or skirts with a French cut aimed at showing off their legs.

If you're not comfortable with the thought of wearing these kinds of costumes, attend a show before you go to any auditions. See how the costumes actually look onstage to the audience. You don't want to be wearing something you don't find acceptable. At the same time, being too rigid about what you will or will not wear limits your chances of finding work.

Dance Work for Men As with female dancers, these days there are jobs for male dancers of every height. And men must also be in great physical condition because their costumes are often just as skimpy as they are for women. Men dancers especially must have good upper body development, as their chests and shoulders are often exposed. Basically they need good shoulders, good pecs, and a tight waistline. Going to a gym on a regular basis is often part of their weekly routine.

As with women dancers, if you're a male dancer interested in working in Las Vegas but the idea of wearing a G-string and little else bothers you, go to an actual performance and see what it looks like from the audience's perspective. Limiting the types of costumes you will agree to wear will limit the number of jobs you'll be able to find.

The Audition Process

If you're specialized in your talents, Vegas is definitely a place where you can find work. There are a few new shows that are like Broadway revues, where you have to both sing and dance, but these are the exception. In Vegas, singers basically sing and dancers dance. If a singer has to make any movements, they're pretty simple. And only rarely are dancers asked to sing. You don't have to be a triple threat to have successful career in Vegas like you do in New York. Just keep in mind that you may not want to stay in Vegas forever. If musical theater in New York or other theater centers is your main goal, then you must develop your talents in all three areas of voice, dance, and acting. No matter what your job in Vegas, keep up your studies while you're there so you can prepare yourself for your future moves.

The audition process is simple. If you're going to a dance call, be prepared to dance. Just make sure to take everything you might need in your dance bag. Don't expect to sing. All the dancers are usually auditioned in the same room at the same time. The director or choreographer takes everyone up on stage, goes over a combination, then breaks the large group down into smaller groups who then do the dance steps. After the audition, you might be offered a job right there and then, or you might be called back to audition further on another day.

If you're auditioning as a singer, be prepared to sing. Like dancers, singers are usually all auditioned in the same room, but unlike dancers, they go onstage one at a time to perform. Also unlike dancers, who are not asked to sing, singers are sometimes asked to perform a simple dance combination—no heavy-duty dance steps, but something to show they know how to move onstage.

Makeup, Hair, and Clothing Some of the rules we have discussed about auditioning for theater jobs do not apply to auditioning in Vegas, especially for women. Vegas directors want to know what their performers will look like onstage. So women should not show up at Vegas auditions looking as much as possible like their headshots. They should always look glamorous, auditioning in full makeup and with their hair up. They should wear a very French-cut leotard that flatters their skin tone and eyes. They should never wear black. Instead, they should wear striking colors, something the casting people will find memorable so they can say, "We want to see that girl in yellow!" Women should also wear fish net stockings, as they are very flattering to the legs, and two-inch heel character shoes, which will make them look taller. As with any other audition, if you do get called back, wear the same outfit the second time around.

Some tips about makeup: Never wear a pastel-colored lipstick. Always wear bright red. And don't forget the lip gloss. False eyelashes aren't a bad idea, either, as you want to look as glamorous as possible. Don't wear street makeup, and apply your makeup a bit more heavily than usual. At auditions some Las Vegas directors like to put on all the lights without any filters, and once those lights hit you, you don't want to turn white or appear completely washed out.

Men don't have to wear makeup to auditions, but they should wear dance outfits that shows off the best physical attributes of their bodies—say a muscle shirt with close-fitting jazz pants, and jazz shoes. Never show up looking sloppy. The first impression is very important, so look smart and act professionally at all times.

Unions, Agents, and Earnings

Only a few shows—*Forever Plaid*, for example—in Vegas are Equity. Therefore, for the most part, you do not need to be a member of a performing union or have an agent to find work as an ensemble performer (chorus, lead singer, dancer) there. Because of this, Vegas is an ideal place to launch your career, to build up your resume, and to network. The people you meet in Vegas can be very helpful later on in your career, if you decide to make the move to New York.

Most of the time, for long-running shows, you will be employed directly by the hotel where you perform. As a hotel employee, you will get health insurance, a vacation package, and perhaps one free meal a day. For some shows you will be hired by an outside producer. In that case the benefits package, if any, will be different and the producer will tell you what your tax status is.

Wages for chorus performers currently run around $600 to $800 a week. Pay for specialty or principal performers is higher.

A Final Word About Vegas Work

The future for performers working in Vegas looks bright. A lot of new hotels are being built, which means more work for singers and dancers. In addition, the variety of types of work is expanding. Many of the new hotels are abandoning the standard Vegas table showroom look of the past, and going for the New York-style theater look. Some of the showrooms in the older hotels are being renovated, and also trending toward theater-style seating, with just a few tables.

Some theater professionals tend to put Vegas work down, as if it's not good enough for serious performers. Don't buy into this nonsense. Work is work, and, in this business, being employed is the name of the game. There are terrific shows and opportunities in Las Vegas. If you're one of the performers who decides to experience and take advantage of what it has to offer, you'll never regret it. It's a road that can lead you directly to Broadway.

13

MOVING INTO THEATER WORK

OK, we've talked about theater-related venues in Chapter 12—those that will help you build your resume and make contacts when you're just starting out. Maybe you're ready to move on from theme park work, cruise lines, or Las Vegas shows. Or maybe you're a "theater snob," one of those young performers who would give practically anything to sing and/or dance on the stage of a legitimate theater and don't want to explore other kinds of theater-related work.

In either case, this chapter applies to you. In it, I'll discuss the ins and outs of every theater experience you'll encounter: community theater, dinner theater, summer stock, regional theater, national touring companies, off-off-Broadway, and off-Broadway. I'll describe how and where to find jobs, what producers and directors are looking for in performers, how to prepare for auditions, and what you can expect to earn. I'll also discuss the jobs of swing performers and dance captains, two positions in theater work that beginners may not know too much about. (I'll discuss working on Broadway in Chapter 14.)

Are you ready? Let's go!

COMMUNITY THEATER

Community theater is run by and for people living in an area (town or city) who have a casual or a vocational interest in theater. Generally, no pay is involved. But as I showed in the case of high school performance (in Chapter 12), community theater is worth exploring as a way for young people to do roles in theater productions for the first time. Depending on the director and the quality of the work the theater produces, it can be a wonderful start.

The most important advantage of community theater is that it gets young performers used to being onstage and helps them develop their performing skills before live audiences. It also helps them learn how to audition, how to get to rehearsals on time, how to prepare for performances, how to work as part of a team, and how to cope with rejection when that issue comes up. Young performers will grow with this experience, picking up the basic skills they will need to pursue a show business career, and as they mature they will be able to move toward actual employment in the theater world.

Community theater also serves a social function, providing an outlet for people of all ages to come together and enjoy themselves within a theatrical environment. For kids it is a safe and positive environment as well, which will allow them to grow as individuals and performers.

And the disadvantages to working in community theater? There are none, but many times kids with no performing skills are pushed to attend auditions by Mom and Dad, even though performing may not interest them or be the field they want to pursue professionally. Under these circumstances, it's a total waste of time for everyone involved. Performing should be the performer's idea, as I've said elsewhere-not something only the parents want.

What to Look for in a Community Theater

If you're a teenager and interested in participating in your local community theater, or if you're a parent and your son or daughter wants to participate, there are several things to keep in mind. All young performers-to-be, in the formative stages of their lives both physically and emotionally, need to be in a supportive setting where they'll be learning and absorbing the craft of acting, dancing, and singing—instead of just getting up, reciting lines, and being the center of attention. So when thinking about auditioning for a community theater, ask yourself the following questions:

* What is the reputation of the theater? Theater *tends* to operate in a liberal environment, not a conservative one. Is there anything about the organization—its politics, its personalities, and so on—that might make the performer feel uncomfortable or regret getting involved? You want to avoid being shocked or disappointed somewhere down the line. So investigate the community theater to make sure everything associated with it is within your comfort zone. If anything conflicts with your values, look elsewhere for the young performer's initial theater experience.
* How good is the director and how does she or he work with young people?
* How does the theater handle rehearsals? How are they scheduled? If rehearsals are supposed to be on Monday, Wednesday, and Friday from 6 to 9 P.M., does the theater adhere to that agenda? Or is the theater disorganized? Does it constantly change rehearsal days, putting the lives of cast members—and the lives of the parents of cast members—constantly in chaos?
* Students, of course, have their school commitments: Will rehearsals and performances allow the student to have a life outside the theater, or will it take up all of his or her time for the next ten weeks?
* What responsibilities will parents have? Will there be any financial or time obligations?
* Most importantly, what will the young performer learn from the experience? Will it be of benefit educationally, in terms of a performing career? Let me emphasize that the experience may be fun, but it won't be worth much if he or she doesn't learn anything. In my opinion, education has to be the main goal. Young people need to be in a situation that produces growth and helps them on their journey of discovery as performers.

Finding Out About Auditions

The simplest way to find out about auditions is to phone your community theater and ask about them. Also ask the theater to put you on its audition mailing list. Most community theaters list auditions in the entertainment section of their local newspapers for several weeks when they are starting to prepare new shows. They may also run announcements in other local publications, such as specialty newsletters or magazines.

DINNER THEATER

You'll find dinner theaters all across the country. Wherever you live, the possibilities of finding one in which to work, close to your home, are in your favor. Dinner theaters are known for producing high-quality musicals, original shows, straight plays, children's theater, and revues. They offer young performers a chance to work and refine their craft in a professional or semiprofessional setting.

Types of Dinner Theater

There are two types of dinner theater. The first is where the audience is seated at tables in the theater where the show is to be presented. Sometimes audience members are served dinner by the cast members, sometimes by a waiting staff separate from the cast, and sometimes they serve themselves from a buffet and bring the food back to their tables. After dinner, the tables are cleared and the show begins. As a rule, dessert and drinks are not served during the performance, but instead during intermissions.

The second type of dinner theater is where dinner is served in one room, and after the meal the audience then moves to a theater space to watch the show.

In addition, there are both Equity and non-Equity dinner theaters. Some Equity dinner theaters require all cast members to be part of the Actors' Equity Association. If you are not a member of Equity, you may still be able to land a job there, working toward your Equity card through the Equity Membership Candidate Program (see Chapter 9). Other Equity dinner theaters simply hire Equity guest artists or star performers for their shows, while the rest of the cast is non-Equity.

Most dinner theaters run year-round, although a few limit their seasons to the summer only. Productions may run from as few as forty performances to as many as a hundred fifty, depending on the theater.

If you are considering auditioning for a dinner theater, there are some questions you ought to ask. First, if a theater is non-Equity, the most important question for you to ask is what other responsibilities you might be assigned. At some theaters, you'll be required to serve dinner, while at others it will be optional. The thought of waiting on tables may not appeal to you—serving food, being sociable with the audience, and dealing with the bills, along with getting ready for the show and actually performing, may be more than you're willing to do. But you should take into account the tips you'll receive, which will substantially increase your income over the pay you'll receive for just performing in the show. Know what you're getting into ahead of time so you won't regret it later.

Also, if the theater you'll be working for is out of town, ask about housing, transportation, and food stipends. Your salary may not cover your expenses if you have to pay for everything out of your own pocket.

Auditions

Most dinner theaters advertise their auditions in their local newspapers. If the theater you're interested in is located in another town or city, call the theater directly and ask to be put on its audition mailing list. You can also subscribe to newspapers and other publications in the town or city where the theater is located.

Some dinner theaters will let you submit your picture and resume along with a cover letter explaining the type of work you're interested in, while others will not. Some theaters will accept promotional tapes, others won't. But most dinner theaters don't appreciate performers just stopping by or trying to convince the casting people to hire them over the phone.

Some dinner theaters cast their own shows, while others do their casting through various organizations like the Regional Theater Conference or the National Dinner Theater Association. Most auditions are held at the theater where the show will be playing.

These days most dinner theaters cast show-by-show, using mostly local performers, but occasionally looking for talent from out of town. Others are more repertory in nature, tending to use the same pool of performers for all their shows. Finding work with the latter type of theater may not be easy.

Preparing to audition for a dinner theater is basically no different from preparing for any other kind of theater audition. Just remember to be prepared—if you're a dancer, make sure you have everything you need in your dance bag, and if you're a singer, be prepared to sing a song appropriate to the kind of show you're trying out for. Present yourself as a professional, and you'll be treated as one.

Salaries

If the dinner theater you're interested in is an Equity one, its pay scale is determined by the salary provisions of its Equity contract and its size. Pay at both Equity and non-Equity theaters runs from $175 to $250 a week at the low end to around $600 a week at the high end.

SUMMER STOCK

For performers just starting out in the musical theater business, summer stock can be a valuable tool. It is not only a valuable learning and performing experience, but a good way to network and meet extremely valuable contacts who can be helpful in establishing a successful career in musical theater.

Kinds of Summer Stock Theaters

There are many different types of summer stock theaters, so you'll have to choose one that best serves your needs and enables you to grow in the direction you want to go.

Some are affiliated with a performing union, and others are not. Some are not affiliated with a performing union, but *are* affiliated with unions representing stage hands or musicians. Some are not affiliated with unions at all. Some theaters offer beginners a program in which they receive training as interns or apprentices without any pay, while others will hire beginners as paid cast members if they're good enough but offer no further training. Occasionally, you'll find a mixture of the two. Most summer stock theaters mount all their productions independently, but some have a mixed season where they mount a couple of productions themselves but bring in touring shows as well.

The kinds of contracts summer stock theaters offer performers also vary tremendously, from the standard performing union contracts to nonunion contracts with all kinds of provisions written into them.

The sizes of summer stock venues vary as well, from small theaters seating only a hundred or so to huge amphitheaters able to accommodate audiences in the thousands. Some theaters have live orchestras, while others use taped music. Some theaters specialize in large-scale, standard musicals, others in straight plays, with the occasional small musical. There are even outdoor venues that put on a single show for the entire summer.

Finding the Right Kind of Theater

As you can see, you'll encounter quite a variety of formats, rules, and demands if you decide to pursue summer stock. This means you should do some research to decide which venue is best for you.

If you're interested in a theater located near you, talk to people who have worked there. Find out about work conditions and how performers are treated by the theater's management. Make sure the theater puts on the kinds of plays you're interested in, and that you'll gain a variety of performing experiences that will stand you in good stead in the future.

There are horror stories about some summer stock theaters where beginners are expected to sleep on the premises and perform in up to four shows concurrently, where there are no designated rest breaks, or where the paychecks bounce. You want to avoid that kind of situation. On the other hand, there are some great theaters out there to work for, like Music Theatre of Wichita, Kansas, which brings in a different director and choreographer for each show. This allows young performers to experience a variety of production styles, teaching methods, and working situations. And since the people brought in come from some of the important musical theater centers like New York, it allows beginners to start building the network of contacts they'll need in the future.

Equity Versus Non-Equity Theaters

As a beginner, your best bets are to find work at an Equity theater as an Equity Member Candidate working toward your membership in Equity, or at a non-Equity theater that hires guest Equity performers. Either is preferable to working in totally nonunion shows. I'm not saying that you won't get valuable experience working in a theater that's entirely nonunion, but such theaters offer few protections in regard to working conditions and pay. As a nonunion performer, you won't be covered by union provisions even at theaters having a union affiliation. But the union affiliation usually indicates better working conditions for everyone.

Auditions

While some summer stock theaters do mailings to colleges and universities, the best source for finding out about summer stock jobs is the *Summer Theatre Directory* (see the Appendix), which provides listings of theaters state by state, including information on theater size, union affiliation, salary ranges, transportation and housing stipends, months of operation, the types of shows each theater does, and (if available) the names of the specific shows to be performed the next season. The listings also provide vital audition data such as the names of producers, directors, choreographers, and casting people, phone numbers and mailing addresses, and breakdowns of how many performers each theater expects to hire for the next summer season. You'll find out how large a theater is, the salary range, and what they provide in the way of transportation and housing. Of course, summer stock auditions are also listed in that old reliable, *Back Stage*.

Applying for an Audition   Once you've decided on the theater you'd like to work for, what next? Every theater has different guidelines regarding applications, and specific deadlines by which it must receive your picture and resume. If the casting people like what you send and are interested in auditioning you, they'll set up an appointment time at a regional site closest to your hometown during their national audition tour or will notify you of the open call at their theater. Some theaters participate in what is known as regional combined auditions, in which the producers and directors of many summer stock theaters attend one large audition at which they all cast for the next season at one time. Whatever the audition process, just remember that summer stock theaters rarely audition via promotional videotapes, so you should be prepared to do some traveling if your theater of choice isn't located near where you live.

Your cover letter (see Chapter 8) should be friendly and detailed. Describe carefully the kind of work you're interested in. Show that you've researched summer stock theaters and know what you're talking about in regard to working at that particular theater. From you're resume it will be clear that you're just starting out, but if your letter is professional in tone, the casting people will take your application to work at the theater seriously.

Mail your cover letter, resume, and picture to the theaters that interest you no later than the end of January for the following summer season. Most summer stock theaters receive around 2000 or 3000 applications each season, and screen those down to 750 or so performers they ask to audition. That means 60 to 75 percent of all applications are eliminated right off the top, making it doubly important that you get it right in the material you send. The criteria casting people use in eliminating applications include the following:

Not having the proper background or skills to play the roles that are being cast for. Make sure you know the plays and musicals the theater will be putting on, and pitch your resume and cover letter accordingly.

Bad working attitudes, unpleasant personalities, and bad tempers. This mostly applies to applications from performers who have worked for directors, producers, or choreographers in the past, or performers whose bad reputations are widely known in the business. As a newcomer, this most likely will not apply to you. But that makes it all the more important to come off as professional in your cover letter and resume. This can be the start of a good reputation as someone people will enjoy working with.

If an applicant is an acquaintance of someone the director, producer, or chore-ographer has worked with previously, he or she will likely get a second look. So in your cover letter make sure to mention anyone whom you know, so long as the working relationship was an amicable one.

Once the applications have been winnowed down, those that are left will be contacted to schedule audition times. Most auditions begin in February, and wrap up no later than April.

The application process for combined regional auditions is similar to that for individual theater auditions, but you'll have to fill out an initial application form and pay a fee.

The Audition Process As a performer in summer stock, you have to be proficient in all three performing fields of singing, acting, and dancing. Each person is usually given five minutes for the singing and acting segment of the audition. The performer comes in and is asked to sing two songs, neither of which should last longer than sixty or ninety seconds. Then, during the remaining two or three minutes, the performer is asked to read some dialogue. If this is not dialogue you have prepared ahead of time but a script the casting people hand you, you must be able to quickly assess the character you're portraying. Who is saying the lines? Does the reading require a certain accent, age, or attitude? You have to be able to convey a lot, instantly.

At some point during the day, there will usually be an open dance call in which everyone is auditioned at the same time. Callbacks are sometimes held later the same day, and sometimes on later days.

At auditions, summer stock directors and production staff members focus first on finding performers who have the talents they need for the shows they will be producing the next season. Second, they look for people with a good attitude. They don't want troublemakers who will cause conflict during the summer.

The rehearsal and performance schedules are quick in summer stock. This mandates that everyone work together as a team, from the highest-ranking Equity star to the most inexperienced apprentice still attending high school. If you're not a team player, no matter how talented you are as a performer, summer stock theater will have no use for you—and summer stock casting people are good at spotting this ability to work as part of a team early in the audition process.

As I've said, summer stock theaters, especially those that are Equity, look for performers who can sing, dance, and act. You can be stronger in one area than the others, but you need to be competent in all three. This is because as a nonunion cast member more than likely you'll be hired as a member of the chorus, where everybody needs to be a triple threat.

In addition, the casting people for summer stock theaters look for people who have done their homework in regard to the shows they're trying out for. So make sure you know the productions the theaters are casting for, and before auditioning read up on them. If a show is on film, rent the video; if its soundtrack has been recorded, buy the tape or CD. Research like that will help you in the audition, and will be noticed by the people who do the hiring.

What Summer Stock Can Teach You

Because summer stock requires learning and performing a lot of material in a condensed period of time, it pushes people toward becoming well-rounded and versatile performers, as well as quick studies. Remember, in just one season, you might find yourself performing in *Crazy for You* and *Oklahoma!*, two dramatically different dance shows with wildly varying stylistic demands.

Some summer stock theaters offer classes one evening a week. These classes teach performers all kinds of useful things, including how to write resumes, how to select good audition material, how to avoid unscrupulous managers, when to join a union, even how to do taxes. Thus, for beginners, working at these theaters provides not only the experience of performing before live audiences, but the opportunity for personal learning and growth. Occasionally, even the guest artists get involved in teaching the classes.

Working in summer stock is also an excellent way of networking. Beginners will be meeting many people who can be of help later on in building successful careers, and should use every day to add new names to their contact sheets or address books.

Salaries

No, you won't get rich doing summer stock. Here's the rundown on pay scales: In some theaters, nonunion performers don't get paid at all—they just get on-the-job experience, the chance to network, and a credit to add to their resumes. At theaters where they do get paid, the average nonunion performer makes $50 a week at the low end to $250 a week at the high end. Equity performers make the Equity minimum for the theater where they work, which depends on the Equity contract pay provisions and the size of the house. Principal performers usually have agents who negotiate their contracts and pay.

Despite the lack of good pay, I don't think young performers should pass up the chance to do summer stock. Remember, training in your craft, adding to your resume, networking, and building a list of contacts are some of the most valuable activities that you as a beginner can engage in to help ensure a long and prosperous career in musical theater.

REGIONAL THEATER

Regional theater is a movement that began some thirty years ago, involving twenty or thirty theaters around the country supported mostly by government and foundation money. Regional theaters differ from community theaters in that the latter are, by and large, nonprofessional in nature, geared to serve the needs of people in a region who love to work in theater for the sake of working in theater, rather than for the sake of pursuing a professional theater career. The aim of the regional theater movement, on the other hand, has been to create professional venues whose focus is regional and which will develop pools of local talent rather than importing performers, directors, and other theater professionals from New York or Hollywood.

Regional theater these days is more active than ever. Currently there are over two hundred regional theaters nationwide, some union and others nonunion, ranging in size from small venues seating around three hundred to large ones seating over a thousand and specializing in everything from musical theater to puppet shows. Recent statistics from Actors' Equity show that regional theaters currently employ more performers than Broadway, indicating their importance as the backbone of employment opportunities for professional theatrical talent.

Regional theater can help you on your road to Broadway in several ways. The primary benefit is the performing experience you'll gain, which is at a higher level than that offered by community theater or even college and university theater programs. While community and college theaters offer valid work and opportunities to explore and expand your talents as a performer, you will eventually hit a glass ceiling beyond which you cannot go. In regional theater you'll find work that challenges and stretches you as a performer. A second benefit has to do with networking. In community theater you may find yourself working with dentists or car salesmen who pursue acting in their spare time, and in college drama programs you'll be working with students who are beginners like yourself, and who are just as likely to change their majors to business or some type of technical field as they are to remain in the performing field. But in regional theater you'll actually find yourself working with other professional performers. This will not only teach you something about being a professional performer yourself, but offer you contacts with those who already know their way around the industry and may be of help to you in building your career.

Types of Regional Theaters

Regional theaters are categorized by the League of Regional Theaters (LORT) as level A, B, C, or D. These categories are based on actual box office receipts, averaged over three complete fiscal years. LORT A theaters bring in the highest box office receipts, while LORT D theaters bring in the lowest. Clearly the categories are also related to theater size. As an example, a theater on the high end, like the main stage of the Guthrie Theater in Minneapolis, Minnesota, is considered LORT A, and seats 1300 people. Its second stage, called the "Lab," seats 300 and is categorized as LORT D. The Long Wharf Theater in New Haven, Connecticut, also has two stages, but one is categorized as LORT C and the other as LORT D. This means neither brings in as high a level of cash receipts as the main stage at the Guthrie, and also that neither seats as large an audience as the Guthrie's main stage.

Note that LORT categories refer only to the size of box office receipts and the number of seats, not the quality of productions. Some plays lend themselves to large theaters and stages, and others to smaller venues. You probably wouldn't find a two-character play being performed at a LORT A theater since the small-scale setting of a LORT C or D stage would be more likely to provide the intimacy such a production requires. Likewise you wouldn't find a full-scale musical like *Oklahoma!* being put on at a LORT D theater. But the quality of both productions could be equally high.

Another distinction between various regional theaters is whether they are union-affiliated or not. Again, this has nothing to do with quality of productions. The issues here are differences in pay scales and adhering to performing union work rules. There are some wonderful nonunion regional venues, such as the Pollard Theater, in Guthrie, Oklahoma, that are committed to producing quality work.

Starting Out in Regional Theater

You may find an opportunity to go from a college theater program to an internship or, through a successful audition, a paying job at a regional theater. You'll find some stark differences in these two types of theater experience. First, in regional theater the competition for roles is more intense than it is in the educational theater. The turnover in roles is faster. Your chance of landing roles depends on your abilities, but also on how well you work with directors, producers, and other performers. You have the opportunity to learn how to interact in a professional way—something you'll need to know to further your career.

If you attend the performing arts program of a university, make sure it's one with good teachers who know the ropes of the professional theater world. University training is good, but there are an awful lot of people coming out of universities unprepared to work professionally.

Students in college or university performing arts programs are often permitted to sink to their level of ability and to remain there indefinitely without learning the professional skills they will need to survive in the world of professional theater. Just be aware that in a university theater setting, you can find yourself in a situation that will poorly prepare you for your professional one later on. For instance, a student with great ability in the program may get all the lead roles. This means that either he or she is already beyond the level of training that can be offered at that institution, or the school has an abundance of students who don't have much previous training. This does none of the students much good. The students with less training are shut out of important roles, while those being handed all the lead roles don't learn how to compete effectively with those as talented or well trained as themselves. Likewise, even if students are cast at their level of ability, beginners may be placed in the "back row," so to speak, where they can hardly be seen at all. And because of the time put into preparing university productions, once you're placed in the back row, you may be forgotten completely. Young performers in regional theater, on the other hand, find themselves forced to develop their skills and abilities. It can be a big change-but, of course, it is one that can only help their careers later on.

If you do find yourself performing at a regional theater right off, you probably won't start out as an Equity performer, but finding work as a nonunion cast member in an Equity theater can be very valuable to your career. Again, you'll be working in a professional environment. You'll learn the Equity rules and how a professional theater operates. This experience can only benefit you, helping you to build up contacts with people in the industry.

Let's face it, theater is really a big club, or lots of small ones, and people tend to hire people they know. If you're really serious about your career as a performer, regional theater is a good route to gain admission to the right theater "club"—the one with the best contacts to help you become upwardly mobile in the theater world. In regional theater, you'll find actors at the Mark Taper Forum who are in contact with the Guthrie Theater who are in touch with the Alley and the Hartford, and so on. At the upper levels of the theater world, everybody knows everybody else, and if *you* know the right people it will certainly put you in a place where agents, directors, and producers will come to see your work.

Regional theater provides you with the opportunity to perform in front of live audiences and get paid for the experience. You'll learn what it's like to deal with a long-running production, honing your performance skills along the way.

Resident Companies

There used to be a time when regional theaters commonly had resident companies, or a group of actors who, for one specific season, signed a contract and made up the cast for all the shows. A female performer in that situation might find herself playing everyone from Nora in *Brighton Beach Memoirs* to Fanny Brice in *Funny Girl* to Daisy in *Driving Miss Daisy!* That is, actors were exposed to a wide range of roles as part of the company. Today, most regional theaters no longer have resident companies per se, and don't sign year-long or seasonal contracts with actors. Instead, they hire actors according to the production, job by job. If the role is right for you, you'll be cast; otherwise, it's on to the next show.

Regional Theater and the Triple Threat

As we've learned throughout this book, it's good to be a triple threat whatever jobs you audition for, and regional theater is no exception. The more things you can do, and the more flexible you are in terms of your training, skills, talent, and experience, the more qualified you'll be for different kinds of jobs and the more likely you'll be able to land the jobs you want when they come along.

Say you play the banjo, and come across a super role as a banjo player. You have a leg up on the competition. Obviously, going out and taking a crash course in banjo playing when such a role comes up isn't practical. What *is* practical, however, is deciding which skills are stage-appropriate, and setting out to acquire them if you don't already have them, or improve them if you already have the rudiments. These skills can include basic stage abilities you may not have developed thoroughly yet, like acting, dancing, or singing, or more exotic abilities like juggling, performing as a clown, gymnastics, fencing, and so on. You can also add specialized skills in the major areas, including tap, ballet, jazz, classical acting, and dialects. The more you have to offer, the more likely you'll fit in with some casting director's idea of what he or she is looking for. The whole secret of being successful is knowing how to combine luck, talent, professionalism, perseverance, and luck. Notice that luck appears at the beginning and the end of that short list. Think about it.

Auditioning for Regional Theater

Some regional theaters do their auditions at the theaters themselves, others do them at theater conferences, while still others do them through university/resident theater association auditions. Some regional theaters complain that when they look for talent at outside venues, they can't find the kinds of performers they need. Because of that, they just audition locally.

There are many ways for you to find out about regional theater auditions. Some theaters place notices in the local newspapers. You can also call the theaters directly and ask about openings. If told that the theater keeps an active file of performers, send along a headshot and resume, accompanied by a cover letter describing the kind of roles you're interested in, so the theater can notify you about auditions. Another good source of information is the *Regional Theatre Directory*, compiled and edited by Jill Charles (see the Appendix).

Regional theater auditions are, for the most part, less stressful than those for Broadway shows, simply because fewer people attend them. However, there are still some pointers to remember. First, if you're auditioning for a particular role, and the director asks if you're interested in another, it's all right to say no. If, on the other hand, you say that you are interested in the other role, then two weeks later you take another job elsewhere and aren't available to perform it, there will be a black mark on your record. While it won't be harmful at the moment because you already have a job, it could damage future job opportunities at the theater where you were offered the role, with the director running the show, or even with other directors or producers who hear about the incident.

Auditioning is an inexact science, both for performers and for casting people, and directors look at everything they can to decide who they want to hire. They pay attention to how you dress and present yourself, if you have poise, if you're prepared for any contingency. For example, say you come in with a tape, and the house tape deck isn't working properly. If you can say, "I have my own deck here. Let me set it up so you can hear my tape," the director will note that you are someone on their toes. Remember to always present yourself as if you had never seen the director or other casting staff before, even if you know them well. You don't want to insult them by treating the audition casually, as if you're just walking through the process. Always show the proper respect.

Rehearsals

In regional theater, for the most part you'll be doing shows that have already been mounted, in which case it doesn't take as long to work out the kinks of the production. Usually, depending on how much money the company has budgeted and how long the run will be, rehearsals will last a week or two.

Earnings

In Equity theaters, the pay will range from minimums of $500 to $700 a week on up, depending on the category of the theater. In nonunion theaters, the pay can be just about anything, so make sure to settle that question before signing your contract.

NATIONAL TOURING COMPANIES

A national touring company is a show which, in its entirety, plays a number of theaters in a variety of cities. The entire show travels to a new town daily, weekly, or monthly, doing the very same show, repeatedly. The tour can continue for years, or be of very short duration.

A national tour is a great job, because it offers some of the best pay in the business. During the tour, not only are you paid a salary, but the company pays you a per diem rate, covering meals and lodging. This "allowance" lets a performer go on tour and build a healthy bank account. Because of this, many Broadway performers will leave New York to participate in a show's national tour, simply for the money. Tours are great in other ways too. If you love to travel, and know how to get along with people in travel situations, it's a great way to see the country, or even the world. At the end of the tour or after a long while on the road, you may be happy to come home again, but you will still have enjoyed a wide variety of experiences, going places, seeing things, and meeting people, that would not have been possible if you hadn't been on the tour.

Types of Tours

There are a lot of different types of national tours. The most important breakdown is probably Equity versus non-Equity tours. But there are other distinctions too.

Equity (or Union) Tours One type of tour you may find yourself doing is every performer's dream, the first national touring company of a Broadway show. *Ragtime* is a prime example. This type of show travels to a city, loads in, and stays there for two or three months. The reason everyone loves doing the first national tour of a Broadway production is because it's the first time a particular show will be seen around the world, and a lot of media attention is focused on it.

A second type of tour you may find yourself doing is known as a "bus and truck" tour. Actors' Equity defines a bus and truck tour as one which uses buses and trucks to transport a show from one city or town to another for a series of consecutive engagements, a majority of which are one week or less in duration. You might find yourself playing a theater for two or three days, then getting on a bus and moving to a new location where you'll perform another few days, then getting on a bus and moving on . . . and so on.

A third type of tour is called a "split week" tour. As defined by Actors' Equity, a split week tour means (a) a majority of the total weeks of the tour are engagements of less than one week, (b) at least 80 percent of the total weeks of the tour involve engagements of one week or less in duration, (c) no more than 20 percent of the total weeks of the tour involve engagements longer than one week in duration, (d) no single engagement is longer than four weeks in duration, and (e) no actor's total compensation, for any week of the tour, is more than $10,000 per week.

Shows usually enter the category of bus and truck or split week, playing a slew of one-nighters, when they have gotten old and the audience wishing to see them has diminished. Take well-known musicals like *Cats* and *Miss Saigon*, for example. When they began touring, they would play for many months at one location before moving on to another city because their ticket sales supported such long stays. But as the years went by, fewer people around the country went to see either show, whether as repeats or even first-time attendees. So as their touring audiences decreased, so did the length of time they stayed in any one city. Nowadays, when *Cats* plays around the country, it's not uncommon for it to run for just a few nights at a theater before packing up and heading elsewhere.

Non-Equity (or Nonunion) Tours The first national touring companies for Broadway shows are never nonunion. That means bus and truck and the split week are the most common types of tours you'll find in non-Equity companies.

What to Expect on a Tour

On Equity tours, how you are treated is governed by Equity rules as expressed in the Equity contract you sign. This means the touring company is legally obligated to treat you in certain ways. And Equity has rules covering everything—from the amount of time you have off between performances, to safe and sanitary conditions in the theaters where you perform, dressing room rules, the rest periods you must be allowed during performances, and tentative route sheets that must be attached to your contract. Essentially, you are protected from everything that could go wrong, across the board. In a union show, if you don't receive your paycheck, or if the stage is made of concrete, you can call your union representative for help. If you're cast in an Equity show, there may be deputies (union representatives) for chorus singers and chorus dancers, in addition to deputies for principal actors. Deputies are cast members selected for the post through a vote by all the cast members at the first rehearsal. Because most cast members don't want to be a deputy, it's up to you to accept or decline any nomination. The individual selected has the duty and obligation to report any noncompliance with the agreements and rules that govern employment under the production contract with Actors' Equity. Every Equity house has to meet this requirement, with the deputy acting as the liaison between the show and the union.

On nonunion tours, your working conditions and the way you will be treated by theaters and production companies on will depend on the company you work for instead of an Equity contract. If the company wanted, it could put up a show in the morning, have you perform it that evening, then load up and travel all night to get to the next town by morning, where the process would start all over again, and you would have to go along with it.

Production companies *can* do this, although usually they don't. Obviously, these kinds of producers would be found out in a hurry if they treated their people so poorly, and wouldn't remain in business for long. For that reason, performers usually don't have to worry about extremely outrageous working conditions. Most nonunion tours try to follow the same guidelines as union shows, and I have heard very good things about several nonunion companies such as Troika and Jericko. Still, when the stories about other companies are bad, they're really bad. Because of this, it's very important for young performers who are thinking about touring with nonunion companies to check into the reputations of the companies they're thinking of signing with. If you're interested in going on a tour, ask around. Pay attention to word of mouth, and to the experiences of other performers.

Transportation

Some union tours fly performers between states and then bus them to different locations within each state. But flying versus being bused depends on where the bookings are, the contractual provisions regarding transportation, and the budget the production has to work with.

As I noted earlier, some tours, particularly non-Equity shows, primarily use buses because (1) they don't have the time to fly performers around, and doing so would conflict with the show's itinerary, especially when doing bus-and-truck or split-week tours, or 2) they don't have the budget to pay for air travel. Busing a cast is a lot cheaper than flying them to each location, and every company is going to trim costs wherever it can.

The Experience of Being on Tour

To be honest, touring can be a bit stressful, and that's where a good attitude comes into play. Working, living, traveling, and socializing together week after week means the members of a show actually become a close-knit family. This being the case, it's important that you as a member of a touring cast be pleasant to be around and have a good reputation. As this unit travels around the country, you will find yourself

Grease! *companies, like Troika Productions, offer young performers the chance to tour nationally in nonunion productions, gain experience, and build their resumes doing good-quality shows.*

having little contact with people other than those in the cast. They'll be all you have, and like family members who are forced together for an extended period of time, it can get tense. Anytime you're thrust together with people you don't like, or have little in common with besides the job, you really have to make an effort to get along. The best scenario might be for you to have a best friend on the tour, another performer whom you auditioned, and were cast, with. That way you would have someone you know, like, and trust to share time and expenses with. Even if there are some individuals on the tour you just don't like—and there will be—don't create unnecessary friction. You may find yourself working with them again in the future.

Taking Classes on Tour Just because you're on the road, don't think you should stop your training or practicing. Many performers think that once they land a job, they're set for life. They don't look ahead to the future, where they'll have to audition for new roles with new demands, and where if they're unprepared, they'll lose out on landing those jobs. As a performer, it's important that you stay prepared and in shape, whether that means taking a ballet barre daily by yourself, having someone in the show conduct a daily class, or attending a good studio in each city where you're performing. I realize that it may be hard to bridge the gap between fatigue and practice, but you should really try to do it.

Keeping a Show "Tight" In every show, everyone in the cast has to give it their all, one hundred percent, every time they walk out on the stage. It's hard to do a show the same way, night after night, for six months, especially if you're locked into the same theater the whole time. One thing that helps keep a touring show fresh is that when the cast arrives in a new city, the performers must block the show onto the new stage. In each theater they have to make small adjustments, since what worked onstage in one town may not work in the next one. That alone can keep your work fresh and exciting.

In any show you do, you'll get notes from the dance captain or the stage manager. If necessary, a clean-up rehearsal will be called. If you're one of those performers who are persistently sloppy, you will receive a warning, and be written up to Actors' Equity. Whether you're on a union or a nonunion tour, it's wise to always do your best. Remember, performing is a job, not a hobby, and you'll want to be able to find work when the current show closes.

Your Obligations While on Tour

Usually, for a national tour, you'll sign a six month contract. Because you're out on the road, it costs the production company money for a replacement if you decide to leave. If you quit, the company would have to rehearse someone in New York, or wherever its logistical hub is, and then send the person out to the company and rehearse her or him some more on the road. That's why most companies don't do month-to-month contracts. They prefer that performers stay with shows for a specific, longer-term length of time. And remember, while your contract may run from six months to a year, with a four-week "out" clause, you won't be able to use that clause before the end of your term.

Aside from contractual obligations, whether you're doing an Equity or a non-Equity production, you may be asked to volunteer to do some publicity as part of your job, such as appearing on an early morning TV or radio show, giving newspaper interviews, or performing in a publicity stunt at a local shopping mall. This extra effort shouldn't be a big deal to you, and you really shouldn't make an issue of it. Be a team player, and don't argue. You don't want people shaking their heads, refusing to work with you again.

Per Diems and Salaries

A per diem is an allotment of money you receive each day while on the road, basically for food and lodging. Transportation is almost always supplied by the company, so your per diem won't be used for that. It can be a very good deal, and, if used wisely, it's usually more than you need to pay your living expenses on a tour. Living off your per diem, and banking your paycheck, should be your goal. You can easily do that by living simply while on the road: not eating at fancy, expensive restaurants every day, not choosing the most expensive hotel off the list of hotels the production manager will supply you with in each city. You can also save money by having a roommate to split the hotel bill with, by not going crazy partying all the time, and by not getting involved with the use of alcohol, or worse yet, drugs. It seems many performers get involved with illegal drugs, cocaine being at the top of the list. But don't be foolish and reckless about how you live your life on tour. You won't just ruin your finances—you may also ruin your health and your career.

At the time of this book's publication, salaries for performers on Equity tours were running anywhere from $650 to $1100 a week, and the per diem was $100 a day, or $700 a week. Obviously, if you're smart with your money, you can make a pretty good living by doing union tours. Nonunion shows pay less, but you can use the experience to build up your resume so you can land leading parts, which pay more. Keep in mind that as a beginner in Equity shows, you would not get leading roles for quite some time.

While you're out on the road, the production company will mail the company manager all the pay checks, usually on a Thursday, so that you can get your check to the bank on Friday, a bank which the company manager will have made arrangements with to cash the checks. In this way, you can have some walking-around money.

SWING PERFORMERS AND DANCE CAPTAINS

I said at the start of this chapter that I'd discuss the jobs of swing performers and dance captains. What are these two positions and what kind of theater work do they entail?

Swing Performers

A "*swing*," as the job is often called, is an individual cast to understudy all or some members of the ensemble. In a musical like *Tommy*, there may be two or three swings. Swings have to know how many people they cover, and all the "tracks" of each of those cast members, throughout the show, which means how the performers move on stage, or their blocking, for the duration of the show. If you're hired as a swing, you must keep a book of each character's tracks and write them out. In this way you can study them and memorize them. In a featured show, like *Tommy*, this can be quite a job, since every character has different tracks. In a nonfeatured show, such as the *Will Rogers Follies*, being a swing is easier since just about every character does the same thing. Everyone dances the same choreography, and the differences between what performers do are basically just a question of where they stand onstage.

Not everyone makes a good swing. The work is stressful, and you must be able to handle pressure. You have to be willing to work very hard, and, at the same time, not expect any credit for it. You won't be opening on opening night. You are merely there to replace any of the people you cover, at any time, and you must know all of their parts well. If you don't, you could hurt people on stage or get hurt yourself. Because of all the pressure, if you're not good at retaining information, this job isn't for you.

Once performers have worked as swings, it's only natural that producers and directors may peg them as swings. It can be very hard to break out of that stereotype, and for that reason many performers will not swing shows. And the job has other downsides from the point of view of most performers. For instance, swings must attend all the understudy rehearsals. In effect, they're in rehearsal all the time. Unlike the other chorus members, who come in and work three hours a day, swings work every night and rehearse twice a week during the day, not to mention matinees twice a week.

Swings don't have the same life as other cast members. It's a big commitment, and if you're considering as job as a swing. you will have to decide if the mental strain and stress is worth it.

Despite the perceived negatives, there is a good side to being a swing. Swings get paid a bit more for their work than other cast members. They learn a lot of parts from the shows they swing. This makes them very valuable performers. If you accept a job as a swing, you'll never get bored or tired of the show in the same way that members of the regular cast may, because you will always be doing a different role. That keeps the job very challenging and stimulating. Also swings are a hard-to-find commodity. Once producers and directors know you have done this duty before and are good at it, they'll seek you out to work in their shows. You probably will never be out of work.

Dance Captains

Being a *dance captain* is a big commitment. A dance captain watches the show and keeps it clean. He or she is in charge of taking and giving notes to the performers.

Other responsibilities may include teaching the show to new members. It's a big responsibility, and dance captains must have great people skills. Otherwise, the cast members are going to dislike you—and many dance captains *are* disliked. And nine times out of ten, the people running shows also want dance captains to swing.

On the upside, dance captain is a great job to learn from, and if you ever get a chance to do it, jump at it. When the choreographer is in town, you'll take notes for him or her. You'll learn to recognize all the seemingly small details, the important elements, that make a musical special, that you may never have previously thought about. Your whole perspective on whatever show you're working in will open up and you'll start to understand all the parts of that show, including its technical aspects, not just one part of it.

Just keep in mind that the jobs of swing and dance captain are both driven by the clock, and require strong commitment. Definitely, they are not for everyone.

OFF-OFF-BROADWAY

The idea of off-off-Broadway really started in the late 1950s and early 1960s, with Cafe Cino and Cafe La MaMa, in Greenwich Village—tiny venues that were able to do shows that were considered too avant garde, risqué, or risky for commercial producers.

From the start, off-off-Broadway was considered neither amateur or professional, just a haven for different types of shows done on shoestring budgets. Writers who wanted to experiment with their new work would hold readings and do just the first act of a play, or develop it more fully. Off-off-Broadway was the place to do this. It was risk-free theatrical environment, where playwrights had nothing to lose.

Many writers sprouted from these types of theaters in the 1960s, notably Sam Shepard and Lanford Wilson. Gerald M. Berkowitz, in his book *New Broadways*, reminds us that the Broadway hit musical *A Chorus Line* began in a series of off-off-Broadway workshops and improvisational sessions, during which the real-life, personal experiences of several Broadway dancers were combined and developed into a script.

Most off-off-Broadway theaters lose money. Actors usually do not get paid in their shows, but the costs of running these theaters in New York—including rent, insurance, and utilities—are astronomical. As a result, the theaters are usually run as nonprofit institutions and survive financially through grants and private contributions.

Very few off-off-Broadway theaters survive for very long, but there are still plenty of them around. They seat audiences of ninety-nine people or less and are located all over New York. They also offer very interesting kinds of work for beginning performers: original works of all types, dramas, musicals, reviews, one acters, full-length shows. But they play for only three or four weeks, then close.

Just remember that performers usually don't get paid in off-off-Broadway theaters. If the theaters pay anyone, it's likely to be the administrative or technical staff, and even those people don't get much, more like stipends than salaries.

Showcases

A *showcase* is an off-off-Broadway show that plays up to sixteen performances, after which it closes and a new show is mounted. Showcases are produced on shoestring budgets. You can find out about auditions for them in *Back Stage*, which lists the names of these shows, gives a breakdown of the roles being cast, and describes whether each show is Equity or non-Equity and whether performers are paid or not.

If you are not an Equity member, you can still show up at the open calls for Equity showcases, even though you usually won't be considered. Non-Equity showcases, on the other hand, can only hire non-Equity performers. If a show is non-Equity and becomes successful, the theater has the option to extend the run. If it's an Equity showcase, according to Equity rules it must close after sixteen performances or the actors must begin receiving compensation.

Doing an Equity Showcase

If the off-off-Broadway theater is Equity, and performs under an Equity showcase code, the theater must abide by certain rules and restrictions in how it treats performers. Initially, performers can perform for free, but as already noted, after sixteen performances, they must be paid. There are also Equity rules regarding how long performers can rehearse. And if an Equity show moves from off-off-Broadway to off-Broadway, Equity rules state that either (1) performers must be offered the same role in the off-Broadway production, or (2) if they are not, they must receive financial compensation equaling the amount they would have received during the rehearsal period prior to the show opening off-Broadway.

Why Perform in Off-off-Broadway Productions?

There are a number of reasons you might find these nonpaying jobs worthwhile. Performing in an off-off-Broadway show is a great way to get an agent or casting director to see your work, although you should remember to invite such people only if you're proud of both the show and your work in it. A bad show isn't going to impress anyone, or help you attain what you set out to do.

Another reason to do an off-off-Broadway show is if you're particularly interested in a certain project in the hopes that it will make the leap to off-Broadway. While it doesn't happen often, it does happen. And if it does move to off-Broadway, you'll start getting paid.

Doing off-off-Broadway is also a way to keep your skills honed, and provides experience when you're not working regularly. These show don't run forever, so they don't represent an enormous commitment of time.

If you're a young person coming to New York City for the first time, right out of college, just keep in mind that for a while you can probably expect to get cast *only* in off-off-Broadway shows. Throughout this book, I have been insisting that you not come straight to New York after graduation, but build your resume by doing a variety of jobs in summer stock, regional theater, dinner theater, national non-Equity tours, on cruise ships, and so on. In that way, once you arrive in New York you'll be qualified for other kinds of work and your reasons for doing off-off-Broadway will involve more than just the desperation of needing to find a job.

Auditioning

Jeffrey Corrick, artistic director of the Wings Theater, in New York, says, "The pool of talent in New York is incredible. The talent that comes down to off-off-Broadway is better than the professional talent you'll get in the Midwest." Because of that, it's important that when you audition for an off-off-Broadway theater, you treat it as if you were auditioning for Broadway. Don't think of it as anything less. When auditioning, be prepared. Off-off-Broadway directors see the same bad habits all directors see— young beginners who show up at auditions with no songs to sing, actors who forget their monologues halfway through the tryout, or inexperienced performers who walk up to piano players with unintelligible pieces of music and ask them to transpose everything down an octave—and they don't like it any better. Even though giving the worst audition of your life at an off-off-Broadway theater won't bar you from success at other auditions, it marks you as unprofessional, and tells everyone who sees you that you're not yet ready for a New York job.

OFF-BROADWAY

Off-Broadway is Broadway, just smaller. The seating capacity of off-Broadway theaters ranges from 100 to 499 seats, and the shows are usually new ones that haven't been previously performed for the New York theater-going public.

Unlike off-off-Broadway, where performers work for free in order to get agents and casting directors to see their work, off-Broadway is a professional venue: Not only do people come to see your work, but you get paid to perform. Off-Broadway theaters are union-affiliated, so you must be a member of Actors' Equity, but if you land a job there, you can quit waiting tables for a minimum wage and tips.

Working in off-Broadway shows will advance your career. They look great on your resume, and agents, managers, and casting directors will take you seriously and be more interested in watching your work when invited to do so.

Most Broadway productions first see production off-Broadway or in an outstanding regional theater some distance from New York. Sometimes shows are picked up from off-off-Broadway, but that rarely happens. There are so many off-off-Broadway theaters out there, and so many of the productions are bad, that only if a show is selling out and creating a buzz among members of the theater community, generating some word of mouth, will you find a producer interested in moving the show.

Off-Broadway shows usually have small casts, perhaps nine performers or less. I'm talking about shows like *You're a Good Man, Charlie Brown, Nunsense, Stupid Kids*, or what is the longest-running off-Broadway production of them all, *The*

Fantasticks. These shows, for one reason or another, just are not able to play or survive on Broadway. Perhaps they're too intimate to be on a large stage, or perhaps they're not able to attract a diverse enough audience. In any case, they're able to sell out off-Broadway houses, sometimes for many years at a time, but they can't sell out a 1200-seat Broadway theater for long enough to make any money.

There is a huge monetary difference between opening a show off-Broadway and opening one on Broadway. Today, a Broadway show can cost millions of dollars, whereas an off-Broadway show can be produced for a few hundred thousand dollars. Ticket prices are different, too. Usually to see an off-Broadway show it costs half what it costs to see a Broadway show.

What is the process it takes to get an off-Broadway show open? In one scenario, after a show is written, the writer or writers look for a producer who likes the script. The producer then gathers all the money needed to open the show, and picks the theater and the opening date. Other times the author or authors hold a backers' audition, trying to put the money package together themselves. At the backers' audition, volunteer actors walk through the whole show, singing all the numbers, and reading through the script. They do everything they can to get the possible backers excited about the project.

Auditioning for an Off-Broadway Show

Auditions for off-Broadway shows are the same as any other auditions in New York. Look in *Back Stage* for the audition notices, or, if you're a member of Actors' Equity, check the callboard at the Equity office. Then show up at the audition, prepared to do your best. If it's an Equity call, and you're non-Equity, show up at the open call if the show has one.

If offered a job, you'll have to join the union. If you do land a job, terrific. If you don't, forget it and keep auditioning for other shows.

Earnings

When doing an off-Broadway show, you can expect to make Equity minimum for the house size. But remember, there are many house sizes, and a different Equity contract covers each size. Depending on the type of contract at the theater where you're working, your weekly pay can be as low as $275, which is not a living wage in New York. Because of this, it can be very difficult to make ends meet performing in an off-Broadway show. You'll have to rely on your determination to make it in the business to help you find a way to make it work. One advantage, though: You won't have to leave town for the gig.

Rehearsals

Because most off-Broadway shows have never been performed before, the rehearsal period may be long and tedious. You may work on a musical number, or some blocking, for an entire day. The very next day, you may show up to rehearse and find out that the director now hates everything done onstage the day before, and wants to start all over from the top. This can be physically and emotionally draining, and requires actors with lots of patience and creativity.

Important Points to Remember

There are kids, all over the country, who get their Equity cards working in dinner theaters in the smaller markets. When they arrive in New York, they really don't have the skills, or the resumes, to compete with the better or more experienced Equity actors there, but they can't work non-Equity because they already have their union cards. This is not a good place to be for a young talent who needs more training and experience. On the other hand, if they arrive in New York as non-Equity performers, they can audition for, and be cast in off-Broadway shows, where they can get exactly the kind of experience they need. If you're planning on moving directly to New York from your hometown or college, keep this is mind. Make sure you're ready to compete in the New York market as a fully trained professional, or you'll run into a lot of problems.

Singers and dancers should be aware of something else. Off-Broadway shows rarely have chorus parts. So, unless you can play leading roles (and that means being a triple threat), you may not find work in these theaters.

14

IN NEW YORK AND OVERSEAS

So you've finished with college, or you're tired of working in the smaller theater venues in the area where you live. You've decided it's time to move to New York and try to break into Broadway. Maybe you've even been offered a part in a theater overseas or with a company that does international tours. This chapter is aimed at helping you make these transitions successfully.

MOVING TO NEW YORK

If you're planning on coming to New York, you need a plan. In fact, you need three or four plans. You can't, all of a sudden, say goodbye to everyone you know, hop a plane, and step onto a Broadway stage. Once you get to New York, you'd better know what to do, and that involves extensive preplanning and research.

Let's consider a few things before you make the move. To start with, it might be wise for your entire family to visit New York together. If that's not feasible, try visiting with a friend. After spending three or four days there, you'll have a better idea of what the city is all about.

On that preliminary visit, you can check out various neighborhoods and look at apartments, see how things work in general, and get an overall picture of the expenses involved in living in New York on a regular basis. Many things in New York are different from the rest of the country. You might reach the conclusion that living there isn't for you and you'd prefer working in musical theater on a smaller scale elsewhere. On the other hand, even individuals afraid of the concept of "New York" often find they're quite comfortable after spending a few days there.

Another issue: Have you planned ahead financially? Do you have the resources to support the move? Jo Rowan, chairperson of dance at the School of American Dance and Arts Management, at Oklahoma City University, says:

> If all you're going to do in New York is move in and get a job as a waiter or a waitress, you should be a waiter at home. Save as much money as you can, and when you hit New York have at least three months' worth of money in the bank, ready to go, so all you have to do is concentrate on getting into show business. Just keep in mind that there's a problem with a cushion, however. The softer the cushion, the softer the attempt to find work as a performer.

As I've stressed before, you should build your resume before coming to the city by doing summer stock, dinner theater, and any other performing jobs that come your way. Work with as many professional directors and choreographers as possible, building up a base of at least twenty contacts in the business that you can ask a favor of, should you ever need to. This is a very important consideration. You don't want to be in New York alone, knowing no one in the theater world. If you show up and nobody knows you, it's not likely that anyone will offer you a job. Performing work just doesn't fall into the laps of beginners. Finding jobs in theater is usually a long, hard struggle, and only the strong survive in this business.

What I'm saying is you must organize your approach to living in New York so it furthers your career. I'll give tips and pointers in the following sections. But don't be timid or afraid to ask questions from anyone else you can who knows about being a performer in New York. Learn everything you can before arriving. It will save you a lot of time and anguish, and help you to open doors and reach your goal sooner rather than later.

Planning Your Arrival

In my opinion, the best plan for moving to New York would be to arrive during the month of February, secure an apartment, and have all your personal affairs in order by the end of the month. This is ideal timing. March is a busy time in the theatrical world of New York because of all the auditions for summer stock and touring companies, and you want to be ready for those.

It's important that you *not* arrive during the summer. First of all, not much happens in New York, theatrically speaking, during that time of the year. Second, because students are out of school or a new crop of them has just graduated, it's difficult then to get an apartment in the city or to locate a regular job to hold you over until your big theatrical break.

Apartment Living in New York

Costs and Locations If you had it easy in your home town and things were pretty much handed to you as far as living conditions were concerned, be prepared for a lifestyle change. You're apt to encounter things you never had to deal with before, and will have to sacrifice in ways you never thought you'd have to.

For one thing, most likely you'll have to live in an apartment, not a house, and you'll have to sign a lease obligating you to pay the rent each month for one or two years, at which time the rent will probably go up. In the "city" itself—which is what the locals call Manhattan—the average rent at the time of publication for this book (late 1999) was $1100 a month for an unfurnished, one-room studio apartment in a safe neighborhood. The rent for a furnished studio apartment in a safe neighborhood was around $2000. These are steep prices, and cheaper apartments might be available. But I advise against renting a place to live in Manhattan just because it's cheap. You could wind up living in an unsafe area by trying to save some money, and that's not a good move when your work hours could be as strange as they are for most performers.

If you don't have a lot of money yourself, but still want to live in Manhattan, the best thing to do is have your parents cosign and take financial responsibility for the lease. Or maybe you can find one or two roommates to share the rent. Just make sure the people are already known to you in some way and trustworthy and reliable. Never take a chance on total strangers.

Short of parents paying for their apartments, when most young performers first move to New York they don't usually live in Manhattan, but instead in one of the outlying boroughs, where rents are cheaper. Transportation is an issue here since you'll have a longer commute to the theater section of Manhattan if you live there. But some of the good areas for you to live include:

* A trendy of section of Brooklyn once called Green Point but now known as South Side. It's safe, and less than thirty minutes from Broadway by subway. It was a working class section of New York, but recently has transformed itself into an artistic haven for young people. As of late 1999 apartments there were renting for $600 to $800 a month.
* The Carroll Gardens and Cobble Hill section of Brooklyn. It's also one of the safer areas of the city, thirty minutes or so away from Broadway by subway, and the rents are cheaper than in Manhattan.
* Various sections of Queens, including Astoria, Kew Gardens, Forest Hills, and Bayside. These are all safe areas and the rents are fairly cheap, but the commutes to Broadway are somewhat longer than from Brooklyn, especially in regard to Bayside, which has no subway service.
* The closer-in communities of Long Island and New Jersey. These can offer a lot of places to live at affordable prices, if you're willing to commute to Manhattan on the Long Island Railroad or New Jersey Transit.

The problem with living in some of these areas is that you have to plan your commuting carefully. If you're waiting tables eight hours a day, taking classes, auditioning, and doing whatever else crops up that you need to do in your Manhattan professional life, you'll have to take everything you need for all those activities every time you leave your apartment—including your full dance bag. You won't be able to run home to take a shower before your next audition or to pick up something that you forgot. You might find you have to warm up your voice by vocalizing on the street as you head toward a theater. The commute might tire you out before your day really gets under way. Keep these things in mind, and realize what you're getting into before committing to an apartment in one of the areas farther away from Broadway.

Subletting One option is to sublet an apartment. This means living in someone else's apartment and paying the rent and utility bills while you occupy it. You'll probably have to sign a sublet agreement, but the arrangement has several advantages for beginners in New York. Many performers get gigs out of town for two or three months at a time; they don't want to give up their apartments permanently because they'll be back, but they don't want to pay the rent while they're gone either.

Subletting allows the person who's out of town to save rent money, and allows the subletter to have the use of an apartment already furnished with furniture, appliances, dishes, and silverware. It also allows you to become familiar with a neighborhood without being committed to living there for a long period of time. In fact, if you sublet several apartments in the course of your first year in New York, it lets you try out several neighborhoods and decide which one you would like best to live in when you rent your own apartment. Subletting also helps you build up references you'll need when you start looking for your own apartment.

Just make sure when you agree to a sublet that it's legal. There are buildings in New York where the practice isn't allowed. And if you're still going to need a roommate to meet the rent, make sure roommates are allowed. You don't want to be evicted.

Finding Out About Apartments and Sublets There are several sources where you can learn about available apartments and sublets. Actors' Equity is one, but you'll need your union card to see their list. *Back Stage* is another. Word of mouth from performers you know is still another. There are also New York papers like the *Village Voice*, *The New York Post*, the *Sunday New York Times*, and *Newsday*. *Newsday* has editions for both Queens and Long Island, which include extensive apartment listings in those areas.

You probably won't have the money to use a relocation company. But there are many brokers in New York who for lower fees than a relocation company can help you find an apartment. You may not want to pay any fee at all, but I recommend using a broker since getting a good apartment in a safe neighborhood is worth the money you'll spend.

The broker's fee will run about 7 percent of your annual rent (keep in mind that you'll also have to cough up an extra month's rent as a security deposit, which the landlord will put in an escrow bank account). Again, just be careful which broker you go to. Brokers can, and will, handle illegal rentals, which means you could get evicted somewhere down the road. Buyer—or in this case renter—beware.

Answering Machines and Services

As a performer looking for work, you want to be reachable if your agent or anyone else needs to contact you immediately. Maybe you need a beeper or pager. If that's not your style, make sure you have an answering machine or a message service.

Even with a machine or answering service, you'll need to retrieve your messages in a timely manner. When your phone is hooked up, you'll be asked if you want voice messaging. My advice is to get it. It's reliable and, personally, I've never had any problems with it. It holds up to a hundred messages for a good number of days before deleting them. You can also decide which messages you want saved and which deleted.

If, instead, you decide to buy an answering machine, get a good one. If it breaks down while you're out of town, you could miss some very important messages. Be wise and spend a few extra bucks. Also, remember that everyone's time is valuable, so don't leave a lengthy or cutesy message on your machine that your agent or a casting director has to suffer through. Make your message simple and professional. If you're a woman living alone, it might be wise to protect yourself by getting a male friend to record your message.

If you have an agent, put his or her name and phone number on your resume. In this way, anyone who wants to get hold of you for a job or an audition will call your agent directly, and not your home number. If you don't have an agent, and don't want to give out your home number, buy a beeper or a cell phone. By carrying it with you at all times, you can be contacted immediately.

You can also hire an answering service. This works in one of two ways. With some services, people call your home phone number. After the phone rings a specific number of times, the service clicks in and answers the call. With other services, you give out the answering service's number, which people call. This is real nice for women. You don't have to give out your home number or list it on your resume. You just call the answering service yourself to check your messages.

Answering services also offer other options you might find helpful, like wakeup calls and call forwarding. Of course, each one adds to the monthly cost, but if you shop around, you can find good deals.

Another good idea is to have an Internet e-mail account. With a notebook computer and a modem, you have portable access to the Internet, where you can contact an endless number of people in the business. By having an e-mail account with an Internet service provider, you can be in touch instantly with friends, agents, and others in the entertainment industry.

Survival Jobs

Unless you are one of the lucky few who comes to New York with a performing job already in hand, or you manage to land performing work that pays right away, you'll need to get a survival job. It takes money to survive in New York, and expenses can pop up when you least expect them. So let's explore some of the employment options that exist in New York.

You don't want just any job. You want one where the people you work for understand your goals and ambitions, and where your working conditions are flexible enough to let you attend auditions when you need to. A flexible schedule is the key, and waiting tables just might not be the way to go. There's a cliché that everyone trying to make it in show business has to be a waiter or waitress. It's not true. You can have your own career on the side that allows you to schedule your time to your benefit. When you're in charge of the clock, you're more prepared, you look and feel better, and you have the time to go to the gym. Being physically and emotionally healthy will certainly help you in the long run.

Geoffrey Johnson, of Johnson-Liff Casting and casting director for *Les Misérables*, notes:

> *Many actors get jobs as waiters or waitresses. Many of them become professional waiters and waitresses and begin to ignore their careers. Then they hear about an audition, say an open call for Les Miz, and they're not prepared. Are they going to get a job in a show that way? I doubt it.*

There are many other ways of earning money while you're waiting for your big break. If you have computer skills, you can find work through a temporary employment agency (these agencies are listed in *Back Stage* as well in the Yellow Pages) and earn $15 to $20 an hour. Temp agencies find that performers are reliable and focused people, and are always happy to find them work. Often, if you have computer or typing skills, you can do the work at home.

If you have a business mind and a skill you're particularly good at, there are virtually unlimited possibilities for making money. You can create your own job. I know someone who's a personal chef. He prepares clients' meals ahead of time and delivers them, for which he gets a weekly salary. A dancer I know got her seamstress license and plans to make dance clothes for herself and others, charging her clients less than if they purchased the clothes in a store.

The good news is that in a city like New York the opportunity to create your own niche is nearly unlimited. And by creating your own job, you'll take control of your time in a way that will allow to pursue your dream of becoming a singer, dancer, and performer as much as you want. You just have to keep in mind that you'll have to market your nonperformance skills as much as you do your performing talents if you're going to make a living by the job you've created.

Publications

In previous chapters I've already mentioned publications like *Back Stage* and *Ross Reports for Television and Film* as primary tools for finding auditions and performing work in New York as well as elsewhere. Here are a couple of others you'll find helpful:

* *The Agencies: What the Actor Needs to Know* (New York edition), is updated monthly, and like *Ross Reports* is sold in Manhattan at Samuel French and at the Drama Bookshop. This well-researched publication provides an overview of every performing arts agency, including the types of performers they specialize in and what they're looking for. (See the Appendix.)

* The *National Casting Guide*. Priced at under $20, this publication will provide you with the names of casting contacts, film commissions and unions, companies that offer performing artist resources, schools, and teachers. It contains many ads for voice mail and answering services, doctors, and dentists located in New York, and is sold in many bookstores. (See the Bibliography section of the Appendix.)

Owning a Car in New York

Will you need a car in New York? If you're even asking this question, it's obvious you've never been to that city. You don't need a car there, nor should you want one. Parking on the street isn't a good idea, the monthly parking garage fees are outrageous, auto insurance is high, the cabbies drive like maniacs, and you can get stuck in traffic trying to get to appointments. Unless you're a student, you must change your car registration and get New York state license plates within thirty days of moving there. Finally, you'll want to invest in some kind of anti-theft device if you're planning to park your car on the streets. For a performer starting out, it's just not wise to have a car in New York.

While New York is a hostile environment for cars, the subway and bus mass transit system more than makes up for it. The cost for one ride, as of 1999, is $1.50, with a free transfer between buses and subways. But you can also buy Metrocards that will allow you unlimited rides for a week or a month, which can add up to considerable savings if you use public transportation often enough.

If you feel unsafe using the subways, here's a word of advice: Don't ride them between 1 A.M. and 5 A.M. And when you ride during the day, sit in the middle car, where the conductor is located.

In Manhattan, usually nothing is so far away that you can't walk. With this in mind, invest in some good walking shoes. If you don't feel like walking on a particular day, or if the weather turns nasty, flag down a cab. You'll arrive at your destination quickly and safely. Remember, if you live outside Manhattan and your rent is running around $800 a month, you'll be able to afford that $10 cab ride when you need it.

Medical Insurance

If you don't have health insurance when you move to New York, be sure you have a plan to cover medical bills should you get sick. Do you have a credit card with a high limit? Union performers don't have to worry about this. In Actors' Equity, once they've worked ten weeks, medical coverage kicks in. But as a beginner you probably won't have that luxury.

What if you do get sick? Where will you get treatment? Most people don't like to open up the Yellow Pages and haphazardly pick a doctor. Early on, after you've moved to New York ask friends and other performers what doctors or clinics they recommend. Also, pay attention to the subway ads. Many doctors and clinics advertise there. Finally, there's a toll-free (1-800) doctor search number in New York. It will steer you to a caregiver in your neighborhood.

Joining a Gym

You're going to want to work out. In fact, it's part of your job as a performer to stay fit. But before you join a gym, consider the angles. It's always better to get a membership toward the end of a month, on the thirtieth or thirty-first. People selling memberships at gyms have quotas to meet. If they don't meet them, their jobs can be jeopardized. If it's been a slow month and they haven't met their quota of, say, signing up twenty new people, they'll be willing to deal. Talk to them on the thirtieth of the month; most likely they'll be desperate to sign people up, and you can strike a fantastic bargain.

Credit and Budgeting

In your show business career, you'll need to know how to budget. Americans are often bad at this, but you don't have to be. It's important to build up your credit references starting at a young age, so having a major credit card is a wise choice to make. But don't use the card recklessly. Use it only for emergencies, not for impulse buying, and try to pay it off every month. Otherwise the interest can snowball and put you in a financial hole that you might not be able to dig out of.

During your career, you'll find yourself in Broadway shows or on national tours. Lots of money will be coming in. You could develop an attitude of "spend it all, live life to the limit." But don't forget, there will also be lean times. You need to save to ensure you have money to fall back on when you're not rolling in dough. How many times have we heard about the seemingly rich star who suddenly went bankrupt, oblivious to what was really going on? Stay grounded in reality. Always have at least three months' income in your bank account to fall back on. Maintain a monthly budget so that you know where the money is going. If you find yourself spending money hand over fist, stop, rethink the situation, and regroup.

As I noted in Chapter 13, when you're out on the road on a national tour, you'll get both a salary and a per diem. The per diem should easily cover your road expenses, such as lodging and meals. Most performers learn to live on their per diems and bank their salaries. If you don't live it up too much, you'll always have money left over. Room with someone else. Don't spend every night at a fancy restaurant or buy rounds of drinks at bars. By developing self-discipline, you'll be able to bring a nice paycheck back home with you.

Those are the major practical matters connected with a move to New York. As for your career, if you are this far along in this book, you have learned what it means to think and behave in a professional manner in seeking opportunities and dealing with show business people. This professionalism extends to the all-important tips on how to audition covered in Chapter 15. Those lessons and one more essential thing will be your key to success in the New York entertainment industry: networking.

You have to get out there, meet people, and become known. It doesn't matter if you're terribly shy and find facing others intimidating. To get anywhere in New York you'll have to interact with people. Meeting people will get you jobs. There's something to be said for those who don't sit around and wait for the phone to ring. Go-getters create their own destinies. If you sit home all the time, timid and nervous, it's not going to happen for you. Nobody is going to come knocking at your door, asking you to please dance in their musical.

However, what if you move to New York and find out you made a mistake—that you don't really belong there? First, give yourself a little time before making a final decision. Go to class. See a show. Remind yourself why you went there in the first place. If, after a fair amount of time, you still feel it's not for you, then consider some of the other job venues discussed in this book. There are countless opportunities out there, and leaving New York certainly doesn't mean you're a failure. It means you have to find your niche in the business via other avenues. You might not wind up on Broadway, but instead find success performing in touring companies or summer stock, or working on cruise ships, at theme parks, or in Las Vegas.

Remember, the options are endless.

Jobs Outside the United States

If you'd like to work outside the United States, there are a lot of musicals and other singing/dancing jobs available through various touring companies. If you don't know what you're doing, however, you could get into trouble. There are issues related to working in other countries that don't apply to stateside jobs, and you need to be aware of them.

At the start of your career, even if you're not intending to go abroad, you should go ahead and get your passport. An overseas opportunity could present itself at any time, so you shouldn't wait until the last minute to obtain that basic document.

Knowing What You're Getting Into

Once you know the country where you'd like to work, collect as much information as possible. Learn about the country itself and the company that will be hiring you. Foreign nations and the companies that operate according to their rules aren't under U.S. or American performing union jurisdiction, and don't offer the same safeguards you're used to here. Some countries barely recognize any human rights. Once there you can't simply say "I'm an American" and expect the same treatment you'd get in Illinois or Colorado. You also have to check out the production company you'll be working for by reading up on it and talking to people who have worked for it previously to know what to expect from it when you get there.

Now there are horror stories about working overseas that have been documented in *Back Stage*. This publication has a superb record for detailing whom you should work for and not work for. Its writers do periodic exposés about some of the abuses. For example, in January 1996, it ran an article titled "International Tours." It discussed a Swiss-based company called Scala Theater, a company with a reputation for not paying performers and, worse yet, leaving them stranded with no way to get home. There was even a bus accident that hurt people in a Scala tour. Scala simply abandoned these performers and left them to their own devices. Examples such as this reinforce the importance of knowing what you're getting into before signing up to work in foreign countries and with foreign production companies.

Always read your contract closely, particularly as it relates to the pay scale. Since foreign companies tend to pay in foreign currencies, find out how much you'll be getting in terms of American dollars. Exchange rates fluctuate constantly, so you'll either want to be paid in American dollars (your best choice) or to convert your pay to dollars as soon as possible. You don't want to deposit your money in the banks of a number of foreign countries. What you thought was a great salary could be wiped out instantly if your money is in the bank of a country whose economic conditions are constantly changing.

Before shipping out, you'll need to totally prepare yourself, making sure you take care of everything you need to take care of and that you've packed everything you need to take along with you. Say you'll be heading out on a cruise ship for an international tour. Since the ship won't be docking at U.S. ports for quite a while, try to take care of all your medical needs before you leave. You might not be able to find proper medical care in a foreign port, so I suggest seeing a doctor for a complete physical before departing. Try to avoid dealing with foreign medical practitioners, where the skill levels and sanitary conditions may not be up to par, or where the doctors don't speak English. The same warnings apply to dentists. If you're taking prescription medication, make sure it's in the original container. You don't want the medicine being seized as some kind of illegal substance or contraband.

Be efficient about what you take with you. You don't want to be lugging excess baggage around. Make versatility the key to your wardrobe, choosing items that you can wash out quickly and easily and use in multiple ways.

If you'll be staying at foreign hotels, be aware that the building codes in most places are different from those in this country, and often the codes that do exist aren't enforced very well. Because of that, at each hotel you should immediately familiarize yourself with the escape routes in case of a fire or other disasters. Preplan for any such possibilities by literally walking the escape routes out of the building to ensure you know how to get out. Also, request a room on one of the lower floors, rather than higher up.

Electrical supplies are often different overseas. While we're used to the 110-volt standard in the United States, many countries use 220 volts. Make sure to bring along an adapter, so you can use your electric razor, hair dryer, or hot plate. Also, find out about the hygienic facilities, such as toilets and showers, and whether you'll need to bring along something as basic as toilet paper.

Study up on the cultural differences you'll encounter. Have some knowledge of the food, customs, and religious beliefs of the country or countries you'll be traveling to. You don't want to offend anyone by mistake. Also note the physical disparities that will exist between you as an American and the people in the other country. Minnie Madden, founder of *Dirt Alert*, makes the following observation in the book *Dancing for a Living*: "Also, be cognizant of the physical differences that exist. For example, if you're a 5'10" blond dancer/singer who's going to Japan, remember that people there tend to be smaller. Finding dance clothing in the right size may be next to impossible." This means you have to plan ahead in terms of the kind of clothing you'll be able to buy for yourself in other countries.

It's especially important to make sure that your contract stipulates you will retain possession of your passport at all times. Many overseas show producers have a habit of holding the passports of performers. It's a common practice. Through experience, they know that performers get homesick or become unhappy with the work. They want to go home. If they have your passport in their hands, it ensures that you'll have to finish out the contract and not hop the next plane back to the States. In this way they maintain control. Unfortunately, it also means you *lose* control.

Before signing the contract, make sure the provision about you holding your own passport is in writing. Saying one thing and doing another is also a common practice in this business. And as another way of protecting yourself, make sure you have a round trip airline ticket on you at all times.

But what happens if you decide to break the contract and leave the show early? There are some producers who will seek to protect themselves by putting certain stipulations in your contract. For example, if you do leave the show early, for whatever reason, you may be responsible for paying for your airfare back to the States. That's not so important if you have a valid ticket on you, as suggested above. But it's just the beginning. In addition, you may have to cover the cost of flying in a new performer from the United States to take your place, as well as the cost of rehearsing that person to get him or her into the flow of the show.

These kinds of financial penalties are one more reason to thoroughly check out the company ahead of time. Not only can paying them be very expensive, but being fined in this way can tarnish your reputation in the business. You should always do your best to finish what you start.

On the other hand, there are disreputable producers who may want you to do things you didn't anticipate when you signed the contract. So check out exactly what you'll be doing in the job. Will there be any nudity involved? If so, to what extent? Will there be any extra duties in addition to your main stage job? Scrutinize the contract you're offered by any foreign production company, whether you think it's reputable or not, and insist that the company supply you with the names and telephone numbers of people who have worked for it whom you can contact. If at all possible, you want the unfiltered truth.

In conclusion, traveling abroad is one of the pluses of being a performer. Just make sure you do your homework ahead of time. If you do, it should be a pleasant experience, and one that you'll remember without regrets for the rest of your life.

15

AUDITIONING

We've discussed auditions in many chapters of this book. When it comes to auditioning, whether you are in New York or anywhere else, there's no such thing as a seasoned pro. So this chapter is devoted just to the subject of auditions.

No one ever gets good enough that he or she can stop practicing. Whether you think a particular job is right for you or not, you should attend as many auditions as possible. The experience is different for everybody and, like anything else, the more you do it, the better you'll get. Even so, some performers get nervous before an audition and manifest stress in different ways. Some have trouble breathing, often to the point of nausea. Others feel the psychological pressure of rejection, despite the fact that being cut is almost never personal. If you're new to the scene, you should go on those first few auditions without the expectation of getting a job. Instead, look at them as learning experiences that will help you in the future—as experiences that are getting you in front of the people who might hire you somewhere later down the line. You're showing your face not only to those auditioning you, but to those auditioning alongside you. You may not be right for these first parts you're trying out for, but these initial efforts are getting you noticed—and that's just where someone starting out needs to be.

To make those first few auditions successful, remember to be properly prepared. Any time you walk into an audition room, you'll be sized up in the first thirty seconds. This is when people get their first impressions of you, and those impressions are how you'll be remembered, so make sure to take all the steps necessary to make a favorable impression. Have a current picture and resume with you. Always wear the right clothes required for the audition. Whether you're a singer or a dancer, be prepared to sing sixteen bars each of two songs—something up-tempo, along with a ballad. If you're a singer, always bring dance clothes, and if you're a dancer, bring a nice outfit to change into. As soon as you leave the audition, wipe it from your mind until you get a callback. If that callback doesn't come, don't waste a lot of energy wondering why. Maybe you weren't the right height or the right size for the costume. Maybe it was something else. The reasons you weren't called back can be endless, so don't beat yourself up over it.

WHO WILL BE WATCHING YOU AUDITION

You really shouldn't worry about who's watching. It could be anyone from the casting director to the entire production staff, depending on the job, the locale, and the budget. Instead, concentrate on having a good time and doing your best.

To quote Broadway and film dancer Jack Tygett once again, "Go to auditions with humility. When you perform well, it will be that much more than they expect."

Usually, at the initial call when you're getting typed out, you'll have no idea who the people watching you are. If you make it to the first callback, however, that's when they'll introduce themselves. Just be aware that anyone could be there, including the director, the subdirector, the choreographer, the choreographer's assistants, the music director, the producer, and people from the theater's main office. If it's a new show, the writers may be in attendance.

Keep a log of every audition you attend, updating it with the names of the people who were there, other performers you met, how you did, and any other information you think may help you in the future. Learn to start recognizing the power people of the business. If you've auditioned three times for Geoffrey Johnson, one of New York's biggest casting directors, and you still don't know who he is, maybe you need to brush up on who's who.

AUDITION NOTICES

Your first encounter with auditions will involve casting notices or job listings of auditions in trade papers like *Back Stage* and *Dirt Alert*. On the Internet, you can find them listed in *Playbill Online*. Others sources of audition notices include dance studios, the entertainment section in local newspapers, and word of mouth. The notice should provide you with all the information you need, such as who is holding the audition, the name of the show, a description of the roles being cast for (what parts are actually open), and audition time(s) and location(s).

So that you can become familiar with the format and language of such ads, I list a variety of sample audition notices below. They are based upon actual notices and represent the kind of ads for nonunion and union jobs that appear in publications like *Back Stage*. Most of the nonunion jobs you can obtain by yourself without union affiliation, an agent, or a manager.

Non-Equity Notices

> **"FIDDLER ON THE ROOF"—NATIONAL BUS AND TRUCK TOUR**
> *4/27 & 4/28 at 10 AM and 2 PM at National Tour Theater*
> Jericko Productions will hold auditions for its national bus and truck tour of "Fiddler on the Roof." Rehearsals start Aug 24 and the show opens Sept 17, with a six-month contract. [At this point the notice will give a detailed breakdown of all the characters and state who the casting director and director are.] Open principal auditions will be held Monday, April 27 at 10 AM for women and 2 PM for men. An open chorus call will be held on Tuesday, April 28 at 10 AM for male dancers (ages 20-40) and at 2 PM for women singers (ages 20-50) at National Tour Theater. For principal auditions, be prepared to sing, read, and move. NON-EQUITY PERFORMERS.

"WEST SIDE STORY" TOUR

An open call will be held for the second leg of the American Touring Company of "West Side Story." Jericko Entertainment. [Here the notice lists the members of the production staff.] Rehearsals mid-August: Opens early Sept. and runs through Dec. Non-Equity contract, some salaries are negotiable, plus housing and transportation are provided. Auditions will be held Wednesday, May 6 at 10 AM for female dancers who sing, and Thursday, May 7 at 10:30 AM for male character actors for the "adults" and at 12 noon for singers who dance for the roles of Tony and Maria. Seeking all roles including principals, ensemble, understudies, and swings. All performers (except "adults") should look early 20s, be strong singers, actors, and dancers, as this production uses the original Jerome Robbins choreography. Those auditioning for Tony must prepare "Something's Coming" and "Maria." [The notice then goes on to state what songs those trying out for the other characters should prepare.] All songs must be in show key. Sides for "adults" will be available the morning of the audition. NON-EQUITY PERFORMERS.

Notice that a non-Equity call is exclusively for non-Equity performers. The pay scale will be different from a union show and union rules won't apply, but it's a good way to get your foot in the door and gain the experience you'll need to advance your career.

Equity Notices

B&T "ANNIE"

6/30 at 10AM & 2PM at Broadway House Theater, NYC. A chorus call will be held for future ensemble replacements for the bus and truck production of "Annie" (currently on tour). [Here the notice will list the names of the producer, director, choreographer, and casting director.] Chorus call procedures are not in effect. Auditions will be held at [here the notice will give the address]. Monitor arrives at the half hour. Do not sing from the show. Sing any standard Broadway (e.g., Rodgers and Hammerstein, Jule Styne, Jerry Herman) up-tempo and ballad. You may be asked to dance after singing. Bring two pix & resumes. Equity members of all ethnic backgrounds are encouraged to attend this audition.

EQ. PRODUCTION CONTRACT

Tues. June 30—Equity male singers who dance, 10AM.
Tues. June 30—Equity female singers who dance, 2PM.
Seeking Equity male singers 5'8" or taller who dance and Equity female singers 5'6" or taller who dance.

NY SHAKESPEARE FEST. "ON THE TOWN," B'WAY

7/8 & 7/9 at 10AM & 2PM at [here the notice gives the name of the building or theater and its address], NYC. Equity and non-Equity chorus call will be held for the New York Shakespeare Festival production of "On the Town" (first rehearsal Aug. 10; first performance Oct. 20). NYSF/[here the notice lists members of the production staff]. Chorus call procedures are in effect for Equity call only. Auditions will be held at [here notice gives the address], NYC. Be prepared with 16-bar song selections, up-tempo and ballad, should preferably be from the period (e.g., standards, Gershwin, Porter, Rodgers & Hammerstein, etc.). Bring pix & resumes. Men bring jazz and character shoes. Women bring jazz shoes, character heels, and pointe shoes (optional). The producers are determined to cast a multiracial company. Equity members of all ethnic backgrounds are encouraged to attend these calls. EQ.

PRODUCTION (B'WAY) CONTRACT

Wed. July 8—Equity male dancers who sing and act well, 10AM.
Wed. July 8—Equity female dancers who sing and act well, 2PM.
Thurs. July 9—Open call male dancers who sing and act well, 10AM.
Thurs. July 9—Open call female dancers who sing and act well, 2PM.
Seeking Equity male and female dancers who sing and act well.
Note: Considering casting the role and understudy of IVY (Miss Turnstiles) from these auditions, extremely gifted dancer with a strong classical/ballet background who must be able to act and sing.

An Equity call will either give a separate time for non-Equity talent to audition or will mention that the casting directors will see non-Equity talent if time permits. In the latter case, it means the non-Equity talent will have to wait to audition until all union members have been seen.

DANCE AUDITIONS

What clothes should you wear to an audition? They must be appropriate to the kind of show you're trying out for. So it's important that you do your homework about the show ahead of time. For example, if you're auditioning for *Rent*, you don't want to wear dance clothes—they're not right for the type of performer they're looking for. The same warning applies to *Tommy*. If you're to auditioning for *Crazy for You* or *Cats*, however, dance clothes are not just appropriate, but anything else would be out of place. Ask others who have attended the audition before you go, so you know exactly how to dress.

You should make a checklist of all the appropriate garb and take all of it with you in your dance bag to every audition. If you're missing anything, go out and buy it. For female dancers, according to Erin Robbins, from *Jerome Robbins' Broadway*, that includes ballet slippers, jazz, tap, and character shoes, tennis shoes, and

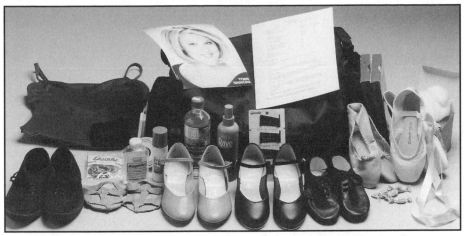

Because women's dance bags contain more items than men's, keep handy a checklist that allows you to keep track of everything and alerts you when an item needs to be replaced.

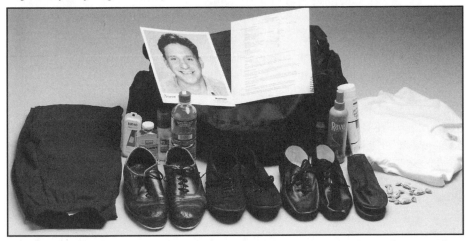

A man's dance bag also needs to be as complete as possible at all times—even when you're on vacation. You'll be prepared for any work-related situation that may suddenly arise.

kneepads: "You never know when you'll get kneework at an audition," he says. "Also, in your dance bag, include a water bottle and an Ace bandage wrap."

Women also should have two different types of leotards in colors that are right for them. Make sure they flatter your figure and fit well, as you don't want to be tugging at them throughout the audition. Have two pairs of tights or fishnets in good condition, with no rips in them. Girls with slightly large hips might want to consider wearing a dance skirt. If you wear a bra under your leotard, make sure it's a sports bra. Remove all your jewelry, and don't forget to have your picture, resume, and vocal selections handy. If you get called back to sing, have a nice outfit specifically for that.

Male dancers should have jazz, tap, ballet, and tennis shoes in their dance bag. Have a water bottle, Ace bandage wraps, kneepads, and a change of clothes for the vocal callback. Dance clothes should consist of your dance belt (undergarment), a pair of jazz pants (tights if you prefer), and a top that flatters your body. Make sure your ensemble is in a color good for you and shows that you're fit. Remember, don't wear baggy clothes, and aim for a clean look.

What to Wear If Asked to Sing

With the exception of a complete dancers' call, where the casting people might stop you and ask you to sing at any particular moment, you'll have time to change before singing. Put some thought into it before showing up at the audition so you can change into something nice, as if you were going to an interview. For women, that might be a dress; for men, it should be a pair of slacks and a shirt.

There are dancers who show up at vocal callbacks in their dance clothes, but it's not a wise thing to do. You want the casting people to know you're as professional about your singing as you are about your dancing. If you sing in your dance clothes, they might think, "Oh, this person's just a dancer who sings a bit."

What to Wear to Callbacks At callbacks, it's important to wear exactly what you wore at the initial audition. The casting people will remember you. It throws them off if at the callback you look completely different than you did at the initial audition, when you caught their interest. You might have found that perfect look the first time out, and that's why they called you back. At the callback they might ask, "Where's that girl in the red leotard? She looked good." But on seeing you in green, they might decide, "No. That won't do." Don't jeopardize the good fortune of being called back by making yourself unrecognizable the second time around. You could lose the job.

The Initial Call

Not all dance auditions are run the same way. While there's a general consistency at, say, Equity calls, variations occur. Nonunion auditions are run the way the director or production staff wants them to run. First, let's go through the audition basics. Later on in the chapter I give examples of different types of auditions and the variations they involve.

When you show up at an initial call, you'll usually sign in with the monitor sitting at the front desk and fill out a form or card. This is standard practice. You'll be asked to supply some information about yourself, as well as to list highlights from your resume. This will be done at the initial call. If the casting people are going to type you out first, they probably won't ask for your picture or resume until the first callback, and if you hand those items over without their being requested, they'll likely just be tossed in the trash. But it's important to have your picture and resume at hand, in case they are requested at this time. As I've said in other chapters, the resume should be glued to the back of your picture, so make sure you print your name on the back of the picture so the casting people will be able to identify you if the resume falls off.

You might be asked to do dance combinations at any audition you attend. So if you feel you're not great at picking up combinations, this may cause you problems. Some choreographers teach at lightning speed, expecting immediate and proficient pickup. All I can tell you is that if you have problems with picking up and there are forty people in the room auditioning for a show, just hope that when the choreographer splits the dancers up into smaller groups to audition you're not in the first group. If you're in one of the latter groups, you'll have some additional time to watch the other dancers as they run through the combination, and you'll be able to think about what you'll need to do before it's your turn to do it. By having time to watch and practice, you'll maximize your chances of making it to the next cut.

At dance calls, I've seen as few as twenty and as many as nine hundred people auditioning. It can be overwhelming, so here are a few pointers to help make the experience easier. You have to get yourself seen early on, and you have to realize that you're being watched the entire time, from learning the combination, to breaking down into smaller groups, to actually auditioning. You can't hide in a corner. You need to be on top of it, right away, because the production staff notices. When the choreographer tells everyone to spread out so he or she can teach the combination, try not to position yourself too far in the back. At most auditions, someone will usually wind up saying, "Can't we change lines? We can't see back here." If, for some reason, the choreographer doesn't change lines, find someone else in the room who's good, and watch him or her to learn what you should do.

Once everyone is spread out, the choreographer, or the choreographer's assistant, will teach a combination to the entire group. It might be ballet, jazz, tap, character—anything—depending on the style of the show. Usually, the audition notice will tell you what kind of dance you'll be doing at the call. It's not carved in stone, however, so be prepared for anything.

After the choreographer or the assistant teaches the combination, everyone will be split into smaller groups. The size of these varies from one audition to another, but usually consists of six dancers each.

The choreographer or assistant then assigns positions to the members of each group, using either your last name or a number assigned to each dancer. If you get a number, memorize it. Once in a group, you'll have either an upstage position or a downstage one. Remember your position so you can get to it quickly when called upon. For those of you who don't know, upstage is away from the audience while downstage is toward the audience.

You'll need to mimic what the choreographer is doing. Tracey Langran, Associate Choreographer for *Tommy*, says: "Dancers tend to be good at duplicating steps during auditions, but too often they don't duplicate the style. Check out what the choreographer is doing. If he or she does an arm in fifth, you do an arm in fifth. If the choreographer throws a head, you throw a head." Often, performers have their own way of dancing, and that can cost them jobs. Musical theater, in particular, is all about style. If you mess up a step, don't get stressed out about it. Just continue on. If you're doing what the choreographer is asking for, a small mistake won't cost you the job. That's what rehearsals are for.

Once the choreographer is done teaching the combination and you've been assigned to your group, get ready to shine. You have to perform the combination instantly and without hesitation. You have to sell it. This is your one chance to nail it and get the job. There are simply too many dancers at every audition for all of them to be hired, and only those that stand out get signed.

It's important to realize that, like every dancer, you have your strong and your weak points, so not every choreographer will like your dancing. Some dancers like to do it all with an edge, hitting every line hard. Some dancers are cool, and make everything look easy. You have to go with your strongest attributes. Sometimes they'll get you the job, other times they won't. Have confidence in yourself and, if you get cut, don't take it personally. The choreographer will be looking for line, proficiency in picking up the combination, showmanship, and, most of all, style.

Remember, from the moment you walk into an audition to the moment you leave, you're being closely watched. While dancing is certainly important, attitude is even more important. If you're a person who's hard to work with, who needs to have things go his or her way, if you can't compromise with others or your ego gets in the way, get out of the business now. Don't waste your time or that of others. A bad reputation never goes unpunished, and soon no one will want to work with you. Have a good attitude. By striking the right balance now, you'll avoid disaster later.

A Word on Being Poorly Prepared Most young dancers new to the business perceive themselves as being better than they are. Then, when they start showing up at auditions, they realize that they can't pick up combinations as quickly as necessary. Lagging behind affects their chances of giving a dynamic audition. Consequently, unless they are exactly the right type for the show, they get cut immediately. It's a harsh lesson, one that demonstrates how unprepared they are to compete for professional work. But nothing says they can't improve with practice, especially by attending a studio that specializes in fast pickup work. It's a skill you can, and have to, learn.

Even worse than not being able to pick up are the dancers who show up at auditions untrained, expecting to find work. They show up with the delusion that they are accomplished artists, when all their training was limited to the Dolly Dinko Remedial Dance Academy. They have no concept about what goes on in the real world, or what's about to take place. They try to fake pirouettes, have no extension, no idea of line, and simply can't keep up.

If you're one of those people, let me offer a piece of advice: Train, train, train. When you think you're pretty decent, train some more. Once you're proficient in ballet, tap, jazz, ballroom, and acrobatic dance, perhaps you'll be ready for a professional dance call. Don't waste precious audition time, or put yourself through unnecessary embarrassment, until then.

Callbacks

If you get past the first cut in a dance call, this is when you'll most likely be asked to sing. If you make that cut, you might have to dance—again and again. There could be as many as seven or eight callbacks to cast a single part in a show. It may take several days, even weeks or months, to cast a show, so don't expect it all to be done in one day.

No matter how many callbacks you attend, you don't have a job until you're offered a contract. Don't get discouraged. If you were meant to get this job, you will. If not, there will be other auditions tomorrow.

VOCAL AUDITIONS

Nobody likes bad singing. You might get away with it in the shower, but at a professional audition you don't want to embarrass yourself and the rest of the people there with an untrained voice. If you can't sing, don't attend vocal calls. If, on the other hand, you can sing professionally, make sure you've prepared yourself thoroughly for the auditions you attend.

Again, what do you wear? As a singer, you have three choices. First, you can go dressed in the period of the show. Second, you can wear something suggestive of the show but not actually of the period to give the casting people an idea of what you would look like costumed in the exact style of the show. Third, you can go in a nice outfit—something that looks good on you—not at all related to the show. Let's explore these choices in detail.

Most directors and producers agree that it's a bad idea to come dressed for the part. Occasionally it works out, but usually it is taken as a sign of desperation. At auditions for *Les Misérables*, many people show up wearing frilly French shirts, while at auditions for *Big River* many people show up in overalls with bare feet. Don't do something like this. It's frowned upon by casting people and will ultimately cost you the job.

The second possibility—coming dressed in a style suggestive of the show, yet not overtly so—is the choice recommended by most performers. For example, if you're a male singer auditioning for *42nd Street*, you might come in a pair of black pants and a nice top, adding suspenders to suggest the style of the 1920s. A female singer might wear a scarf representing that period, a subtle hint.

If you don't want to risk dressing inappropriately for an audition, there is the third possibility—wearing a nice outfit not related to the show at all that makes you look good. A woman might wear a dress or a suit, and perhaps high heels. A man might wear a nice shirt and slacks. Pay attention, though. If the audition notice specifies a certain look, be sure to follow it. And whatever you choose to wear when auditioning for whatever show, remember to make it simple and tasteful.

In regard to callbacks, the same rule applies to singers as to dancers—make sure you wear the same exact outfit that you wore to the initial audition.

Further Advice on Clothes More important than what you wear to an audition is how you wear it. You have to show off your best physical attributes and demonstrate that you're comfortable in your clothes. What you wear affects your attitude.

It's important for young dancers to avoid wearing trendy outfits—something a dancer may think is attractive for himself or herself, but which is totally inappropriate for a particular audition. If you're a female performer and don't like spiked high-heel shoes, then by all means don't wear them to the audition. If you do wear them, you won't be comfortable, you'll walk funny, and you'll be thinking about taking them off the entire time. Also, don't wear skimpy dresses just to show off your figure. If you're a male performer, very baggy pants and huge clunky shoes are not going to put you one step ahead. They'll be a hindrance to your auditions, not a help. As a singer, you should always aim for a more classic look. You want to shine, not lumber around in some ill-fitting outfit.

As a performer, you have to know what looks good on you, what works at an audition, what makes you stand out in a flattering way. You have to know what colors complement your skin tone, eyes, and hair. The point is for the casting people to like what they see and remember you. As the saying goes, if you've got it, flaunt it. If you don't, make the adjustments that will allow you to compete against those that do. If you don't prepare yourself properly for auditions, you'll be cut in a heartbeat.

The Vocal Audition Process

When you arrive at a vocal audition, there will probably be a sign-in sheet. Fill out the requested information and, if you get an index card, fill that out also. The monitor will collect the index cards, along with your picture and resume. After signing in, you may want to find an area away from the audition room to hum a little bit, freshen your makeup, get your music out, and take out your picture and resume if they haven't been asked for yet.

Different vocal auditions are handled in different ways. Sometimes the casting people require singers to enter the audition room one at a time. Other times, the entire group enters the room together, and each singer is called up onstage to sing individually. In yet other vocal auditions, the performers are brought in fifteen at a time, lined up, and typed out. You don't even get to sing at these calls until you're determined to fit the type the casting people are looking for and called back for the actual vocal part of the audition.

The point is, every vocal audition is different. How each one is carried out depends on the job and the time constraints. But no matter how the audition is run, you have to realize that your choice of songs will make or break your chance of being hired.

When you're called on to sing, remember that you are trying to distill everything that marks you as an entertainer and performer into one or two songs. While that may seem impossible, try to convey your potential to those auditioning you. Have both an up-tempo piece and a ballad that shows you and your voice in the best possible light, something that says you're special. You want to give yourself an edge, and the audition provides the perfect forum to do that.

It's best if you can work with a vocal coach to get the right audition material, the right songs for your voice and personality. After you and your coach have determined the best songs for you, go to an arranger and have them arranged in the key in which you sing. Make sure the music is clear and easy for the pianist to read. It takes some money to prepare for vocal auditions, but your career is on the line and, once you have your own arrangements and vocal audition pieces, they're yours for life. You'll probably start out with just a few pieces in your repertoire—most likely old standards. But as you continue to work in the business and have more money to spend on this kind of thing, you can add new pieces to expand your repertoire and keep it current.

As previously mentioned, you should have an up-tempo number and a ballad ready to perform. It will also help to have a contemporary rock and pop song and a 1950s song in your repertoire, to provide enough variety in case the production people ask for other vocal styles. In addition, female singers should be prepared to sing a legitimate song that will show off their head voice and semiclassical vocal range, if called upon to do so. Make sure each selection shows off your vocal range to its best advantage.

Whether it's sheet music bought in a store, copied out of a book, or personally written out by an arranger, your music should be taped together and put in a three-ring binder, with holes punched. In that way, it's not only easy for the accompanist to read, but turning the pages will be hassle-free. When the music is not in a three-ring binder, it sometimes falls off the piano, causing problems for the pianist. Using this type of binder is not only good for the selection of the moment, but for keeping all of your music in one place. In that way, when the casting people ask for your next selection, you can easily access the song and be ready to perform.

Most importantly, make sure all the music for your songs is written out in your key. It shouldn't just have the key written up at the top of the piece, in the hopes that the pianist will be able to transpose it on the spot into the key you need. You don't know who the accompanist at a particular audition will be, and you can never predict his or her skills. It's unprofessional to assume the pianist will be able to do more than sight read whatever music you supply. Also have the beginning of each selection marked with a big written-out "START" and the end with a big written-out "FINISH" or railroad lines (//).

If you're prepared for the audition, you'll have the confidence to do a good job. When your name is called, walk up to the table with a smile and hand the casting people your picture and resume if they haven't already been collected by the monitor. State your name confidently and clearly, and announce the songs you're prepared to sing. The casting people may select the piece they want to hear, or they may respond, "Sing what you like." In the latter case, pick the song that is most comfortable for you to perform. If asked to sing sixteen bars, start at the height of the song. Usually, that's the bridge to the end, the most exciting part of the song with the big finish.

If you are told to pick the song yourself, make sure you select a song in the style of the particular show you're auditioning for, but not one directly from that show unless that is specifically called for in the audition notice. If you're auditioning for *Phantom of the Opera*, how many times do you think the staff will be able to stand hearing "Music of the Night"? Or if you're trying out for *A Chorus Line*, how many times will they like hearing "What I Did for Love"? But also make sure you don't sing something totally inappropriate, like something from *Carousel* if you're trying out for

Rent. Put a little thought ahead of time into choosing the song and pick something fresh and appropriate. That alone can score you points.

When you walk over to the pianist, say hello, smile, and hand her or him your music. Sing a few bars into the pianist's ear to indicate the tempo you want, then move to the center of the stage or room and nod to the pianist when you're ready to start.

If you're choosing the songs, perform your up-tempo song first. As you sing, don't look directly at the director or the staff sitting at the table and, when finished, don't dismiss yourself. Wait for someone to prompt you about what to do next. Play it by ear. Don't be pushy, just relax and give them a moment to decide what they want to do with you. If they cut you off during your song, don't take it personally. Frequently casting people know immediately whether the singers they're auditioning can do what is called for, or not. If they ask you to do something else, great. If they don't, return to the piano player to retrieve your music, thank her or him for accompanying you, and leave. Then just forget about it all. You did your best. Whether you're called back or not is out of your hands.

Everybody needs a job, but you need to look at an audition for what it is. When the notices go out, lots of performers read them and show up to try out. Most of them won't get the jobs. People and job openings aren't always suited to each other. But you will get the ones you're really meant to get. Just do your best each time, and you'll get your share of work.

Directors and producers like performers who come to auditions to be well trained, mature, and prepared for the shows they are trying out for. With that in mind, do some research. If you're auditioning for a show that's already up, familiarize yourself with the score. If it's playing at a theme park, in Las Vegas, or on Broadway, go see it if at all possible. If you haven't explored the part that you're trying out for, you need to know if the voice range is too high or too low for you. There are too many people to count who think they were born to play Tommy, Barnum, or Evita. But if you're a male singer, how can you expect to sing the part of Tommy if you haven't explored the score and found out that Tommy is a tenor? What if you're a baritone? If you're a female singer, you need to know that Evita has a vocal range that not everyone can handle. New York director Jamie Rocco makes the following observation:

> *If someone comes in and starts yelling something inappropriate for their voice—trying to be something that they're not—they generally go on my "not interested" list. On the other hand, if someone comes in and does something exquisitely, I'm going to remember how impressive those three minutes were, as if I were transported out of that audition room and suddenly entertained, touched, or moved. They might not get that job, but may well get another one down the road.*

If the casting people are interested in you, they'll assign you specific songs for the callback. You don't have to rush to learn something from a show the night before

You have to nail down your piece. If you can't do it, don't try. However, if you can entertain or move people with your singing, you'll have made the right impression, and it will pay off for you in the future. So learn how the audition process works. A little homework goes a long way in this business.

AUDITIONS FOR DANCERS AND SINGERS

The way a dance and vocal audition is carried out is based on the show or venue you're auditioning for. They'll all be a little different, so let's look at a few examples to provide an overview of what you might encounter.

Audition Example 1

For some musical theater dance calls, auditions may run like this: The casting people call the dancers up onstage in groups of fifteen, placing them in a straight line across the stage. When it's your turn, you take two steps forward, go from first to fourth, and execute a classic double pirouette. When finished, you state your name and supply any other information asked for. If the casting people ask if you can sing, just answer "Yes" or "No" at this point and step back in line. After everyone in line has finished with the dance steps, the casting people will call out the names of those they're interested in, thank the rest for coming, and dismiss them.

This is exactly the kind of audition shown in the musical *A Chorus Line*. What the casting people did was type the dancers out—that is, decide which ones were among the "types" needed for the show, and which ones were not. Too many people show up at musical theater auditions these days, and the casting staff types performers out to avoid wasting valuable audition time. If you are typed out, it may be because you don't have the right look for the show, or won't fit in the costume already sewn for the part if you're a replacement. There are many reasons why you might be typed out. Don't worry about it, just move on to the next audition.

The people not typed out—those the casting staff kept—will now move on to the next cut, the first callback. That might involve performing a ballet combination, for instance. Then once again the casting people will call out names to remain for the next cut—the jazz cut—thanking the rest and dismissing them. After the jazz cut, certain people will be asked to come back for another callback, scheduled perhaps a few days later. At that session, you might be asked to do the same combinations, perhaps with another count of eight added.

Audition Example 2

When casting for *Rent* in Los Angeles, the show ran notices on television, in the newspapers, on the radio—just about everywhere. The producers were after fresh faces and raw talent, not people with Broadway credits. Over eight hundred people turned out to audition. According to Collun Titmus, a singer who tried out for the show:

> *They had everybody sing sixteen bars, unless they were interested in giving you a part in the show. I sang my entire song, and another song from the show. After that, they gave me all of Mark's and Roger's music and a couple of sides [parts of the show's script]. I had a week to prepare and went back the next week to sing all the solos in the show. A month later, I came in and sang again. In all, it was a three-month process. They just kept narrowing it down, always saying they'd let me know.*

Audition Example 3

During the recasting of *Les Misérables*, all the singers who auditioned were placed in a straight line across the stage. They weren't asked anything, just typed out immediately. You have to remember that if a show is recasting a part for a guy they're replacing who's 5' 7" with dark hair, they need a guy who's 5' 7" with dark hair. In *Miss Saigon*, when singers showed up to try out for the part of Chris, the monitor didn't waste anyone's time. If you didn't fit the description, you were told to leave. It's virtually impossible to predict what's going to happen.

In the trade papers, shows always list an exact breakdown of the parts they're recasting. But because so many people have heard stories about the actor who didn't fit the description, but changed the director's mind on the basis of his or her talent alone, many unsuitable types show up at every audition. They figure they might as well give it a shot and, if they get typed out, so be it. This might work occasionally at auditions for new shows, but never at replacement calls. So don't try it.

Audition Example 4

A cruise ship audition may be different. More than likely the casting people won't type you out. If you're a dancer, you'll go to the dancers' call first. You'll be asked to do a ballet, jazz, or tap combination. Then the staff will ask if anyone sings. If you do, you'll come back to the singers' call. If you make that cut, you'll be asked to return for the next call a few days later, with everyone, the dancers and singers, attending.

Audition Example 5

Disney holds auditions for singers on one day and dancers on another, females in the morning, males in the afternoon. Several days later, they hold callbacks with every-one—singers and dancers, men and women—attending. You might be typed out based on the specific show they're doing. If you're auditioning for a face character (Snow White, Ariel, etc.), the casting staff will have you sing and dance and then take photos of you in the character's wig. If the character requires a certain height, and you're not right for it, you may be considered for another role.

ACTING AUDITIONS FOR CHORUS ROLES

If you're familiar with musical comedies, you know that there are main leads, supporting leads, and minor characters that pop in and out throughout each show. Sometimes, in a chorus call, the director will have the singers/dancers read these minor roles from the script. At other times, these roles aren't cast until the first day of rehearsal. However they're cast, when you audition for these minor roles, your job is to enjoy yourself. That has to be your sole objective. If you go in with the intention of winning the role, you're apt to be disappointed. However, if you go in to have fun and do your best at that moment, you're far more likely to be hired. Why? Because you're more relaxed, have more energy, and aren't afraid to give the audition your all.

When you audition for chorus parts, you'll have just the information from the scene, whatever else the director may throw in, and a few seconds to form a picture of the character in your mind. Let's say the character is a New York City cop. You should ask yourself questions like:

"Who am I playing?"

"How do I let everyone know who this character is in three lines or less?"

"Is the guy from Brooklyn? From Long Island? From New Jersey?"

"Is he going to chew gum?"

Have fun with the tryout. Improvise, interpret the character in your own way. Ask yourself, "What purpose does the cop serve in the scene?" "What does he want? What is his motivation?" "What can I do to instantly transform myself into a cop?" By answering those questions, you'll be able to use the vocal delivery and physical actions best suited to that character at that particular moment. To be memorable, the individual you create has to have energy. Simply put, you'll be more effective if you just let it out.

Because singers and dancers don't always know a lot about acting, remember to read loudly and clearly. Don't upstage yourself, and don't try to memorize the lines. Understand that directors are aware that some singers and dancers panic when asked to act, so don't worry about it. Just do your best.

At an acting audition, you're basically showing the director the range of your technique and that you have the appropriate tools as a performer to make a character come alive. You're fleshing out words into a living, breathing individual. That skill comes from your training and your ability to energize at will, to respond and react to anything at any time.

Directors look for good vocal projection and enunciation. If the role requires a dialect, can you do it? If the part requires physical acting, can you project convincingly? You don't want to produce a lame caricature. Directors also check to see that you don't have the *wrong* accent. For example, a thick Southern drawl won't work in a musical like *Grease!*.

SINGERS AND DANCERS ON VACATION

In the performing arts, you'll find yourself meeting people daily who have possible job connections. You can't predict when you'll be offered a job. So be prepared at all times, even on vacation, and in all places, even Alaska, Germany, or Timbuktu. Always have the tools of your profession with you. A dancer should always take his or her dance bag along on trips, including clothes, shoes, makeup kit, picture, resume, and vocal selections for singing auditions. A singer should always travel with demo tapes—both audio and video—as well as tapes of any recorded performances. Every performer should travel with business cards to hand out, in case you meet someone who wants you to try out for a show. These days, business cards are easy and inexpensive to make on a home computer, so there's no reason to be caught without them.

16

FINAL THOUGHTS

During my own journey in show business, a story was told to me by former Broadway performer Garold Gardner (*Camelot, How to Succeed in Business Without Really Trying,* and *Mata Hari*), now a Las Vegas dance instructor. It concerned the actor Reid Shelton, who played Daddy Warbucks in the Broadway musical *Annie.* Shelton had struggled for thirty years before he got any kind of a lead role on Broadway. Throughout those three decades, he did road companies, bus and trucks, summer stock, and a variety of odd jobs to stay afloat, living in the same, small, one-room apartment, in a big apartment building. In the year before he got the Warbucks role, there were no other roles for him to even audition for. In fact, during those twelve months, his total income was only $6800. As the story goes, once he got the part in *Annie,* he bought the entire apartment building he had been living in. Now that's what I call getting the last laugh.

While his story has a happy ending, its moral is even more important: *If you hang in there long enough, and don't give up, anything is possible.* Today, it seems, if most young performers don't enjoy success immediately, they don't want to be bothered even with trying. I suppose it stems from the desire for instant gratification—a kind of "I want it. Right now!" kind of attitude.

DRIVE AND DETERMINATION

You have to be driven in this profession, you must have a long-term determination to succeed. It's really a magnificent obsession, wanting it more than anything else in the world, because there will always be competition to contend with, a fantastic singer or dancer who wants the job as much as you do. You've got to want to prevail, and commit to your ambition, by staying involved and in touch with the business and the people in it. You have to take classes, learn about the business in depth, network, and do everything else we've discussed in this book—for the duration. If you're wishy-washy about it, if you just want to dabble in show business, then get yourself right over to that burger stand and fill out an application. In my experience, you either have this obsession, or you don't. I don't believe it's something that can be developed. It's there or it isn't.

You'll have to develop a thick skin, because rejection will become commonplace in your life. You'll have to remind yourself constantly that, just because the last fifty producers weren't interested in your talent, it doesn't diminish what you have to offer. Too many performers today head to New York, and after a few rejections, leave it behind forever. Before embarking on your journey, you have to realize, and accept, that you will get turned down—a lot.

Your philosophy has to be that you can do anything. If may be difficult, but if you persist, you can do it. Once you make the decision that this is definitely what you want to do, you'll have to come to terms with the fact that there are other skills you have, other jobs you're qualified for, that you'll have to leave behind. Whether your goal is the Broadway stage or regional theater, all your other options will be closed off. The only way to focus is to put all your energy toward a single objective. You'll have to make decisions, set priorities, and always put your best foot forward. If you don't, if you take the path of least resistance, you'll wind up with a mediocre life.

As we discussed earlier, don't have too big a parachute for yourself. The bigger it is, the more likely you'll be to rely on it. It's human nature. If you attend college and enroll in the musical theater department, and also get your teaching certificate as a music teacher for high school students, or a business degree, you're apt to fall back on those credentials when the going as a performer gets tough, as it will. The idea of a steady job, without constant rejection, and steady pay, is wonderful. And safe. But if you have this obsession of being a professional performer, you won't settle for playing it safe. That's not where real performers find themselves, looking for the easy way out.

If success is what you're after, realize that there is a long haul ahead of you. Those people that "kinda thought" they wanted a show business career will take the easy road to a safe, average destination. Most do. Because you're reading this book, and have made it to this point, I'm assuming you're not average. Expect a lot of aggravation, rejection, and disappointment, for a while, anyway. But if you have the drive to make it, even during those inevitable hard times, you will.

To see your obsession through and succeed in the performance world, you'll have to do certain things, with passion and commitment. They include:

1. Attending daily classes in singing, dancing, and acting, and avoiding excuses to skip them, even once in a while.
2. Thinking about performing, practicing, and what you can do to advance your career, virtually every minute of every day, making performing something that you can't live without.
3. Taking care of yourself, and your body. It has to last a long time.
4. Rethinking your goals and where you want to end up in your life if your idea of socializing includes partying and staying up all night.
5. Realizing that you may have to live under some strenuous conditions and that you won't be getting things handed to you, as when you lived at home.
6. Understanding that you might have to hold down two or three part-time jobs to keep your head above water, financially speaking.

TWO COMMON BEGINNERS' MISTAKES

I once had a student who was about to graduate from high school, and asked her what she planned to do once she was out. She told me she was going to New York, give things a try for six months, and see what happened. My answer to her, and to you, is: "Don't bother." In this business, if you can't commit long term, then head on over to the post office to see if they'll let you sort mail. A performing arts career can't be constrained by time limits.

On the one hand, lightning can strike, and you can achieve your goal immediately. On the other, as with Reid Shelton, it can take thirty years to get the role you deserve.

Are you willing to commit your life to achieving the success you want? If you're just going to "give it a try," as if you were test-driving a car you're not really interested in, don't bother. Get a degree in another field and spare yourself the heartache.

Another student of mine was hanging around the dance studio one day, and I asked what her plans were for the summer. She said she was going to wait tables, save some money, and buy a car. I explained to her that while she was taking orders for steaks and chops, someone else, not quite as talented as she was, would be out there working toward her goal. That person would spend the summer taking classes, and, come fall, would have passed her by in the "success race." "Doesn't it bother you to know that?" I asked. There was no reply.

Each of us feels that we're talented, that we have the skills and drive to succeed. But what most of us forget is that when we reach New York, Los Angeles, Las Vegas, or any other major performing market, there are a thousand other people getting off planes and buses there also, with the same drive and talent. If you're a brain surgeon, you can go into any major city and only be the third best in your profession. Even so, you'll earn a lush living and have a nice house and the respect of your peers. But if you attend an audition for a particular role and come in third, you'll be unemployed.

In this business, only the best make it to number one. If you're one of five hundred people auditioning for the same role, there is only one person you have to beat—the best of the other four hundred ninety-nine. You can forget about the losers who come in unprepared, who don't have their songs memorized or the proper dance clothes to wear. You don't have to beat *them* out, as they've already eliminated themselves from the competition. You just have to vanquish that one individual—the person who *is* prepared and who will get the job if you don't.

In closing, I quote Garold Gardner again:

> *Welcome to the world of the musical. The highs, the lows, the triumphs, and the rejections that go along with it all! Keep your focus, study voice, acting, and dance on a regular basis, and keep your determination in high gear. Remember, you're doing all this wonderful stuff because you love it more than anything.* Now, go get 'em!

I wish the best for each and every one of you. There are doers and there are watchers—don't you sit back passively and watch your dream evaporate. As Mr. Gardner noted above, you have to become an active, energetic participant in your career. Make your dreams come true. Don't lie to yourself, and don't do something that only makes the dreams of someone else come true. Push the guilt aside and make your own way. It's important that you live the life you want. It's the only life you have, and if you waste it, it's gone. Don't let that happen.

I hope this book will be a security blanket for you, something to refer back to whenever you need either information or inspiration. I achieved my dream. Now go out and achieve yours.

APPENDIX

PROFESSIONAL ASSOCIATIONS

Talent Unions

Actors' Equity Association (AEA)
165 West 46th Street
New York, New York 10036
(212) 869-8530

American Federation of Television and Radio
Artists (AFTRA)
260 Madison Avenue, 7th floor
New York, New York 10016
(212) 532-0800

American Guild of Musical Artists (AGMA)
1727 Broadway
New York, New York 10019
(212) 265-3687

American Guild of Variety Artists (AGVA)
184 Fifth Avenue, 6th floor
New York, New York 10010
(212) 675-1003

American Society of Composers, Authors
and Publishers (ASCAP)
Two Music Square West
Nashville, Tennessee 37203
(615) 742-5000

Hebrew Actors Union
31 East 7th Street
New York, New York 10003
(212) 674-1923

Screen Actors Guild (SAG)
1515 Broadway, 44th floor
New York, New York 10036
(212) 944-1030

Other Talent Associations

Casting Society of America (CSA)
311 West 43rd Street
New York, New York 10036
(212) 333-4552

National Association of Talent Representatives
(NATR)
c/o The Gage Group
315 West 57th Street, #48
New York, New York 10019
Attention: Lee Buckler

National Conference of Personal Managers
4619 220th Place
Bayside, New York 11361-3651
(718) 225-5103
Attention: Gerard W. Purcell, National President

PUBLICATIONS

Talent Directory

Academy Players Directory
Academy of Motion Pictures
8949 Wilshire Boulevard
Beverly Hills, California 90211
(310) 247-3058
To be listed in this directory, you must be a
member of any actors' guild or have a SAG
franchised agent. Submissions in September,
January, and May. $25 per category.

Periodicals Listing Current Auditions

Note: When subscribing to any of the following,
always send a check or a money order.

Audition News
156A East Lake Street, Suite 142
Bloomingdale, Illinois 60108
(773) 637-5230
Cost: $24.95 for twelve monthly issues
Covers both union and nonunion employment
opportunities in the Midwest for music, theater,
dance, variety, and modeling.

Back Stage and *Back Stage West*
1515 Broadway
New York, New York 10036
(800) 437-3183
Cost: $84 for fifty-one weekly issues of *Back Stage*;
$79 for fifty-one weekly issues of *Back Stage West*

Cruise Employment Program
P.O. Box 85180
Seattle, Washington 98145-1180

Dirt Alert
2375 E. Tropicana, Suite 6
Las Vegas, Nevada 89119
Cost: $26 for six-month subscription; $52 for
one-year subscription

Publications Listing Miscellaneous Information on the Performing Arts, Including Yearly Auditions

The Dance Directory
P.O. Box 904
New York, New York 10023
(212) 535-3757
Cost: $39.95, plus $4.50 for shipping
Lists detailed information about ballet companies, including their audition requirements, repertoire, salaries, contracts, benefits, and schedules. Updated yearly.

Dance Magazine
P.O. Box 5068
Brentwood, Tennessee 37024-9726
(800) 331-1750
Cost: $34.95 for twelve monthly issues
A magazine for dance-related issues, and a great place to find a thorough listing of all summer programs in dance.

Dance Spirit
P.O. Box 2041
Marion, Ohio 43306-2141
Cost: $12.99 for six bimonthly issues
A magazine for dance, drill, pep, and pom pom squads. Detailed information on training, instruction, and special stories on a variety of subjects.

The Agencies, New York Edition
P.O. Box 3899
Hollywood, CA 90078
(212) 585-4181
Comprehensive listing of performing arts agencies located in New York, providing an overview of the types of performers each agency specializes in and and the type of talent each is looking for. Updated monthly.

Regional Theatre Directory
P.O. Box 519
Dorset, Vermont 05251
(802) 867-2223
Cost: $16.95
Information on four hundred thirty Equity and non-Equity regional and dinner theaters. Published each May. Lists Fall-Winter-Spring employment opportunities for performers, directors, designers, technicians, and management. Also lists student internship opportunities. Contains an appendix listing career development resources and service organizations.

Ross Reports for Television and Film
P.O. Box 5018
Brentwood, Tennessee 37024-5018
(800) 817-3273
Cost: $50.00 for twelve monthly issues

Summer Theatre Directory
P.O. Box 519
Dorset, Vermont 05251
(802) 867-2223
Cost: $16.95

NATIONAL DANCE ORGANIZATIONS

Dance Educators of America
P.O. Box 607
Pelham, New York 10803
(800) 229-3868

Dance Masters of America
214-10 41st Avenue
Bayside, New York 11361
(718) 225-4013

DANCE STUDIOS NATIONWIDE

The dance studios listed below are just to get you started. As you attend classes in these studios, you will meet other dancers who will tell you about good classes elsewhere.

Las Vegas

Backstage 1
1942 1/2 East Sahara
Las Vegas, Nevada 89104
(702) 457-7310

Las Vegas Dance Theatre Studio
3248 Civic Center Drive
North Las Vegas, Nevada 89030
(702) 649-3932

Le Tang Academy of Dance
953 East Sahara, #35-B
Las Vegas, Nevada 89104
(702) 892-8499

Los Angeles

Edge Performing Arts Center
1020 North Cole Avenue
Hollywood, California 90038
(323) 962-7733

New York

Alvin Ailey American Dance Center
211 West 61st Street
New York, New York 10023
(212) 767-0940
Modern dance

Broadway Dance Center
221 West 57th Street, 5th floor
New York, New York 10019
(212) 582-9304
Ballet, jazz, tap, ethnic, modern, yoga, aerobics

Isadora Duncan Foundation
for Contemporary Dance
141 West 26th Street
New York, New York 10001
(212) 691-5040

José Limon Dance Foundation
611 Broadway
New York, New York 10012
(212) 777-3353

Martha Graham School
of Contemporary Dance
316 East 63rd Street
New York, New York 10021
(212) 838-5886
Modern dance

Merce Cunningham Dance Studio
55 Bethune Street
New York, New York 10014
(212) 691-9751
Modern dance

Steps Studio
2121 Broadway (at West 74th Street)
New York, New York 10023
(212) 874-2410
Dance in all styles and at all levels

PUBLIC AND PRIVATE PERFORMING ARTS HIGH SCHOOLS

Public—Magnet High Schools

A magnet high school is nothing more than
a public school that stresses training in the
arts. Most of these schools will accept students
from their county or state of residence without
charging tuition. Expect to be well trained by
the time you graduate, as these schools make
you focus on your goals. Some magnet high
schools give out a "special" diploma instead
of a regular high school diploma. You will need
a regular diploma if you plan to pursue higher

education, so be sure to ask. Admission is based
on audition. Some of the bigger magnet high
schools include: Fiorello H. LaGuardia High
School of Performing Arts, New York; The
Los Angeles County High School for the Arts;
Booker T. Washington High School for the
Performing and Visual Arts, Dallas. There are
over one hundred other magnet schools in the
United States. To find one close to you, write to:

Network
35th and S Streets, N.W.
Washington, D.C. 20007

Private—Residential High Schools

Residential high schools are private, and,
therefore, do cost money. Students live in on-
campus dormitories and attend a local high
school for morning academic classes, which
are basically college prep. Afternoon classes
are given over to specific performance training
and evenings are for rehearsals. Scholarships
are available. Some of the more well-known
residential high schools are:

Florida School of the Arts
5001 St. John Avenue
Palatka, Florida 32177
(904) 312-4300

Harrid Conservatory
2285 Potomac Road
Boca Raton, Florida 33431
(561) 997-2677

Idyllwild School of Music and the Arts
P.O. Box 38
Idyllwild, California 92547
(909) 659-2171

Interlochen Arts Academy
P.O. Box 199
Interlochen, Michigan 49643
(616) 276-7472

North Carolina School of the Arts
P.O. Box 12189
Winston-Salem, North Carolina 27199-0520
(800) 282-2787

The Virginia School of the Arts
2240 Rivermont Avenue
Lynchburg, Virginia 24503
(804) 847-8688

Walnut Hill
12 Highland Street
Natick, Massachusetts 01760
(508) 653-4312

COLLEGE, UNIVERSITY, AND CONSERVATORY PERFORMING ARTS PROGRAMS

Publications

Several publications are available to help you choose the program best suited to your needs. They include:

Dance Magazine College Guide
33 West 60th Street
New York, New York 10023
(212) 245-9050
Cost: $20.45, plus any requested shipping or handling
Contains information on over five hundred college and university dance departments, with detailed descriptions of more than one hundred programs. Includes degrees offered, tuition, and performance opportunities. Lists entries by state and country.

Directory of Theater Training Programs
P.O. Box 519
Dorset, Vermont 05251
(802) 867-2223
Cost: $25.95
Profiles four hundred fifty programs at colleges, universities, and conservatories. Detailed information on facilities, faculty, curriculum productions, and philosophy of training. Valuable articles on finding the training program most suitable to your goals.

Peterson's Professional Degree Programs in the Visual and Performing Arts
P.O. Box 2123
Princeton, New Jersey 08543-2123
Cost: $24.95
Can be bought at any bookstore.

Programs

College programs change yearly. What is offered this year can be swept away the next. The colleges and conservatories I have listed below support the philosophies of musical theater. Some are large schools, while others have very small programs. I believe every school is right for certain students. I will not say which school I think is the best because it's relative to who is attending. I will only say that the three schools that have the most students performing professionally on Broadway, and all over the country, are Oklahoma City University, Point Park College, and the University of Cincinnati College Conservatory of Music.

ALABAMA

University of Alabama
P.O. Box 870366
Tuscaloosa, Alabama 35487
(205) 348-7110
Enrollment: Medium

University of Alabama/Birmingham
Birmingham, Alabama 35294
(800) 421-8743
Enrollment: Medium

ARIZONA

Arizona State University
P.O. Box 870304
Tempe, Arizona 85287-0304
(602) 965-5029
Enrollment: Large

CALIFORNIA

California State University at Fullerton
P.O. Box 34080
Fullerton, California 93834-6850
(714) 278-3511
Enrollment: Large

COLORADO

University of Northern Colorado
Greeley, Colorado 80639
(970) 351-2194
Enrollment: Medium

DISTRICT OF COLUMBIA

The American University
4400 Massachusetts Avenue
Washington, D.C. 20016
(202) 885-3429
Enrollment: Medium

The Catholic University of America
Washington, D.C. 20064
(202) 319-5414
Enrollment: Small

Howard University
6th and Fairmont Streets, N.W.
Washington, D.C. 20059
(202) 806-6100
Enrollment: Medium

FLORIDA

Florida School of the Arts
5001 St. John Avenue
Palatka, Florida 32177
(904) 312-4300
Enrollment: Small

Florida State University
Tallahassee, Florida 32306-2008
(850) 644-5548
Enrollment: Large

University of Florida
Gainesville, Florida 32611
(352) 392-1365
Enrollment: Large

University of Miami
P.O. Box 248273
Coral Gables, Florida 33124
(305) 284-4323
Enrollment: Medium

GEORGIA

LaGrange College
LaGrange, Georgia 30240-2999
(706) 812-7256
Enrollment: Small

ILLINOIS

Illinois Wesleyan University
P.O. Box 2900
Bloomington, Illinois 61702-2900
(309) 556-3031
Enrollment: Small

Millikin University
1184 West Main Street
Decatur, Illinois 62522
(217) 424-6210
Enrollment: Small

Roosevelt University
430 South Michigan Avenue
Chicago, Illinois 60605-1394
(312) 341-3515
Enrollment: Small

Southern Illinois University at Edwardsville
P.O. Box 1771
Edwardsville, Illinois 62026-1771
(618) 692-3705
Enrollment: Medium

INDIANA

Ball State University
Muncie, Indiana 47306
(765) 285-8300
Enrollment: Medium

Butler University
4600 Sunset Avenue
Indianapolis, Indiana 46208
(317) 940-9346
Enrollment: Small

KANSAS

Kansas State University
Manhattan, Kansas 66506
(800) 432-8270
Enrollment: Medium

KENTUCKY

Northern Kentucky University
Highland Heights, Kentucky 41099-1007
(800) 637-9948
Enrollment: Medium

MASSACHUSETTS

Boston Conservatory
8 the Fenway
Boston, Massachusetts 02215
(617) 536-6340
Enrollment: Small

Emerson College
100 Beacon Street
Boston, Massachusetts 02128
(617) 824-8600
Enrollment: Small

MICHIGAN

Eastern Michigan University
Ypsilanti, Michigan 48197
(734) 487-0193
Enrollment: Medium

University of Michigan
Ann Arbor, Michigan 48109-1285
(313) 764-7433
Enrollment: Large

MISSOURI

Stephens College
Columbia, Missouri 65215
(800) 876-7207
Enrollment: Small

Webster University
470 East Lockwood Avenue
St. Louis, Missouri 63119-3194
(314) 968-6991
Enrollment: Medium

NEBRASKA

University of Nebraska
P.O. Box 880201
Lincoln, Nebraska 68588-0201
(402) 472-2023
Enrollment: Medium

NEVADA

University of Nevada, Las Vegas
P.O. Box 451021
Las Vegas, Nevada 89154-1021
(702) 895-3443
Enrollment: Medium

NEW HAMPSHIRE

University of New Hampshire
30 College Road
Durham, New Hampshire 03824-3538
(603) 862-1360
Enrollment: Medium

NEW MEXICO

The College of Santa Fe
1600 St. Michael's Drive
Santa Fe, New Mexico 87505
(505) 473-6133
Enrollment: Small

NEW YORK

The American Musical and Dramatic Academy
2109 Broadway
New York, New York 10023
(212) 787-5300
Enrollment: 530

Circle in the Square Theatre School
1633 Broadway
New York, New York 10019-6795
(212) 307-0388
Enrollment: Small

Ithaca College
201 Dillingham Center
Ithaca, New York 14850-7293
(607) 274-3124
Enrollment: Small

State University of New York/Fredonia
Fredonia, New York 14063
(716)673-3596
Enrollment: Small

Syracuse University
820 East Genesee Street
Syracuse, New York 13244-2970
(315) 443-3611
Enrollment: Medium

Tisch School of the Arts
New York University
721 Broadway, 7th Floor
New York, New York 10003-6807
(212) 998-1900
Enrollment: Large

Wagner College
Staten Island, New York 10301
(718) 390-3411
Enrollment: Small

NORTH CAROLINA

Catawba College
Salisbury, North Carolina 28144
(800) 228-2922
Enrollment: Small

East Carolina University
Greenville, North Carolina 27858
(919) 328-6640
Enrollment: Medium

Lees-McRae College
Banner Elk, North Carolina 28604
(800) 280-4562
Enrollment: Small

Mars Hill College
Mars Hill, North Carolina 28754
(800) 543-1514
Enrollment: Small

OHIO

Baldwin-Wallace College
275 Eastland Road
Berea, Ohio 44017
(440) 826-2222
Enrollment: Small

Kent State University
P.O. Box 5190
Kent, Ohio 44242-0001
(330) 672-2444
Enrollment: Medium

University of Akron
354 East Market Street
Akron, Ohio 44325-2502
(330) 972-7948
Enrollment: Medium

University of Cincinnati College-
Conservatory of Music
P.O. Box 210096
Cincinnati, Ohio 45221-0096
(513) 556-9479
Enrollment: Medium

OKLAHOMA

Oklahoma City University
2501 North Blackwelder
Oklahoma City, Oklahoma 73106
(800) 633-7242
Enrollment: Small

University of Oklahoma
563 Elm Avenue, #209
Norman, Oklahoma 73019-0310
(405) 325-4021
Enrollment: Medium

PENNSYLVANIA

Carnegie Mellon University
5000 Forbes Avenue
Pittsburgh, Pennsylvania 15213-3890
(412) 268-2385
Enrollment: Small

University of the Arts
320 South Broad Street
Philadelphia, Pennsylvania 19102
(215) 717-6030
Enrollment: Small

SOUTH CAROLINA

Columbia College
1301 Columbia College Drive
Columbia, South Carolina 29203
(803) 786-3810
Enrollment: Small

TEXAS

Sam Houston State University
Huntsville, Texas 77341-2418
(409) 294-1056
Enrollment: Medium

Southwest Texas State University
601 University Drive
San Marcos, Texas 78666-4616
(512) 245-2364
Enrollment: Medium

UTAH

Brigham Young University
B-380 ASP
Provo, Utah 84602
(801) 378-3777
Enrollment: Large

VIRGINIA

James Madison University
Harrisonburg, Virginia 22807
(540) 568-6147
Enrollment: Medium

Shenandoah University
1460 University Drive
Winchester, Virginia 22601
(540) 665-4581
Enrollment: Small

WISCONSIN

University of Wisconsin/Stevens Point
1801 Franklin Street
Stephens Point, Wisconsin 54481
(715) 346-2441
Enrollment: Small

GREAT BRITAIN
Mountainview Theatre School
104 Crouch Hill
London N8 9EA, Great Britain
(0181) 340-5885
Enrollment: Small

BIBLIOGRAPHY

Alper, Steven M., *Next! Auditioning for the Musical Theater* (Reed Elsevier/Heinemann, New Hampshire, 1995)

Bell, Richard O., *Audition and Scenes from Shakespeare* (Theatre Directories, Dorset, Vermont, 1996) (Includes over 700 monologues and scenes for auditions)

Berkowitz, Gerald, M., *New Broadways* (Applause Books, New York, 1997)

Callan, K., *How to Sell Yourself as an Actor* (Sweden Press, California, 1996)

Charles, Jill, *Regional Theatre Directory* (Theatre Directories, Dorset, Vermont, updated regularly)

Charles, Jill, and Bloom, Tom, *The Actor's Picture and Resume Book* (Theatre Directories, Dorset, Vermont, 1996)

Criscito, Pat, *Designing the Perfect Resume* (Barron's, Happauge, New York, 1995)

Doty, David, *Frommer's New York City* (Simon & Schuster/Macmillan, New York, updated regularly)

Eaker, Sherry (Editor), *Back Stage Handbook for the Performing Artist* (Back Stage Books, New York, 1995)

Early, Barbara, *Finding the Best Dance Instruction* (Betterway Books, Cincinnati, 1992)

Henderson, Laura Browning, *How to Train a Singer* (Parker Publishing Company, West Nyack, New York, 1991)

Henry, Mary Lyn, and Rogers, Lynne, *How to Be a Working Actor* (Back Stage Books, New York, 1994)

Hooks, Ed, *The Audition Book* (Back Stage Books, New York, 1989)

Hooks, Ed, *The Ultimate Scene and Monologue Sourcebook* (Back Stage Books, New York, 1994)

Ito, Robert, and Roetzheim, Bill, *Tumbling* (H. Regnery, Chicago, 1997)

Mayfield, Katherine, *Smart Actors, Foolish Choices* (Back Stage Books, New York, 1996)

McGaw, Charles, *Acting Is Believing* (Rinehart Press, San Francisco, 1966)

Mirault, Dan, *Dancing for a Living* (Rafter Publications, N. Hollywood, 1999)

Oliver, Donald, *How to Audition for the Musical Theatre* (Smith and Kraus, Lyme, New Hampshire, 1995)

Peterson's Professional Degree Programs in the Visual and Performing Arts (Peterson's, Princeton, New Jersey, 1998)

Schwartz, David J., Ph.D., *The Magic of Thinking Big* (Simon & Schuster, New York, 1987)

Shurtleff, Michael, *Audition* (Walker & Company, New York, 1978)

Vando, David (Executive Editor), *The National Casting Guide* (Peter Glenn Publications, New York, 1998)

Wolper, Andrea, *The Actor's City Sourcebook* (Back Stage Books, New York, 1992)

INDEX

ABOUT THE AUTHOR

Since beginning his career as a performer, choreographer, and director two decades ago, Michael Allen has appeared in shows and at festivals internationally and has worked in Las Vegas, Hollywood, and New York alongside show business giants Jerry Lewis, Sammy Davis, Jr., and Milton Berle, to name just a few. He has also appeared at the St. Louis Tap Dance Festival and with the Cleveland Pops Orchestra and the National Repertory Orchestra. Michael was featured at New York's Tap Extravaganza, honoring legends Gene Kelly, Ann Miller, and his mentor and friend Maceo Anderson—the founder and only living member of the Original Four Step Brothers. As a choreographer and director, Michael has staged critically acclaimed productions of *Annie, The Wiz, A Chorus Line, 42nd Street,* and *Evita.*

As artistic director of Kids to Go, in Colorado Springs, he creates diverse and exciting musical theater programs for children 8 to 12. Michael is the owner of a studio specializing in musical theater and he has coached numerous students as a performing arts consultant and dance teacher. He also enjoys nationwide acclaim for for his lifelong dedication to the art of hoofing and trick roping.

Jo Rowan, the chief researcher for this book, trained as a ballet dancer at the School of American Ballet in New York and at the Bolshoi School in Moscow and has performed internationally with ballet and opera companies. Her real love is musical theater, and she has appeared in more than sixty Equity musical productions as a singer, dancer, actress, and comedian. In demand as a master teacher for dance organizations in both this country and abroad, Jo is the chairman of dance at the School of American Dance and Arts Management at Oklahoma City University. She directs the American Spirit Dance Company and writes and directs the annual Oklahoma City Philharmonic Yuletide Festival.